Diversity in Mind and in Action

**Recent Titles in
Race and Ethnicity in Psychology**

Sources of Stress and Relief for African American Women
Catherine Fisher Collins

Playing with Anger: Teaching Coping Skills to African American Boys
through Athletics and Culture
Howard C. Stevenson Jr., editor

The Psychology of Prejudice and Discrimination, Volumes I-IV
Jean Lau Chin, editor

Light, Bright, and Damned Near White
Stephanie R. Bird

Diversity in Mind and in Action

Volume 3

Social Justice Matters!: Social, Psychological, and Political Challenges

EDITED BY JEAN LAU CHIN

Foreword by Joseph E. Trimble

Praeger Perspectives
Race and Ethnicity in Psychology

PRAEGER
An Imprint of ABC-CLIO, LLC

A B C CLIO

Santa Barbara, California • Denver, Colorado • Oxford, England

Library of Congress Cataloging-in-Publication Data

Diversity in mind and in action / edited by Jean Lau Chin ; foreword by Joseph E. Trimble.
      p. cm. — (Praeger perspectives race and ethnicity in psychology)
   Includes bibliographical references and index.
   ISBN 978-0-313-34709-2 (v. 1 : alk. paper) : (978-0-313-34710-8 (e-book) — ISBN 978-0-313-34711-5 (v. 2 : alk. paper) : (978-0-313-34712-2 (e-book) — ISBN 978-0-313-34713-9 (v. 3 : alk. paper) : (978-0-313-34714-6 (e-book) — ISBN 978-0-313-34707-8 (set) : (978-0-313-34708-5 (set e-book)
   1. Prejudices—United States. 2. Intercultural communication—United States. 3. Minorities—Mental health services—Social aspects. 4. Psychiatry, Transcultural—United States. 5. Minorities—Employment—United States. 6. Minorities—Education—United States. I. Chin, Jean Lau.
HM1091.D58 2009
305—dc22   2009000516

13   12   11   10   09   1   2   3   4   5

This book is also available on the World Wide Web as an eBook.
Visit www.abc-clio.com for details.

ABC-CLIO, LLC
130 Cremona Drive, P.O. Box 1911
Santa Barbara, California 93116-1911

This book is printed on acid-free paper (∞)
Manufactured in the United States of America

Contents

Foreword

Within and without the sombre veil of color vast social forces have been at work—efforts for human betterment, movements toward disintegration and despair, tragedies and comedies in social and economic life, and a swaying and lifting and sinking of human hearts which have made this land a land of mingled sorrow and joy, of change and excitement and unrest.

—W.E.B. DuBois (1903, p. 129)

The poignant, profound, and haunting words of the eminent African American scholar, W.E.B. DuBois, set the tone for the contents of these volumes with their emphasis on diversity in mind and action. Indeed, the lives of countless immigrants and those of the indigenous peoples of the Americas are filled with the "swaying and sinking of human hearts" that continue to move to and fro as the populations in the Western Hemisphere swell in number. An afternoon stroll down the busy sidewalks of major cities in North America gives attention to the multitudes of people from different nationalities and ethnocultural populations; the principal elements of diversity in all of its forms rise up when one hears the sounds and tones of various languages, becomes aware of distinctive clothing styles and dress patterns, and observes the manner in which couples stroll along arm-in-arm. The multiplicity of differences is more apparent now than it has ever been. The differences have always been there, but they were suppressed. Often, when diverse groups appeared out in the open, they drew sneers, derision, sarcasm, attacks on the dignity of the people, exclusion, harsh commentary, and outright offensive injustices.

The spectacle created by rapid sociocultural changes is no more evident than in educational institutions. In some school districts around the

United States, for example, there are countless foreign languages and dialects spoken in the homes of the youth. In the southwestern quadrant of the country, Spanish is the lingua franca in homes, communities, religious institutions, and the workplace, but not necessarily in the school systems. Similarly, Canada endorses French and English as the two primary languages of the country. Diversity, as represented by the expression and declaration of one's ethnocultural allegiance and affiliations, is no longer concealed; it's out in the open.

Survey results from the 2000 U.S. Census Bureau, for example, indicate that countless Americans opted to identify an ancestral nationality or ethnic group as significant for them. One of the survey questions in the 2000 form asks, "What is this person's ancestry or ethnic origin?" Eighty percent of the respondents specified their ancestry; 58 percent provided a single ancestry and 22 percent provided multiple ancestries (U.S. Census Bureau, 2004). The specific ancestral or ethnic groups listed reveal an interesting and illuminating pattern, as 42.8 million considered themselves to be of German ancestral background; this figure represents over 15 percent of the total responses. Groups mentioned with over 15 million reporting included Irish (30.5 million), African American (24.9 million), English (24.5 million), American (20.2 million), Mexican (18.4 million), and Italian (15.6 million). Overall, the census item generated some 92 different ancestries with 100,000 or more people belonging to them; furthermore, it generated some 500 different ancestral listings. Additionally, an inspection of the ancestral demographic distributions by U.S. county provided by the Census Bureau shows heavy concentrations of national groups in certain areas of the country; a quick glance at Minnesota, Wisconsin, and the Dakotas shows pockets of people of Nordic and German descent. County maps in Florida, Texas, New Mexico, Arizona, and California show heavy concentrations of descendants from the Caribbean, Mexico, and Central and South America.

There are other powerful influences among the populations of North America that emerge from interethnic marriages and childbearing. In the 2000 census, for example, the Census Bureau asked citizens to indicate their multiethnic affiliation by asking them to check more than one so-called racial category if this was applicable; results from the survey showed that, on average, 2.4 percent of the U.S. population identified with two or more racial groups. Use of the new multiracial item created debates and problems for all who rely on use of census outcomes. The addition of the multiracial category presents difficult tabulation and reporting problems for health care professionals, economists, demographers, social and behavioral scientists and others who use racial categories for their work. Prewitt (2002) pointed out that the addition of the multiracial category represents a "turning point in the measurement of race . . . and . . . the arrival of a multiple-race option in the census classification will so blur racial distinctions in the political and legal spheres and perhaps also in the public consciousness that race classification will gradually disappear" (p. 360).

People from similar ethnocultural heritages tend to cluster in communities; this clustering is most evident when groups migrate to North America and gravitate to an area where people reside who share a common identity, cultural lifeways, values and beliefs, that are unique from the mainstream culture. This resettlement suggests a strong sense of identity and the need for affiliation. The path to like-minded communities also implies that one will find a haven from discrimination and social ostracism, as well as a place where one can feel comfortable expressing one's traditional lifeways and thoughtways. Degrees of subjective self-identity influence the extent to which one seeks social support from peers to validate and substantiate this identity; it's a reciprocal and often negotiated progression, accompanied with rules and acceptable sources of evidence such as language use, family birthrights, physiognomic features, interaction styles, and so on. Social validation brings comfort and reinforcement of one's personal identity. Personal well being is also strengthened and, along with it, the hope that daily life will be free from the suppression of traditions, customs, and beliefs.

But as the landscape changes and culture and diversity become more obvious, people insensitive to these issues must learn to accommodate differences and understand the strengths that differences and diversity provide to society as a whole; history books and chapters tell gripping and chilling stories about what happens when insensible bigots refuse to accommodate differences and, in the process, exert and ultimately abuse their power. Change must occur if we are to avoid any further intergroup and interpersonal conflict. And one of the ways proactive change can occur is through an emphasis on the development of multicultural competence, as suggested in several chapters in these volumes. While there are numerous ways to achieve and define cultural competence, no doubt there is much greater agreement about recognizing instances of multicultural incompetence. The fallout and the untoward consequences of cultural incompetence are unprecedented in the annals of the history of our planet; the emotional, psychological, physical, ecological, and economic costs are extraordinary and often beyond comprehension. Advocating and encouraging cultural competency in every aspect of life can avoid cultural incompetence; many of the chapters in these volumes provide thoughtful guidance and orientation on this topic.

In reading the chapters in the volumes, we should be mindful of the psychosocial complexities of the melting pot theory and the strong influence of individualism in North America. In one of the classic statements on personhood in non-Western cultures, Clifford Geertz (1973), an American cultural anthropologist, reminds us that: "The Western conception of the person as a bounded, unique, more or less integrated motivational and cognitive universe, a dynamic center of awareness, emotion, judgment, and action, organized into a distinctive whole and set contrastively—both against other such wholes and against social and natural background—is however incorrigible it may seem to us, a rather peculiar idea within the context of the world's cultures" (p. 34). His observation is worthy of serious consideration and contemplation as we forge and promote intergroup relationships deriving from respectfulness and civility.

The collection of thoughtful and coherent chapters in the *Diversity in Mind and in Action* collection provides a discourse on an extensive range of topics in the rapidly emerging field of multiculturalism in the social and behavioral sciences, as well as in other academic disciplines. Readers may not agree with some of the concepts, proposals, and arguments. But there may be countless others who have waited for the contents of the volumes to come along to provide them with support and direction. Volumes like these are set out to encourage debate and discussion, especially about the growing multicultural populations of North America where, eventually, no single ethnocultural group will be dominant.

Editor Jean Lau Chin and her hand-picked collection of competent and often inspiring authors are to be heartily congratulated for their stimulating and thought-provoking contributions. Many of the contributions are based on first-hand experiences, while others provide a blend of empirical research findings with practical applications. Examples abound describing the effects of cultural incompetence; their blend with wonderful and insightful examples of how to deal with them add an important dimension to the field. Above all else, however, is the hope provided by the content and flow of the volumes and chapters that intergroup and interethnic relations will improve to eliminate discrimination, prejudice, hatred, incivilities, and the vile and venomous hatred they provoke.

Joseph E. Trimble, PhD
Professor of Psychology
Western Washington University
Bellingham, WA 98225
September 28, 2008

REFERENCES

Du Bois, W. E. B. (1903). *The souls of black folk.* Chicago: A. C. McClurg.

Geertz, C. (1973). *The interpretation of cultures: Selected essays.* New York: Basic Books.

Prewitt, K. (2002). Race in the 2000 census: A turning point. In J. Perlmann & M. C. Waters (Eds.), *The new race question: How the census counts multiracial individuals* (pp. 354–360). New York: Russell Sage Foundation.

U.S. Census Bureau. (2004). *Ancestry: 2000.* Washington, DC: U.S. Department of Commerce, Economic and Statistics Administration.

Preface

This new three-volume set is part of the Praeger Series on Race, Ethnicity, and Psychology. A previous set, *The Psychology of Prejudice and Discrimination*, also edited by Dr. Chin, was named a 2005 Choice Outstanding Academic Title (Chin, 2005b).

Diversity is a hot and contemporary issue. While the successes of the Civil Rights Movement and Women's Movement in the twentieth century led to transformations in U.S. society, diversity remains an issue in the twenty-first century as it becomes even more important for diverse people and communities to live and work together for the common good and mutual survival. Diversity has also become a global issue as advances in technology, transportation, and the Internet have narrowed our borders and made our boundaries more permeable. Internationally, many countries now share the common experiences and problems of increased mobility among its citizens and a more diverse population. We must now address the contemporary issues of diversity and move beyond the melting-pot myth of the twentieth century and the segregationist policies that legislated different paths for people based on their skin color. We are talking about tolerance and cultural competence, and these traits start in our minds. We are saying that *diversity matters!* We must *act* to create equitable work and living environments, and *advocate* to change that which perpetuates the intolerance of difference and diversity.

Diversity is complex. Whereas promoting diversity once meant simply meeting the needs of immigrants and ethnic minorities, and welcoming new and different racial/ethnic groups into our communities and institutions, promoting diversity now means much more. We must address the differences between new immigrants and those racial/ethnic minority

groups born and bred in the United States. We must expand our definitions of diversity to include not only race and ethnicity, but also gender,
sexual orientation, religion, and disability. Moreover, it has become clear
that our identities do not manifest themselves in isolation, and we must
understand the complexity of how they interact. Our attention to diversity must also grapple with the issues of multiculturalism, both within the
United States and in a global society.

Diversity must also be placed in a historical context. The melting-pot
myth in America reflects a time in which the dominant group in the
United States was white and middle class; those in positions of power
were white men; the social ideal was to call on a nation to unite. Technology, terrorism, and continued immigration changed all that. We have
become increasingly global and diverse. Even our labeling of groups has
evolved, and must be placed in a historical context. It is more difficult to
label African Americans, Latin Americans, Asian Americans, and American Indians, the four historical groups of color, as minority groups. The
individual labels changed through the preference to avoid the stigma of
marginalization and racism inherent in the labels of "Negro," "Oriental,"
and "Indian."

Diversity is both a state of mind and a stance of action. How we conduct
ourselves as responsible citizens, and how we practice as ethical professionals amid a diverse population, community, and society is central in
this conversation. This volume set, *Diversity in Mind and in Action*, intends
to address just that. How do we grapple with inequity in our institutions
and workplaces? How do we honor our multiple identities? How do we
confront the adverse consequences of privilege and power that favor
some groups while oppressing others? How do we transform the bias in
our minds and actions that lead to disparities and incompetence in the
delivery of services? How do we recognize the narrowness of our borders
and our interdependence within a global society?

This set organizes each volume by major themes related to diversity
and multiculturalism that beset today's society. Volume 1 addresses the
themes of identity and how individuals and groups identify with one
another based on race, ethnicity, country of origin, gender, sexual orientation, and religion, often cutting across geographic boundaries and professional affiliations. Volume 2 addresses disparities in health and mental
health, and how our care delivery systems are often biased in providing
differential access to care for different groups. Diversity as a matter of ethics and cultural competence is the theme. The climate and contexts of our
educational institutions and workplaces in which diverse groups learn,
work, and live will be discussed, as well as diversity and leadership. Diversity matters! Volume 3 discusses the themes of social justice, power,
and oppression, which are associated with racism, classism, and social
privilege. Social, political, and psychological challenges face us as we seek
strategies and solutions to create social institutions that honor diversity,

and are the training grounds for diverse citizens living together with differences of perspectives, origins, and persuasions. This is social change and advocacy. It is a contemporary view of diversity amid a historical context.

Contributors to this set provide a framework not only for understanding diversity, but also for acting together in transforming our society and its institutions to create equity for diverse groups. All volumes are anchored in a global perspective, attend to issues of difference, and contribute to a *vision for diversity in mind and action*—a vision to honor diversity, and of a society where all groups can co-exist while respecting differences; where our institutions will no longer be biased against any one group over another, and will be culturally competent in serving their diverse needs.

Key Questions at the end of each volume are intended to make the set useful for training by educators and professionals, as well as for further inquiry by a broader audience addressing diversity in contemporary society. Each chapter author has contributed a key question to promote discussion and challenge thinking based on the theme and key issue or main focus of the chapter. These have been compiled as a table at the end of each volume to be used as exercises.

ACKNOWLEDGMENTS

I would like to acknowledge my family, and especially my mother, an immigrant from Nanking, China, from whom I gained valuable insights about our journey in life. I documented her narrative in *Learning from My Mother's Voice* (Chin, 2005a) and learned important lessons, with her as my mentor, about the importance of resiliency and endurance. These serve as lifelong lessons for us to continue that struggle and goal toward inclusion and equity and of valuing the differences that make us human and humane.

I am also grateful to my graduate assistants who contributed to this volume set including Gideon Kim, Kirsten Petersen, and especially Jessica Shimberg, who toiled together to bring together the contributions of this diverse groups of authors.

Jean Lau Chin

REFERENCES

Chin, J. L. (2005a). *Learning from my mother's voice: Family legend and the Chinese American experience.* New York: Teacher's College Press.

Chin, J. L. (Ed.). (2005b). *The psychology of prejudice and discrimination.* Westport, CT: Praeger Publishers.

Introduction to Volume 3: Social Justice Matters!: Social, Psychological, and Political Challenges

Diversity is a social justice issue. It is about power and oppression associated with racism, classism, and social privilege. We are faced with social, political, and psychological challenges as we seek strategies and solutions to create social institutions that honor diversity, and are the training grounds for diverse citizens living together with different perspectives, origins, and persuasions. It is about social change and advocacy. Diversity is about contemporary society consisting of people living and working together amidst political, economic, psychological, and social contexts drawing on historical perspectives.

We can learn much about a country and its citizens by examining its legislative history and political past. In the enactment of legislation on affirmative action, anti-discrimination and antiharassment (e.g., Title IX is a law passed in 1972 that requires gender equity for boys and girls in every educational program that receives federal funding), the United States demonstrated its commitment to diversity. At the same time, it enacted legislation that limited the civil rights of some of its citizens and gave differential treatment to its citizens based on race and color. These acts mirrored public sentiment toward people of color, LGBTQ persons, and ableism. In its actions, the government mirrored the national mindset based on the prevailing majority of white middle-class Americans. These actions created marginalized and oppressed groups; they mirrored the mindset that some are more equal than others, and that resources could be rationed to a privileged set. While history and American ideals suggest that we welcomed diversity, prohibited harassment, and strived to create a just and equal society, the government's actions said otherwise. In the twenty-first century, the national debate on undocumented immigrants has resurrected a sentiment of fear, anger, and outrage toward the outsider found in the nineteenth and twentieth centuries—the new immigrant is depicted as inferior, evil and menacing in robbing so-called bonafide U.S. citizens of their rightful place in the sun. This hardly reflects the fact that all except the Native Americans were once immigrants; all sought a better life in the so-called promised land to escape poverty, starvation, persecution, war, and asylum. How quickly our perspectives have narrowed, the subjectivity of our truth that sees criminality in the acts that brought ourselves and our ancestors to this country, how quickly we close the door on those who escaped persecution because they were different only to demand a unitary perspective that would establish a regime from which we and our ancestors escaped.

We need to advocate for diverse perspectives and promote diversity. We need a public policy that captures a humane sense (Fassinger, 2008). However, the importance of attending to diversity brings with it many challenges. Diverse groups who do not make up the majority often experience bias in society and institutions, inequities associated with power, oppression or simply ignorance. Privilege associated with being in the majority, being male, white, or middle class often operates outside conscious awareness. Despite significant gains made in raising awareness of disparities and promoting the importance of attention to diversity, many continue to behave as if we are or should live in a color-blind society, and that issues of race and culture are inconsequential to education, service delivery, workforce environments, management and leadership, and communities. Stereotypes are often perpetuated in the service of knowing diverse racial and ethnic minority groups. The inappropriate use of power serves to oppress; those in power or those who enjoy a privileged existence often fail to recognize the adverse consequences of their behaviors. Social, political and psychological consequences often result from the inattention to diversity; strategies and solutions are needed to eliminate these inequities.

As racial and ethnic minority groups now make up a growing fabric of U.S.-born Americans, a shift in attention to immigration has occurred. This has created a tension within groups as the needs of newcomers or "international students" are viewed as different from the needs of racial and ethnic minority groups who are born in the United States. New issues are also emerging as negative attention to so-called illegal aliens is highlighted despite the fact that they make up a small percentage of those entering the United States. How do we address diversity in this changing environment?

The rise of terrorism in the twenty-first century affects us all; the consequences of trauma are now widespread and on a global scale. Some have argued that diversity and international issues are different. Multiculturalism and diversity have become a priority in the United States because underserved and victimized racial and ethnic minority groups do not have equal access. A shift to internationalism has been criticized for not addressing issues of social justice, inequities of social class, and racial and ethnic discrimination. This volume will look at the trends in today's world and use strength-based models to promote diversity in the twenty-first century.

As we look at cultural diversity in the United States, fusion cuisines and new American cuisine reflect the integration of cultures through its food—something we could not have achieved a decade ago. This is different from earlier restaurant cuisines that emphasized the ethnic authenticity. Now the cultural blend markets something for everyone. Looking at diversity within a global and international perspective is a twenty-first century phenomenon. In prior times, we talked about what the United States has done. Now we must look at how countries around the world are also becoming increasingly diverse with regard to their populations. With advances in travel and communications, countries throughout the world are beginning to see changes in the make-up of their citizens. Moreover, multinational corporations create new cultures in their host countries that could well mirror the colonization of past centuries. Responsible government is needed to ensure that citizens are not exploited as government officials look to accumulate wealth.

The chapters in Volume 3 address social justice as diversity in action. Diversity is not new, but we face new challenges with changing demographics, evolving global economies, and diverse communities, not only here in the United States, but also throughout the world. The chapters address aversive racism, threats to diversity from economic globalization, and legislative and political issues of immigration policies, affirmative action, and health care reform. However, new issues arise such as the rise in trauma and violence, our aging population, and their differential impact on racial and ethnic minorities. Diversity is now more complex than simply looking at our racial and ethnic minority populations. It also includes our attention to interactive variables such as disability, LGTBQ, religious groups, women, and other populations that have been marginalized by our systems.

This conference logo was adopted from a model of instruction developed by Dobbins, Malloy, Thompson, Adams, and Cimbora (2007) with the input of the Aspirations to Actualization Conference committee. It reflects an educational and research approach in which social responsibility is the foundation of diversity competence in professional psychology education.

Now we have new groups also demanding that our government and societal institutions recognize their uniqueness and differences. No longer are we confined to race and ethnicity as dimensions of diversity, but its intersection with other identities that go beyond age, sexual orientation, gender, and ability status. We need to stand ready to face these challenges in the future.

REFERENCES

Dobbins, J. E., Malloy, K., Thompson, V., Adams, D., & Cimbora, D. (2007, August 15). *Aspirations to actualization conference committee kick off.* Paper presented at the NCSPP Summer Meeting, San Francisco.

Fassinger, R. (2008). Workplace diversity and public policy: Challenges and opportunities for psychology. *American Psychologist, 63*(4), 252–268.

CHAPTER 1

Social Justice: Diversity in Action

Marcia Moody, Miguel Ybarra, and Nina Nabors

HISTORICAL OVERVIEW

A review of the social justice movement must consider philosophical, sociopolitical, educational, and psychosocial influences with the understanding that presenting a precise history of the movement is challenging given there is a lack of consensus regarding even the meaning of social justice (Choules, 2007; Furman & Gruenewald, 2004). Philosophers and social scientists focus on themes of justice, equality, liberty, distribution of wealth, and merit (Crosby & Franco, 2003; Toens, 2007; van Gorder, 2007). Educational discourses revolve around organizational structures, policies, and pedagogical strategies that promote critical consciousness and parity in academic achievement (Asher, 2007; Brookfield, 1995; Brown, 2004). Mental health practitioners and scholars have considered social justice implications related to personal and group identities, mental health delivery systems, institutional structures, professional practices, and multiple other areas (Constantine, Hage, Kindaichi, & Bryant, 2007; Cross, 1991; Goodman et al., 2004; Kiselica, 2004). While the diverse influences on social justice have been noted, this treatise will narrow the focus to multicultural education and multicultural counseling recognizing that parallel sociopolitical civil rights movements existed in the United States and elsewhere.

It is often difficult to explain concisely and succinctly what is meant by *multiculturalism*, however David Hoopes (1979) proposes a seminal conceptualization that captures the complexity of multicultural processes. His *Intercultural Learning Process* model delineates internal mechanisms that define and stabilize identity using a developmental framework.

The first stage of the model, *ethnocentrism*, is defined as an intolerance and perhaps aggression toward members of other groups. The second stage, *awareness*, is characterized by an acknowledgement that other cultures exist as well as the awareness of one's own culture as one of many. The third stage, *understanding*, is described as the acquisition of knowledge and information about other cultures on a rational and cognitive level. The fourth stage is *acceptance and respect (tolerance)*; during this phase, "acceptance" refers to the validation of other cultures without comparing or judging them against one's own culture. The fifth stage, *appreciating/valuing*, is expressed as an understanding that all cultures have their own strengths and weaknesses leading to a consideration of cultural norms and traits in terms of one's own identity and values. The last two stages are *selective adoption* that involves adopting new attitudes and behaviors from other cultures and *multiculturalism*, the ideal state of an ongoing process whereby a person is able to feel comfortable in, and communicate effectively with people from, many cultures and in multiple situations. This model illustrates the complexities of becoming multicultural and emphasizes that the development of multicultural attitudes, skills, and behaviors can be a lifelong learning process.

The multicultural movement has its roots in the civil rights movement of the 1950s and 1960s (Abreu, Chung, & Atkinson, 2000; Arredondo & Perez, 2003; Ogbu, 1992; Reid & Kampfe, 2000) and has facilitated social change within many disciplines, including the professions of psychology and education. However, it can reasonably be argued that the issue of coping with a pluralistic society has been historically addressed by those without power in the United States. Accordingly, multiculturalism, a precursor to the social justice movement, has addressed issues of inequity and given voice to those who have been marginalized due to race/ethnicity, class, gender, sexual orientation, age, and other social and/or demographic categories.

A general "awareness" of multiculturalism emerged in the United States in the late 1960s steeped in a consciousness of social and cultural differences. Two educational movements emerged that launched reforms to broaden pedagogical approaches and made them more inclusive: the ethnic studies movement and what was referred to as "multiethnic" education (Sheets, 2003). The first major ethnic studies programs in the country were established at San Francisco State University in 1969. These programs laid the foundation for ethnic studies, women's studies, and other academic programs throughout the United States that still persist today (Kowlski, 2000; Ogbu, 1992; Sheets, 2003).

A key figure in the K-12 reform movement was Paulo Freire (1921–1997), a Brazilian educator whose groundbreaking 1970 book, *The Pedagogy of the Oppressed*, led the way for inclusive, multicultural pedagogy (Brookfield, 1995; van Gorder, 2007). Freire's work was an outgrowth of the *Frankfurt School*, a term that describes social science scholars affiliated with the Institutes for Social Research in post–World War I Germany. Members of the Frankfurt School embraced neo-Marxist philosophy and posited the term "critical theory," which called for radical social change to counter the presumed oppressive and passive nature of traditional scientific and literary approaches (Chen, 2005; Hague, 2007; North, 2006; Sayles-Hannon, 2007).

Freirean pedagogy is referred to as *popular education* in Latin America and is commonly called *critical pedagogy* in the West. The term critical pedagogy was originally coined by Henry Giroux in his1983 publication *Theory and Resistance in Education* (Chen, 2005). Popular education was tied to social change movements that arose from working with disenfranchised groups to challenge the status quo to create a fair and just society. The unique curriculum of this approach is derived from the lived experiences of those involved in social justice movements and focuses on strategies used to combat oppression, linking teaching and learning to activism (Choules, 2007).

The multicultural counseling movement paralleled the multicultural education movement. An impetus for this attention was the predominance of theories developed by and normed on whites as well as clinical samples of people of color resulting in excessive pathologizing of the latter. A concern also existed over mental health practices that were discriminatory and served to further marginalize already disenfranchised groups.

During the civil rights era, psychologists from various cultural and ethic backgrounds advocated for recognition and equal representation within the American Psychological Association (APA) (Abreu et al., 2000). This advocacy for inclusion within the larger professional organization led to the creation of the Association of Black Psychologists, the Association of Psychologist por La Raza, the Asian American Psychological Association, and the Society of Indian Psychologists (Abreu et al., 2000). It was after the establishment of these groups that the APA supported the creation of the Office of Ethnic Minority Affairs in 1979, the Board of Ethnic Minority Affairs in 1981, and the Division of Ethnic Minority Affairs (Division 45) in 1986. The requirement of appropriate education and training in the provision of culturally relevant clinical services has since been codified by the APA and the Council for Accreditation of Counseling and Related Educational Programs (CACREP). Reid and Kampfe (2000) stress that this movement was further refined in the 1980s and 1990s because a broader cross-section of the population participated not only in the development of theory but also in the provision of clinical services (e.g., gays, lesbians, and bisexuals; women).

Recently, greater attention has been devoted to the development of cultural competencies. However, it can be argued that authentic multiculturalism cannot exist without social justice, as discrimination and prejudice are inherently a part of the life-experience for all marginalized groups (Vera & Speight, 2003). Accordingly, of the 31 multicultural counseling competencies that were adopted by the Association of Multicultural Counseling and Development, Arredondo (as cited in Vera & Speight, 2003) identifies seven that focus on issues of social justice. One important aspect that seems to tie these particular competencies together is a need for self-reflection and self-awareness (Constantine, Hage, Kindaichi, & Bryant, 2007; Vera & Speight, 2003).

In addition to the advocacy work done within professional associations, there is a vast body of multicultural literature. Pioneering work in the area of black racial identity emerged in the 1970s paralleling the Black Power Movement. Theorists like William Cross (1971, 1991) investigated the processes for developing affirmative ethnic identities (Chizhik & Chizhik, 2002). While work in this area was originally focused on identity development of people of color, it has since expanded to include whites (Dass-Brailsford, 2007; Helms & Carter, 1991; Helms & Cook, 1999); women (Gilligan, 1982; Moradi, 2005); gays, lesbians, and bisexuals (Cass, 1979; McCarn & Fassinger, 1996; Mosher, 2001; Robertson, 2004); those who have religious/spiritual identities (Faiver, Ingersoll, O'Brien, & McNally, 2001; Richards & Bergin, 2000; Ripley, Jackson, & Tatum, 2007), and members of other social groups. Criticisms of the identity literature include a tendency to generalize simplistic notions of identity reinforcing stereotypes that all members of a particular group are the same, the creation of tensions between separatist and alliance ideologies, and the emphasis on individual development that fails to take into account systemic factors that perpetuate and sustain inequalities (Chicago Cultural Studies Group, 1992; Perrons & Skyers, 2003).

In contrast to much of the identity work that highlights oppressive forces and contact with members of dominant groups, is the literature on white privilege. White privilege is often a difficult topic for people to address as it is possible some individuals may equate the concept of privilege with a politically correct application or with an expectation of guilt that may threaten an already established identity (Branscombe, Schmitt, & Schiffhauer, 2007). McIntosh (1990) discusses the concept of privilege as conferred (unearned) power and dominance. This work has certainly led to an evolution in the meta-cognitive examination of multiculturalism and social justice as evidenced by a growing body of empirical work. For instance, Branscombe et al. reveal that white Americans may respond with an increase in racism not simply when addressing privilege, but when status or position due to that privilege is threatened. However, a more structured and supportive learning process has been shown to increase the likelihood that participants would be willing to take action in addressing racism and white privilege (Kernahan & Davis, 2007; Niehuis, 2005). Another example of the mounting research on white privilege research is a qualitative analysis of white counseling students' written reactions to a list of McIntosh's privileges. Three major themes of awareness are identified: none, demonstrated awareness, and profound awareness accompanied by proactive attempts to eradicate privilege (Ancis & Szymanski, 2001).

While there are numerous multicultural conceptions and applications that have informed the modern day social justice movement, there is no universal shared meaning about what actually constitutes "social justice." However, theoretical frameworks do share common social justice themes of critical reflection, critical consciousness, social change, and social activism. A highlight of these theories is presented in the next section.

SOCIAL JUSTICE THEORIES

Much like multiculturalism and diversity, there are a vast number of social justice conceptualizations. These include philosophical foundations (Vera & Speight, 2003), sociopolitical frameworks (Furman & Gruenewald, 2004; Toens, 2007; Vera & Speight, 2003), and pedagogical theories (Brown, 2004; Furman & Gruenewald, 2004; Weil, 1993) making social justice challenging to define, describe, and operationalize. Social justice principles can be traced back to pioneers such as Marx, who embraced socialism as a socioeconomic system in which goods and services are distributed and shared equally without regard for an individual's class standing. Other pioneers include Locke, who espouses a libertarian justice model that focuses on individual freedoms and outcomes, and Rousseau, who expands on libertarian principles to include governmental policies that protect civil rights (Vera & Speight, 2003).

Examples of sociopolitical frameworks that incorporate social justice themes include Marshall's emphasis on welfare as a social right, a perspective that was popular in Europe and the United States in the post–World War II era as well as three so-called theoretical interventions adopted by Haberman, Honneth, and Fraser that challenge the notion that the government is solely responsible for the welfare of its citizens (Toens, 2007, p. 166). Haberman, like Marshall, endorses the welfare state as long as there are opportunities for public discourse and democratic decision-making. Honneth's critical theory addresses the sociopolitical context that influences discourse, emphasizing power differentials due to "misrecognition" (Toens, 2007, p. 169) defined as disempowerment typically associated with social class and work status, a term more commonly referred to as marginalization, only misrecognition is primarily associated with an individual's social class and employment status. Fraser's model of participatory parity (Toens, 2007) and Young's model of communitarian justice (Vera & Speight, 2003) expand on the concept of misrecognition to include injustices based on other social group memberships (e.g., race/ethnicity, sex/gender roles, and sexual orientation). Honneth, Fraser, and Young all agree that inclusiveness is a critical foundation for promoting social justice (Toens, 2007).

Other sociopolitical social justice frameworks include the *ecofeminism* and *ecojustice* perspectives, which are focused on environmental issues that result in oppressive practices. Ecofeminism investigates the relationship between "ecological exploitation" and "patriarchal, capitalistic societies" (Furman & Gruenewald, 2004, p. 56) whereas ecojustice has a broader focus consisting of four primary educational and political goals:

1. Understanding the relationships between ecological and cultural systems, specifically, between the domination of nature and of oppressed groups;
2. Addressing environmental racism, including the geographical dimension of social justice and environmental pollution;
3. Revitalizing the noncommodified traditions of different racial and ethnic groups and communities, especially those traditions that support ecological sustainability; and
4. Reconceiving and adapting our lifestyles in ways that will not jeopardize the environment for future generations (Furman & Gruenewald, 2004, p. 55).

Nearly all social justice pedagogical theories incorporate the tenets of critical pedagogy that is rooted in the intellectual traditions of Hegel and Marx as well as Freire (Brookfield, 1995). Critical pedagogy actually encompasses multiple paradigms that are derived from analyses of how social statuses (e.g., race/ethnicity, class, and gender) have shaped public policies, particularly educational practices. Common themes of theories derived from critical pedagogy include critical reflection for members of dominant social and economic groups, empowerment of historically disenfranchised groups, dialogues among equals, and social action (Chen, 2005; Choules, 2007; Giroux, 2006). A sampling of pedagogical theories that incorporate social justice themes include *critical multicultural literacy, critical humanism, critical pedagogy of place,* and Brown's (2004) t*ripartite theoretical framework.*

Critical Multicultural Literacy has three primary goals aimed at developing critical consciousness: (a) increased awareness that facilitates higher-level thinking about multicultural issues; (b) personal connections that foster dialogues about the lived experiences of students with particular emphasis on those who have been disenfranchised; and (c) active learning that includes advocacy work geared towards combating oppression (Weil, 1993). Critical humanist perspectives incorporate constructivist principles that emphasize how individuals process information by making their own meanings based on prior knowledge and previous experiences. Constructivism also highlights the role of sociocultural, economic, and political forces in shaping the generation and consumption of knowledge. Critical humanism stresses that social structures are inherently value-laden and reflect inequities that are embedded in society. Learners are therefore prompted to become social change agents to help overcome these inequities (Furman & Gruenewald, 2004).

Critical pedagogy of place is an outgrowth of the ecojustice perspective that incorporates socioecological justice in response to environments that have been contaminated or abused through human actions (or inactions). The goals of this perspective include the concepts of *decolonization* and *ecological reinhabitation*. Berg and Dasmann (cited in Furman & Gruenewald, 2004) define reinhabitation as "learning to live-in-place in an area that has been disrupted and injured through past exploitation" (p. 58). bell hooks (as cited in Furman & Gruenewald, 2004) defines decolonization as a "process of cultural and historical liberation; an act of confrontation with a dominant system of thought" (p. 58). These two goals are designed to provide support and empowerment to those who have been victimized by environmental problems caused by colonization and practices that caused psychological and/or physical harm to community members. Examples include individuals who have contracted chronic illnesses or incurred injuries because of environmental contaminants and those who have been displaced due to adverse environmental conditions resulting in loss of property and land, languages, community ties, and sustainable relationships with community surroundings (Furman & Gruenewald, 2004, p. 56).

The tripartite theoretical framework proposed by Brown (2004) draws from adult learning, transformative learning, and critical social theory. Adult learning theory, referred to as "andragogy," was a term used by Malcolm Knowles, who published a seminal book in 1970 entitled *The Modern Practice of Adult Education: Andragogy Versus Pedagogy*. Knowles published another work in 1980, called *The Modern Practice of Adult Education*, which contrasts the learning assumptions of pedagogy, characterized as subject-centered pedagogy, with those of andragogy, characterized as learner-centered instructional practices. Hallmarks of andragogy are basic assumptions regarding adult learners, such as adults are self-aware and self-directed, adults' life and work experiences inform the learning process, adults are intrinsically motivated to learn, and adults prefer experiential and applied learning (Brown, 2004; Forrest & Peterson, 2006). Mezirow's theory of transformative learning seeks to shape learners' worldviews through processes of critical reflection and rational discourse. Mezirow proposes ideal conditions for rational discourse that include the need to "have accurate and complete information, be free from coercion and distorting self-conception . . . be open to alternative perspectives . . . and have equal opportunity to participate" (Brown, 2004, p. 85). Critical theory (previously described in this chapter) emphasizes social transformation and calls for educators to serve as social change agents.

Most theories of social justice fall into two categories. The first group consists of "scientific" theories that are subject to rules of evidence as articulated by Popper, who was concerned with testing predictions to either affirm or falsify them. The second category of theories are those that are practical and action oriented (i.e., theories that provide guidance and directives for combating injustices). Caputo (2007) further refines this dichotomous categorization of social justice theories by describing three types: (a) *positive social theories* that follow the tradition of the natural sciences and are verifiable through hypothesis testing procedures; (b) *interpretive social theories* that emphasize anthropological perspectives of culture using standard scientific approaches that incorporate the interpretive and allegedly "value free" nature of social analyses; and (c) *evaluative social theories* that reject the assumptions of positivist "objectivity" and interpretive "value neutrality" and instead are based on philosophical or moral principles.

All categories of social justice theories have both strengths and weaknesses. Positive social theories have been criticized for their lack of social utility, relevance, and ability to provide concrete solutions to solve societal problems, but are considered "legitimate" (at least in academic circles) because of the empirical support that validates their authenticity and allows for generalizable applications. Interpretive approaches are challenged by the notion that they represent value neutral concepts and practices when, in fact, no scholarly endeavors are completely value free given the social hierarchies and residual influences of oppression that are still a part of the academy. Yet interpretive theories offer scientifically validated models and practices that are informed by cultural perspectives and principles as well as practices that address inequities. Evaluative social theories are sometimes prematurely embraced without regard for empirical validation or generalizability, yet they allow for the voices of those who have historically been disenfranchised to be heard.

Given these strengths and limitations, many scholars have endorsed eclectic or integrative approaches for generating theories. One example is Unger's conceptualization of a social justice "super theory," which is a combination of multiple theories and practical applications that are informed by historical occurrences and institutional norms that could possibly limit progressive social and political action (Caputo, 2007). Another example is the merging of micro-level analyses dedicated to investigating and interpreting individual decision making (without regard for contextual variables) and macro theories that are derived from systemic and institutional analyses (Mouzelis as cited in Caputo, 2007). The micro/macro integration represents a comprehensive approach to theory building that incorporates economic, political, educational, and relational factors as well as individual and institutional values (Caputo, 2007). Both Unger and Mouzelis retain the scientific validity of positive and interpretive theories while also taking the philosophical influences of evaluative theories into consideration. They also believe that social justice theories should make a difference in the lives of people by providing concepts and strategies for promoting positive social change.

While many philosophies and paradigms derived from social justice principles are conceptual, there is a growing body of empirical evidence that validates social justice ideologies and frameworks. The next section presents a sampling of this evidence, highlighting recent social justice research.

SOCIAL JUSTICE AND RESEARCH

The literature is replete with theoretical discussions of social justice and social change. Few empirical studies, however, address the impact or the application of social justice with regard to various aspects of society.

Empirical evidence of the impact of social justice is primarily concentrated in the educational arena. Several studies of children show that engaged learning is positively correlated with feelings of belonging and being able to relate to curriculum and pedagogical strategies that reflect their lived experiences (Shields, 2004). Efforts to transform education with respect to social justice have also been demonstrated with high-school students (Cammarota, 2007; Kraft, 2007). Cammarota integrates a social justice education project into the curriculum of "at risk" Latino high-school students. The project taught the students about various aspects of social justice specifically related to their own futures, including a focus on personal history, oppression, and critical thinking about their lives and the lives of people in their communities. At the end of the two-year project, Cammarota reports that the students who participated in the social justice education project had significantly lower drop-out rates, higher graduation rates and were more likely to pass advanced classes in high school. As a pilot project, Cammarota illustrates the impact of socially relevant education on student success.

Using ethnography, Kraft (2007) examines the impact of a model for teaching social justice on high-school students at two public schools. The teaching social justice model comprises three main components. The first component involves integrating social justice issues throughout the school curriculum (history, English, science) and places emphasis on race, social class, gender, and other areas of oppression. The second component involved utilizing socially relevant teaching practices, including an inclusive curriculum with diverse assignments (essays, personal reflections, art, and other creative projects). The third component was the most important piece, creating a socially just community. The schools created a culture of respect, honesty, and value for others that students were then encouraged to adopt and practice, both during school hours and in their personal lives. Kraft discovered that the model led to an increase in interest, knowledge, and participation in social justice activities and illustrated a method for creating social change agents.

Transformational education through social justice teaching is also an important focus within higher education. Researchers report that positive attitudes towards social justice have increased in college students in recent years (Anderson & Bryjak, 1989). Several researchers have developed curriculum to educate college learners about the need for social justice

(Enns & Sinacore, 2005) and these efforts have raised the social awareness of students, according to researchers (Gazel, 2007; Van Voorhis &
Hostetter, 2006). Nilsson and Schmidt (2005) examine the impact of several variables, including social concern, worldview, political interest,
and problem solving on social justice advocacy for counseling graduate
students. The desire to engage in social advocacy and political interest
were much more likely to lead to social justice activism. Broido's phenomenological study (Edwards, 2006) finds that variables related to having
precollege egalitarian values and participating in activities that presented
opportunities to serve as advocates are associated with college students'
identity development as social justice allies.

In addition to the educational arena, researchers have assessed the specific impact of social justice through the "belief in a just world phenomenon" such that good and bad things happen to people based on their
deservedness (Aguiar, Vala, & Correia, 2008; Alves & Correia, 2008; Edlund, Sagarin, & Johnson, 2007; Van Voorhis & Hostetter, 2006). Alves and
Correia (2008) demonstrated that the stronger the belief in a just world,
the better one's social standing, which implies that belief in a just world is
a socially-desirable characteristic. Aguiar et al. (2008) assesses the strength
of the "Belief in the Just World" phenomenon using scenarios of victimization of individuals who belong either to the perceived in-group or the
perceived out-group. The researchers reveal that the participants struggle
more with the belief in a just world when the victim belongs to the in-
group. Edlund et al. (2007) evaluate the relationship between the belief
in a just world phenomenon and reciprocity, and report that participants
with a stronger belief in a just world feel more obligated to reciprocate
good deeds than those with weaker beliefs. These studies illustrate the
complexity of empirically demonstrating social justice theories. While the
majority of studies focus on the impact of social justice in the education
arena, efforts are currently underway that illustrate the impact of social
justice theories on social change.

SOCIAL JUSTICE AND SOCIAL CHANGE: TAKING ACTION

Terms like *diversity* and *multicultural* have been difficult to define
given the various educational, vocational, social, political, legal, and
global environments in which they are employed. Similarly, *social justice* has multiple definitions that vary depending on the context. Young,
cited in Speight and Vera (2004), defines social justice as "the elimination
of institutional domination and oppression" (p. 111). Other definitions
include the themes of "full and equal participation of all groups in a
society" (Bell as cited in Speight & Vera, 2004, p. 259), "a fundamental valuing of fairness and equity in resources, rights, and treatment for
marginalized individuals and groups of people who do not share equal

power in society" (Constantine, Hage, Kindaichi, & Bryant, 2007, p. 24), and "an ideal condition in which members of society have the same basic rights, protections, opportunities, obligations, and social benefits" (Barker as cited in Banerjee, 2005, p. 451).

While there is clearly a consensus amongst those who offer definitions of social justice that the aspirational goal is to give equal opportunities to all people, regardless of racial, class, sex, or ability, rarely do definitions of social justice offer strategies for accomplishing this monumental task. Moreover, no evidence exists in the history of humanity that *any* society was *ever* successful in establishing equitable treatment and distribution of resources to *all* of its citizens (and noncitizens). Further, it is unclear whether most modern nation-states would thrive if resources were literally distributed equitably across all groups.

While some would argue that the problem lies in certain economic systems and therefore dismantling the infrastructures that maintain unjust practices is the solution, this stance will not be debated here as it falls beyond the scope of this chapter to consider the "ideal" political and economic systems to support social justice tenets. Instead, strategies for working and improving extant systems will be explored.

When reviewing social justice definitions and theories, the major problems of these conceptualizations include: (a) vague and broad terminology that refers to the liberation of *all* people, which is unrealistic and daunting; (b) failure to adequately delineate concrete strategies for including members of disenfranchised groups in classroom dialogues, public policy forums, sustainability initiatives, political processes, and cross-cultural platforms; (c) politicized and narrow conceptualizations of social justice interventions that result in polarization and marginalization of those who do not endorse U.S. political views; and (d) U.S.-centric notions about what the core social justice issues are resulting in a lack of global generalizability.

Strategies for responding to these challenges consist of:

1. Adaptation of more precise terminology to discuss social justice conceptualizations and advocacy strategies;
2. Strategic institutional planning (e.g., educational institutions, businesses, political entities, nonprofit organizations, community-based organizations, religious/spiritual communities, etc.) at the local, state, and national levels that includes realistic and measureable outcomes designed to address social, political, and economic injustices;
3. Intentional outreach for social justice advocacy work that is organized and facilitated by members of disenfranchised groups and culturally competent parties;
4. Establishment of interdisciplinary coalitions that include members of dominant groups as well as those who have historically been marginalized with both parties sharing common visions and strategies for combating injustices at the local, state, national, and international levels;

5. National and international summits linked with local efforts to generate fiscal and human resources that facilitate the creation of infrastructures (within the interdisciplinary coalitions previously described) dedicated to social justice theory, research, training, and applied practice;

6. Adaption of theory, research, and practice (generated through interdisciplinary and collaborative coalition building that includes members of disenfranchised groups) as a part of educational and training programs in K-12, postsecondary, vocational education, nonprofit, industrial, community-based, religious/spiritual, and other settings; and

7. Creation of political coalitions, political action committees, and international organizations (that cross party lines) to engage in advocacy work in local, state, and national legislative arenas.

Many current initiatives and trends reflect the aforementioned strategies, especially in terms of education and training. Vera and Speight (2003) make a distinction between *mandatory ethics,* "actions taken to avoid breaking the rules" and *aspirational ethics,* "actions taken toward attaining the highest possible standard" (p. 257). They caution mental health professionals to move away from interventions that fall into the category of mandatory ethics (e.g., remedial therapeutic approaches and the delineation of multicultural counseling competencies that offer few strategies for operationalizing social justice) toward initiatives that are more consistent with aspirational ethics, such as training programs that require community outreach, preventative mental health services, and advocacy work.

Educators like Brookfield (1995) and Shields (2004) discuss *pathologies of silence* that are described as "misguided attempts to act justly, to display empathy, and to create democratic and optimistic educational communities" (Shields, 2004, p. 117). The misguided attempts revolve around treating differences as deficits; that is, blaming the lived experiences of disadvantaged children, young people, and adults rather than recognizing the institutional structures and barriers that inhibit student learning.

Furman and Gruenewald (2004) propose a socioecological perspective and a critical pedagogy of place that challenges the assumptions of traditional education rooted in Western traditions that overemphasize school underachievement as an indicator of social injustice, individual accomplishments, competitive processes, and technological advancements as barometers of success and progress. In contrast to these traditions, the socioecological approach is based on: (a) an inclusive application of diversity initiatives that emphasizes the interdependence of humankind; (b) an understanding of the linkages between the environment and the domination and exploitation of people; (c) active approaches to sustainability at local and global levels; and (d) the willingness to challenge Western values and norms, especially the assumption that there is a direct relationship between technological literacy and progress.

Blustein, McWhirter, and Perry (2005) use the emancipatory communitarian (EC) framework for psychology practice postulated by Prilleltensky to make practices in vocational psychology more consistent with social justice tenets. The EC approach espouses interventions at both individual and systemic levels in recognition of the need to go beyond traditional mental health services and advocate for social change through the empowerment of individuals and groups. Blustein et al. make specific recommendations to help transform vocational psychology that include:

Recommendation 1: Strive to incorporate democratic participation among stakeholders and participants throughout research and delivery of interventions.

Recommendation 2: Strive to engage in the process of research and practice that starts from the bottom and is simultaneously worked down from the top (e.g., grassroots level social action groups, participatory-action research, and consciousness-raising).

Recommendation 3: Strive to instill a critical consciousness; not just among the powerless, but also among the powerful and privileged.

Recommendation 4: Incorporate social advocacy and activism into our notions of research and practice. (Blustein et al., 2005, pp. 164–168)

Nancy Fraser's model of status recognition (Perrons & Skyers, 2003) is derived from analyses of relationships between economic systems and cultural injustice. She critiques redistribution programs that stigmatize recipients and inadvertently reinforce notions of inferiority based on social statuses like race and class without regard for the processes that originally created the inequities. One remedy to this dilemma is to include those who have historically been excluded as part of political discourse. In order to avoid marginalization, all parties involved in these political discourses should have equal social standing by ensuring that everyone has information as well as the power to exercise influence in their communities. That is, those who have been disenfranchised must be in a position to take ownership of political and economic processes. They must also have power and authority to influence resource allocation.

While there are similarities and differences between these models, the goal of each is to demonstrate the manner in which social justice is conceptualized and implemented in society. Which model would be most likely to succeed has yet to be empirically determined.

FUTURE DIRECTIONS

Much progress has been made in the social justice arena since the civil rights movements of the 1960s, laying a solid foundation for continued progress in the United States and elsewhere. For instance, formal degree courses are offered in social justice studies at institutions like Brock University and the University of Windsor in Ontario, Canada. U.S. institutions such as Georgetown University in Washington, D.C., and Loyola College in Maryland have centers for social justice research, teaching, and service; and this is just a small sampling of postsecondary opportunities for earning degrees in social justice throughout the world.

Social justice models and research are increasingly becoming more action oriented in response to the call to connect scholarship with advocacy work. Community organizations, and religious and spiritual bodies like the Bahá'í Faith and Unitarian Universalism embrace unity themes that promote social action as an outgrowth of faith and commitment.

Despite the progress that has been made, areas for growth still exist, especially in terms of consolidating and expanding paradigms and movements so that there is increased conceptual continuity and shared power. As we continue to develop models, theories, and practices that are solidified by well-designed studies, we must ask the following questions to inform our work:

1. How have my own cultural lenses biased my thoughts and actions and, as a result, limited the generalizability of this approach to social justice?
2. Who are the key "players" of this project and if it is a relatively homogenous group consisting primarily of academics and practitioners, how can others from diverse social groups be included?
3. What actions will result from this project and what are the measureable short- and long-term outcomes that will demonstrate that progress has been made?
4. How does this conceptualization, research, and/or project fit in with extant literature and social justice work at local, state, national, and international levels?
5. How is this work going to be documented, written, and disseminated to ensure that it makes a difference in the lives of multiple constituents, especially those who are outside of the academy and communities of practice?
6. How can this conceptualization, study, and/or advocacy work be adapted for use in public policy and community development work?
7. What changes in the system that supported this work are implicated in the theories, models, and applications of this project? What are the next steps to advocate for these proposed changes?
8. Where are the potential funders and other empowered stakeholders who can help advance the social justice agenda that is articulated in this project? What plans are in place to solicit their assistance?
9. Who are the people who can carry on the legacy of this project? What steps have been taken to develop individuals and groups that are the benefactors of this initiative to take ownership and continue the work?

Many barriers are in place to prevent us from responding to these questions, including a Western bias (for those of us in the West). One challenge to this bias is the recognition that we cannot make significant progress as individuals and instead need to connect with others, including those who have been disenfranchised and those who are in power to effect social change. Another obstacle is the assumption that a "one size fits all approach" is the answer. One theory or program cannot possibly solve the problems of people worldwide. In fact, a collection of work from one country will not suffice. As proposed by Unger (Caputo, 2007), so-called super theories that are derived from integrated theoretical and applied approaches are needed. Even these super theories will need to be adaptive so that they translate to diverse stakeholders who are often constrained by institutional, political, economic, and social barriers. In addition, concepts from multicultural pedagogy, including developmental instructional approaches, can be adapted to inform teaching and training efforts outside of educational settings (Edwards, 2006; Hoopes, 1979).

Another barrier is the nature of many social justice movements worldwide that pit those in power against those who have historically been disempowered; when in many instances, the former are the very people in positions to support advocacy initiatives. Strategies that have been recommended in this chapter to include those who have historically been marginalized can also be used to reach out to those in power, including liberal, moderate, and conservative politicians; business leaders, top administrators in K-12 as well as postsecondary institutions; and others who are able to facilitate individual and institutional changes to further social justice agendas.

In conclusion, consistent with the suggestions offered in this chapter about drafting realistic and measureable outcomes, here are a few tangible goals that could be included as action items for social justice agendas:

1. Editors of professional publications could encourage and, in some instances, mandate that theorists, researchers, and practitioners include social justice applications as part of findings and/or recommendations (Gainor, 2005). One concrete method for attaining this is the addition of psychopolitical *validity* espoused by Prilleltensky as a criterion for evaluating research and practice in training programs. Psychopolitical validity assesses the extent to which studies and interventions have a positive impact on the social conditions of those who have been disadvantaged (Blustein et al., 2005).
2. Social justice work such as teaching, service, and research could be part of the criteria for reappointment, promotion, tenure decisions, and accreditation standards in postsecondary institutions, especially at colleges and universities that have social justice values and missions (Gainor, 2005; Palmer, 2004).
3. Establish interdisciplinary relationships for the purposes of theory building, research productivity, and coalition building for all foundations to social justice advocacy work (Borgen, 2005; Palmer, 2004).
4. Connect outcomes (based on research) to social justice initiatives to demonstrate the efficacy of the interventions and solutions your proposal/project offers when soliciting fiscal and human resources.
5. Actively participate in professional associations; local, state, national, and international organizations; community groups; religious/spiritual communities; and other entities that can effect social change with goals of supporting existing social justice initiatives and helping to launch new ones.

REFERENCES

Abreu, J. M., Chung, R. H. G., & Atkinson, D. R. (2000). Multicultural counseling training: Past, present, and future directions. *The Counseling Psychologist, 28*, 641–656.

Aguiar, P., Vala, J., & Correia, I. (2008). Justice in our world and in that of others: Belief in a just world and reactions to victims. *Social Justice Research, 21*, 50–68.

Alves, H., & Correia, I. (2008). On the normativity of expressing the belief in a just world: Empirical evidence. *Social Justice Research, 21*, 106–118.

Ancis, J. R., & Szymanski, D. M. (2001). Awareness of White privilege among counseling trainees. *The Counseling Psychologist, 29*, 548–569.

Anderson, J. B., & Bryjak, G. J. (1989). Out of the tower and into the street: University students and social justice issues. *Educational Research Quarterly, 13*, 47–56.

Arredondo, P., & Perez, P. (2003). Expanding multicultural competence through social justice leadership. *The Counseling Psychologist, 31*, 282–289.

Asher, N. (2007). Made in the (multicultural) USA: Unpacking tensions of race, culture, gender, and sexuality in education. *Educational Researcher, 36*, 65–73.

Banerjee, M. M. (2005). Applying Rawlsian social justice to welfare reform: An unexpected finding for social work. *Journal of Sociology and Social Welfare, 32*, 35–57.

Blustein, D. L., McWhirter, E. H., & Perry, J. C. (2005). An emancipatory communitarian approach to vocational development theory, research, and practice. *The Counseling Psychologist, 33*, 141–179.

Borgen, F. H. (2005). Advancing social justice in vocational theory, research, and practice. *The Counseling Psychologist, 33*, 197–206.

Branscombe, N. R., Schmitt, M. T., & Schiffhauer, K. (2007). Racial attitudes in response to thoughts of white privilege. *European Journal of Social Psychology, 37*, 203–215.

Brookfield, S. D. (1995). *Becoming a critically reflective teacher*. San Francisco: Jossey-Bass.

Brown, K. M. (2004). Leadership for social justice and equity: Weaving a transformative framework and pedagogy. *Educational Administration Quarterly, 40*, 77–108.

Cammarota, J. (2007). A social justice approach to achievement: Guiding Latina/o students toward educational attainment with a challenging, socially relevant curriculum. *Equity & Excellence in Education, 40*, 87–96.

Caputo, R. K. (2007). Social theory and its relation to social problems: An essay about theory and research with social justice in mind. *Journal of Sociological & Social Welfare, 34*, 43–61.

Cass, V. C. (1979). Homosexuality identity formation: A theoretical model. *Journal of Homosexuality, 4*, 218–235.

Chen, H. (2005). The rationale for critical pedagogy in facilitating cultural identity development. *Curriculum and Teaching Dialogue, 11*–22.

Chicago Cultural Studies Group. (1992). Critical multiculturalism. *Critical Inquiry, 18*, 530–555.

Chizhik, E. W., & Chizhik, A. W. (2002). A path to social change: Examining students' responsibility, opportunity, and emotion toward social justice. *Education and Urban Society, 34,* 283–297.

Choules, K. (2007). Social change education: Content matters. *Adult Education Quarterly, 57,* 159–176.

Constantine, M. G., Hage, S. M., Kindaichi, M. M., & Bryant, R. M. (2007). Social justice and multicultural issues: Implications for the practice and training of counselors and counseling psychologists. *Journal of Counseling and Development, 85,* 24–29.

Crosby, F. J., & Franco, J. L. (2003). Connections between the ivory tower and the multicolored world: Linking abstract theories of social justice to the rough and tumble of affirmative action. *Personality and Social Psychology Review, 7,* 362–373.

Cross, W. E., Jr. (1971). The negro-to-black conversion experience: Toward a psychology of Black liberation. *Black World, 20,* 13–27.

Cross, W. E., Jr. (1991). *Shades of black: Diversity in African American identity.* Philadelphia, PA: Temple University Press.

Dass-Brailsford, P. (2007). Racial identity change among White graduate students. *Journal of Transformative Education, 5,* 59–78.

Edlund, J. E., Sagarin, B. J., & Johnson, B. S. (2007). Reciprocity and the belief in a just world. *Personality and Individual Differences, 43,* 589–596.

Edwards, K. E. (2006). Aspiring social justice ally identity development: A conceptual model. *NASPA Journal, 43,* 39–60.

Enns, C. Z., & Sinacore, A. L. (2005). *Teaching and social justice: Integrating multicultural and feminist theories in the classroom.* Washington DC: American Psychological Association.

Faiver, C., Ingersoll, R. E., O'Brien, E., & McNally, C. (2001). *Explorations in counseling and spirituality.* Belmont, CA: Brooks/Cole.

Forrest III, S. P., & Peterson, T. O. (2006). It's called andragogy. *Academy of Management Learning & Education, 5,* 113–122.

Furman, G. C., & Gruenewald, D. A. (2004). Expanding the landscape of social justice: A critical ecological analysis. *Educational Administration Quarterly, 40,* 47–76.

Gainor, K. A. (2005). Social justice: The moral imperative of vocational psychology. *The Counseling Psychologist, 33,* 180–188.

Gazel, J. (2007). Walking the talk: Multiracial discourses, realities, and pedagogy. *American Behavioral Scientist, 51,* 532–550.

Gilligan, C. (1982). *In a different voice: Psychological theory and women's development.* Cambridge, MA: Harvard University Press.

Giroux, H. A. (2006). Academic freedom under fire: The case for critical pedagogy. *College Literature, 33,* 1042.

Goodman, L. A., Liang, B., Helms, J. E., Latta, R. E., Sparks, E., & Weintraub, S. R. (2004). Training counseling psychologists as social justice agents: Feminist and multicultural principles in action. *The Counseling Psychologist, 32,* 793–837.

Hague, E. (2007). Critical pedagogy in English for academic purposes and the possibility for "tactics" of resistance. *Pedagogy, Culture, and Society, 15,* 83–106.

Helms, J. E., & Carter, R. T. (1991). Relationships of White and Black racial identity attitudes and demographic similarity to counseling preferences. *Journal of Counseling Psychology, 38,* 446–457.

Helms, J. E., & Cook, D. A. (1999). *Using race and culture in counseling and psychotherapy.* Needham Heights, MA: Allyn & Bacon.

Hoopes, D. S. (1979). Intercultural communication concepts and the psychology of intercultural experience. In M. D. Pusch (Ed.), *Multicultural education: A cross cultural training approach.* LaGrange Park: IL: Intercultural Network.

Kernahan, C., & Davis, T. (2007). Changing perspective: How learning about racism influences student awareness and emotion. *Teaching of Psychology, 34,* 49–52.

Kiselica, M. S. (2004). When duty calls: The implications of social justice work for policy, education, and practice in the mental health professions. *The Counseling Psychologist, 32,* 838–854.

Kowlaski, R. M. (2000). Including gender, race, and ethnicity in psychology content courses. *Teaching of Psychology, 27*(1), 18–24.

Kraft, M. (2007). Toward a school-wide model of teaching for social justice: An examination of the best practices of two small public schools. *Equity & Excellence in Education, 40,* 77–86.

McCarn, S. R., & Fassinger, R. E. (1996). Revisioning sexual minority identity formation: A new model of lesbian identity and its implications. *The Counseling Psychologist, 24,* 508–534.

McIntosh, P. (1990). White privilege: Unpacking the invisible knapsack. *Independent School, 49,* 31–36.

Moradi, B. (2005). Advancing womanist identity development: Where we are and where we need to go. *The Counseling Psychologist, 33,* 225–253.

Mosher, C. M. (2001). The social implications of sexual identity formation and the coming out process: A review of the theoretical and empirical literature. *The Family Journal, 9,* 164–172.

Niehuis, S. (2005). Helping white students explore white privilege outside the classroom. *North American Journal of Psychology, 7,* 481–492.

Nilsson, J. E., & Schmidt, C. K. (2005). Social justice advocacy among graduate students in counseling: An initial exploration. *Journal of College Student Development, 46,* 267–279.

North, C. E. (2006). More than words? Delving into the substantive meaning(s) of "social justice" in education. *Review of Educational Research, 76,* 507–535.

Ogbu, J. U. (1992). Understanding cultural diversity and learning. *Educational Researcher, 21,* 5–14.

Palmer, L. K. (2004). The call to social justice: A multidiscipline agenda. *The Counseling Psychologist, 32,* 879–885.

Perrons, D., & Skyers, S. (2003). Empowerment through participation? Conceptual explorations and a case study. *International Journal of Urban and Regional Research, 27,* 265–285.

Reid, C., & Kampfe, C. (2000). Multicultural issues. In A. Sales (Ed.), *Substance abuse and counseling* (pp. 2–20), Greensboro, NC: ERIC Counseling and Student Services.

Richards, P. S., & Bergin, A. E. (2000). *Handbook of psychotherapy and religious diversity.* Washington, DC: American Psychological Association.

Ripley, J. S., Jackson, L. D., & Tatum, R. L. (2007). A development model of supervisee religious and spiritual development. *Journal of Psychology and Christianity, 26,* 296–306.

Robertson, P. K. (2004). The historical effects of depathologizing homosexuality on the practice of counseling. *The Family Journal, 12,* 163–169.

Sayles-Hannon, S. J. (2007). Feminist and liberatory pedagogies: Journey toward synthesis. *The International Journal of Diversity in Organisations, Communities, and Nations, 7,* 33–42.

Sheets, R. H. (2003). Competency vs. good intensions: diversity ideologies and teacher potential. *Qualitative Studies in Education, 16,* 111–120.

Shields, C. M. (2004). Dialogic leadership for social justice: Overcoming pathologies of silence. *Educational Administration Quarterly, 40,* 109–132.

Speight, S. L., & Vera, E. M. (2004). A social justice agenda: Ready, or not? *The Counseling Psychologist, 32,* 109–118.

Toens, K. (2007). The dilemma of regress: Social justice and democracy in recent critical theory. *European Journal of Political Theory, 6,* 160–179.

van Gorder, A. C. (2007). Pedagogy for the children of the oppressors: Liberative education for social justice among the world's privileged. *Journal of Transformative Education, 5,* 8–32.

Van Voorhis, R. M., & Hostetter, C. (2006). The impact of MSW education on social worker empowerment and commitment to client empowerment through social justice advocacy. *Journal of Social Work Education, 42,* 105–121.

Vera, E. M., & Speight, S. L. (2003). Multicultural competence, social justice, and counseling psychology: Expanding our roles. *The Counseling Psychologist, 31,* 253–272.

Weil, D. (1993). Towards a critical multicultural literacy: Advancing an education for liberation. *Roeper Review, 15,* 211–218.

CHAPTER 2

Aversive Racism—How Unconscious Bias Influences Behavior: Implications for Legal, Employment, and Health Care Contexts

John F. Dovidio, Samuel L. Gaertner, Louis A. Penner, Adam R. Pearson, and Wynne E. Norton

Over 100 years ago, in his classic book *The Souls of Black Folk*, W.E.B. DuBois (1903/1986) observed: "The problem of the twentieth century is the problem of the color line" (p. 372). On the one hand, consistent declines in the overt expression of racial prejudice among whites and increasing endorsement of egalitarianism as a central cultural value (Bobo, 2001) seem to challenge the validity of DuBois's proposition. Indeed, the nomination of Barack Obama for president of the United States by a major political party and his eventual election victory are landmark events that shatter a major historical racial barrier. On the other hand, significant and pervasive economic and social disparities between blacks and whites in the United States make DuBois's observation prophetic.

In this chapter, we explore the current status and psychological nature of racial bias in the United States. We propose that current racial attitudes of whites toward blacks in the United States are fundamentally ambivalent, characterized by a widespread contemporary form of bias associated with aversive racism, and we consider its influence on the behavior of whites toward blacks. The central question we address is, how can well-intentioned people inadvertently and subtly discriminate to contribute to racial disparities? We hypothesize that the ambivalence reflected in aversive racism can offer broader insights for understanding racial disparities, bias in interracial interactions, and ultimately race relations.

In this chapter, we mainly focus on white-black relations in the United States. We recognize that other forms of intergroup relations, both within the United States and internationally, merit theoretical and empirical attention, particularly when considering the changing demographics in the United States and trends in international immigration. In addition, within white-black relations, our emphasis is on the impact of whites' attitudes on race relations. We acknowledge that the attitudes of blacks are also important, but because whites have the major share of resources and social power in U.S. society, their attitudes are particularly influential for causing, and potentially ameliorating, racial disparities. In this chapter, we first discuss the existence of a contemporary form of racial attitudes and aversive racism among whites. We then explain how aversive racism is manifested in subtle forms of discrimination that can have significant consequences for outcomes for blacks, as well as for the dynamics of inter-racial interactions. After that, we explore the implications of aversive racism for understanding racial disparities in legal, employment, and health care contexts. We conclude by reviewing ways of combating the subtle bias associated with aversive racism.

THE NATURE OF AVERSIVE RACISM

Research from the 1920s through the 1950s typically portrayed prejudice as psychopathology (Dovidio, 2001). However, stimulated by develop-ments in the area of social cognition, by the mid 1960s and early 1970s, much more emphasis was devoted to recognizing how *normal* cognitive (e.g., social categorization), motivational (e.g., needs for status), and socio-cultural (e.g., social transmission of stereotypes) processes contribute to the development of whites' biases toward blacks (see Dovidio, 2001; Dovidio & Gaertner, 2004). For instance, people automatically distinguish others on the basis of race, and this social categorization spontaneously activates more positive feelings and beliefs about in-group members ("we's") than out-group members ("they's") (see Gaertner & Dovidio, 2000, for a review). In addition, whites automatically activate stereotypes of whites as intelli-gent, successful, and educated, and of blacks as aggressive, impulsive, and lazy (Blair, 2001). Intergroup processes, such as system-justifying ideolo-gies as well as perceived competition over material resources, can also form a basis for negative racial attitudes (see Sidanius & Pratto, 1999).

Kovel (1970) distinguishes between dominative racism, which is the old-fashioned, blatant form, and aversive racism. Aversive racism reflects a fundamental conflict between whites' denial of personal prejudice and the negative feelings toward and beliefs about blacks, which may be unconscious, that result in the normal psychological processes that pro-mote racial bias (Gaertner & Dovidio, 1986). Because of current cultural values in the United States, most whites have strong convictions concern-ing fairness, justice, and racial equality. Overt expressions of prejudice in the United States have declined significantly over the past 40 years. As Bobo (2001) concludes in his review of trends in racial attitudes, "the single clearest trend in studies of racial attitudes has involved a steady and sweeping movement toward general endorsement of the principles of racial equality and integration" (p. 269). However, because of the range of normal psychological processes that promote intergroup biases, most whites also develop unconscious negative beliefs and attitudes about blacks, as well as negative feelings. However, the negative feelings that aversive racists have toward blacks do not reflect open hostility or hatred. Instead, the reactions of aversive racists may involve discomfort, anxiety, or fear. That is, they find blacks "aversive," while at the same time they find any suggestion that they might be prejudiced "aversive" as well.

Aversive racists are presumed to have egalitarian conscious, or explicit, attitudes but negative unconscious, or implicit, racial attitudes (Dovidio & Gaertner, 2004). Explicit attitudes operate in a conscious mode and are exemplified by traditional, self-report measures. Implicit attitudes, in contrast, are evaluations and beliefs that are automatically activated by the mere presence (actual or symbolic) of the attitude object. They commonly function in an unconscious fashion. Implicit attitudes and stereotypes are typically assessed using response latency procedures, memory tasks, physiological measures (e.g., galvanic skin response), and indirect self-report measures (e.g., involving attributional biases). The Implicit Association Test (IAT; Greenwald, McGhee, & Schwartz, 1998), for example, taps the different stereotypic or evaluative (e.g., good-bad) associations that people have with racial groups (but of which they may be unaware) on the basis of the general finding that people make decisions about pairs of stimuli that are similar in valence faster than they make decisions about pairs that differ in valence.

Techniques for assessing implicit attitudes are particularly useful for distinguishing between aversive racists, who endorse egalitarian views and nonprejudiced ideologies but harbor implicit racial biases, and nonprejudiced people, who also endorse egalitarian values but do not have significant implicit prejudice or stereotypes. Consistent with the aversive racism framework, for example, the majority of whites in the United States appear nonprejudiced on self-report (explicit) measures of prejudice, whereas a very large proportion of whites also demonstrate implicit racial biases. Overall, whites' generally negative implicit attitudes are largely dissociated from their typically more positive overt expressions of their attitudes toward blacks (Dovidio, Kawakami, & Beach, 2001). Thus, a substantial portion of whites are characterized by aversive racism.

CONSEQUENCES OF AVERSIVE RACISM

In contrast to the traditional form of racism, which is blatant and expressed openly and directly, aversive racism operates in subtle and indirect ways. Specifically, whereas old-fashioned racists exhibit a direct and overt pattern of discrimination, the actions of aversive racists may appear more variable and inconsistent. Sometimes they discriminate (manifesting their negative feelings), and sometimes they do not (reflecting their egalitarian beliefs). Nevertheless, their discriminatory behavior is predictable.

Because aversive racists consciously recognize and endorse egalitarian values and because they truly aspire to be nonprejudiced, they will *not* act inappropriately in situations with strong social norms when discrimination would be obvious to others and to themselves. Specifically, when they are presented with a situation in which the normatively appropriate response is clear, in which right and wrong are clearly defined, aversive racists will not discriminate against blacks. In these contexts, aversive racists will be especially motivated to avoid feelings, beliefs, and behaviors that could be associated with racist intent. Wrongdoing of this type would directly threaten their nonprejudiced self-image. However, aversive racists still possess unconscious negative feelings and beliefs, which will eventually be expressed but in subtle, indirect, and rationalizable ways. For instance, discrimination will occur in situations in which normative structure is weak, when the guidelines for appropriate behavior are vague, or when the basis for social judgment is ambiguous. In addition, discrimination will occur when an aversive racist can justify or rationalize a negative response on the basis of some factor other than race. Under these circumstances, aversive racists may engage in behaviors that ultimately harm blacks but in ways that allow whites to maintain their self-image as nonprejudiced and that insulate them from recognizing that their behavior is not colorblind.

Much of the research on aversive racism focuses on the orientation of whites toward blacks in the United States, but similar processes are found for the attitudes of members of dominant groups in other countries with strong contemporary egalitarian values and discriminatory histories or policies (e.g., Hodson, Hooper, Dovidio, & Gaertner, 2005). Despite its subtle expression, the consequences of aversive racism are as significant and pernicious as those of the traditional, overt form.

For instance, one of our early experiments (Gaertner & Dovidio, 1977) demonstrates how aversive racism can operate in fairly dramatic ways. In a scenario inspired by an incident in the mid-1960s in which 38 people witnessed the stabbing of a woman, Kitty Genovese, without a single bystander intervening to help, we created a situation in the laboratory in which white participants witnessed a staged emergency involving a black or a white victim. We led some of our participants to believe that they were the only witness to this emergency, while we led others to believe there were other white people who also witnessed the emergency, each isolated in a separate room within the laboratory.

As we predicted, when white participants believed they were the only witness and bore full responsibility for intervening, they helped both white and black victims very frequently (over 85 percent of the time) and equivalently. There was no evidence of blatant racism. In contrast, when they thought other witnesses were in the vicinity and they could rationalize a decision not to help on the basis of some factor other than race, they helped black victims only half as often as they helped white victims

(37.5% versus 75%). This research, therefore, shows that although the bias may be subtle and the people involved may be well-intentioned, its consequences may be severe.

We, and others, find considerable additional empirical support for the aversive racism framework across a range of other paradigms and participant populations. These situations include nonemergency scenarios both inside and outside the laboratory, college admissions and other consequential decisions (see Dovidio & Gaertner, 2004). In addition, in a recent study (Pearson, Dovidio, & Pratto, 2007) we report, as hypothesized within the aversive racism framework, that whereas blatant prejudice is characterized by feelings of antipathy and hate, the subtle bias associated with aversive racism is "cooler" and less affective in nature.

We further propose that because the subtle bias associated with aversive racism occurs without personal awareness and the actions can be attributed, even by observers, to factors other than race, the influence of aversive racism commonly goes unrecognized by whites. As a consequence, whereas blatant expressions of prejudice, such as hate crimes, are readily identified and inhibited by social sanctions, aversive racism is likely to persist relatively unchallenged over time. For instance, Saucier, Miller, and Doucet (2005) report a meta-analysis of 31 experiments conducted over the past 40 years that examined race and whites' helping behavior. Across these studies, Saucier et al. reveal that a pattern of discrimination reflective of aversive racism remained stable over time. Saucier et al. summarize, "the results of this meta-analysis generally supported the predictions for aversive racism theory" (p. 13), and ask, "is racism still a problem in our society? . . . Racism and expressions of discrimination against blacks can and will exist as long as individuals harbor negativity toward blacks at the implicit level" (p. 14).

We propose that prejudice not only systematically influences intergroup *outcomes* but also intergroup *interactions*. In particular, the dissociation between negative implicit attitudes and egalitarian explicit attitudes experienced by aversive racists can have a significant impact on how whites and blacks interact in ways that contribute substantially to misunderstandings in intergroup interactions.

BIAS AND INTERRACIAL INTERACTION

Implicit and explicit attitudes can influence behavior in different ways and under diverse conditions (Dovidio, Kawakami, Johnson, Johnson, & Howard, 1997; Fazio, Jackson, Dunton, & Williams, 1995). Explicit attitudes shape deliberative, well-considered responses for which people have the motivation and opportunity to weigh the costs and benefits of various courses of action. Implicit attitudes influence responses that are more difficult to monitor and control. For example, whereas self-reported prejudice predicts overt expressions of bias, measures of implicit attitudes predict whites' biases in nonverbal behaviors, such as measures of interest (e.g., eye contact), anxiety (e.g., rate of eye blinking), and other cues of friendliness (Dovidio et al., 1997; Fazio et al., 1995). Thus, the relative impact of implicit and explicit attitudes is a function of the situational context, individuals' motivation and opportunity to engage in deliberative processes, and the nature of the behavioral response.

The nature of contemporary racial prejudice in the United States is particularly problematic with respect to producing and perpetuating misunderstandings in interracial interactions. Dovidio, Kawakami, and Gaertner (2002) reveal that whites and blacks have different interpretations of the feelings and actions demonstrated by whites during interracial interactions. Whites have full access to their explicit attitudes and are able to monitor and control their more overt and deliberative behaviors, which are generally expressed in a nonprejudiced and nondiscriminatory way. However, whites do not have full access to their implicit attitudes, which tend to be reflected in their less easily deliberative and controlled behaviors (e.g., nonverbal behaviors).

Perceptions of whites about how they are behaving or how they are perceived by others are based more on their explicit attitudes and overt behaviors, such as the verbal content of their interaction with blacks, and less on their implicit attitudes or less deliberative behaviors. In contrast, the perspective of black interaction partners in these interracial interactions allows them to attend to both the spontaneous (e.g., nonverbal) and deliberative (e.g., verbal) behaviors of whites. To the extent that the black partners attend to whites' nonverbal behaviors, which may signal more negativity than their verbal behaviors, blacks are likely to form more negative impressions of the encounter and be less satisfied with the interaction compared with whites. One fundamental implication of these processes is that whites and blacks are likely to form very different perceptions of race relations, with blacks developing a general sense of distrust of whites (Dovidio, Gaertner, Kawakami, & Hodson, 2002).

IMPLICATIONS OF AVERSIVE RACISM IN LEGAL, EMPLOYMENT, AND HEALTH CARE SETTINGS

Blacks and whites have fundamentally different realities and experiences in the United States. Significant racial disparities exist in legal outcomes, economic opportunity and achievement, and health and health care. In this section, we consider the potential influence of aversive racism in these three fundamental spheres of social life and well-being in the United States. We draw on direct experimental research, our own as well as by others, as well as archival evidence to make a case that aversive racism may play a critical, but largely unrecognized, role in shaping racial disparities in these domains.

Legal Contexts

Traditionally, blacks and whites have not been treated equally under the law (Sidanius & Pratto, 1999). Across time and locations in the United States, blacks have been more likely to be perceived by jurors as guilty, more likely to be convicted of crimes, and, if convicted, sentenced to longer terms for similar crimes, particularly if the victim is white. Although there is some evidence that disparities in judicial outcomes are declining (see Sommers & Ellsworth, 2001), aversive racism may be contributing to the persistence of these disparities.

Three studies represent conceptual replications of the operation of aversive racism in legal decision making over a 25-year period. Faranda and Gaertner (1979) investigated whether being exposed to inadmissible incriminating evidence would have a more negative influence on whites' judgments of black than white defendants. Participants were not exposed to inadmissible evidence (the defendant's confession to a third party), which they were instructed to ignore. This research also tested the hypothesis that this bias could take different forms: Whereas the racial biases of those who are likely to have traditionally racist attitudes (high authoritarians) would reflect primarily antiblack biases, the racial biases of those who are likely to exhibit aversive racism (low authoritarians) would mainly represent pro-white biases.

As expected, both high- and low-authoritarian participants displayed racial bias in their judgments of guilt, but they did so in different ways. High authoritarians were more certain of the black defendant's guilt when they were exposed to the inadmissible evidence than when they were not presented with this testimony. For the white defendant, however, high authoritarians followed the judge's instructions appropriately. Low-authoritarian participants, in contrast, followed the judge's instructions about ignoring the inadmissible testimony when the defendant was black. However, they were biased *in favor of* the white defendant when the inadmissible evidence was presented. Thus, low-authoritarian participants demonstrated a pro–in-group bias.

More than 15 years later, Johnson, Whitestone, Jackson, and Gatto (1995) further examined the impact of the introduction of inadmissible evidence that was damaging to a defendant's case on whites' judgments of a black or white defendant's guilt. No differences in judgments of guilt occurred as a function of defendant's race when all the evidence presented was admissible. However, consistent with the aversive racism framework, the presentation of inadmissible evidence increased judgments of guilt when the defendant was black but not when the defendant was white.

We conducted another study along these lines in the United Kingdom (Hodson et al., 2005), involving inadmissible incriminating DNA evidence. Paralleling the earlier findings, we report that white participants appropriately corrected their judgments for white defendants by effectively discounting the inadmissible evidence, judging the defendant as less guilty when the damaging evidence was inadmissible than when it was admissible. In contrast, white participants had difficulty suppressing the inadmissible evidence when the defendant was black; they demonstrated a rebound effect, tending to judge the black defendant as more guilty when the evidence was inadmissible than when it was admissible.

Thus, three experiments that used similar paradigms over a span of over 25 years obtained evidence of a subtle but persistent pattern of discrimination predicted by the aversive racism framework. Several other studies of legal decision making have also yielded evidence consistent with the proposition that whites' biases against blacks will be more pronounced when they have an apparently nonrace-related justification for judging a black defendant guilty or sentencing them more severely (Knight, Guiliano, & Sanchez-Ross, 2001). However, also consistent with the aversive racism framework, when testimony is included that racial bias may be involved in the allegations against a black defendant, whites no longer racially discriminate (Sommers & Ellsworth, 2000).

Employment Decisions

The racial gap in median family income has been substantial and enduring over time. The ratio of white family income relative to black family income was 1.73 ($21,904/$12,674) in 1980, 1.72 ($36,915/$21,423) in 1990, 1.57 ($53,029/$33,676) in 2000, and 1.67 ($59,317/35,464) in 2005. Across the same period, the unemployment rate for blacks has hovered around double that of whites: 2.27 (14.3%/6.3%) in 1980, 2.38 (11.4%/4.8%) in 1990, 1.55 (7.6%/4.9%) in 1995, 2.17 (10.4%/4.8%) in 2000, and 1.96 (10.0%/5.1%) in 2005 (U.S. Census Bureau, 2008).

Whereas the evidence indicating the persistence of the effects of aversive racism in whites' helping behavior and juridic decisions have relied on conceptual replications across time and different locations, we have further evidence in employment contexts involving a direct procedural replication (Dovidio & Gaertner, 2000). We used exactly the same paradigm with students from the same college in 1989 and 1999. Participants at these two different points in time were asked to assist in deciding which applicants should be hired as a Resident Advisor in one of the college's large dormitories. They were given background information, including a résumé and excerpts from an interview, indicating (as pretested) that the applicant had very weak, moderate (arguably qualified), or very strong qualifications for the position. Information on the résumé revealed the race of the candidate as black or white. Our prediction, based on the aversive racism framework, was that bias would not be expressed when the candidate was clearly qualified or unqualified for a position, because the appropriate decision would be obvious. However, bias was expected when the appropriate decision was unclear, when the candidate had moderate qualifications.

Consistent with the aversive racism framework, when the candidates' credentials clearly qualified them for the position (strong qualifications) or the credentials clearly were not appropriate (weak qualifications), no discrimination was seen against the black candidate. However, when candidates' qualifications for the position were less obvious and the appropriate decision was more ambiguous (moderate qualifications), white participants recommended the black candidate significantly less often than the white candidate with exactly the same credentials. Moreover, when we compared the responses of participants in 1989 and 1999, whereas overt expressions of prejudice (measured by items on a self-report prejudice scale) declined over this 10-year period, the pattern of subtle discrimination in selection decisions remained essentially unchanged.

More recently, Otero and Dovidio (2005) conceptually replicated this research with human resource professionals in Puerto Rico, focusing on the moderate qualifications and strong qualifications conditions. The findings illustrate the generalizability and persistence of these effects even among experienced professionals in the field. When the applicant had strong qualifications, blacks and whites received equivalently strong recommendations for hiring. However, when the applicant had only moderate qualifications, black candidates were recommended significantly less strongly than white candidates.

Overall, these studies show that, in contrast to the dramatic decline in overt expressions of prejudice, subtle forms of discrimination outlined in the aversive racism framework continue to exist, apparently largely unabated. As we noted earlier, one reason for the persistence of these types of bias is that they are largely shaped by unconscious processes. A recent series of experiments by Son Hing, Chung-Yan, Hamilton, and Zanna (2008) concerning another form of racial bias, prejudice and discrimination against Asian job applicants in Canada, speaks directly to this issue. These researchers also manipulated the strength of qualifications for a white or Asian job candidate. Similar to our findings, more bias was seen against Asian relative to white job applicants when the candidate had moderate qualifications (allowing a nonrace-related excuse for not hiring the person) than when the candidate had very strong credentials. Moreover, Son Hing et al. obtained direct evidence of the role of implicit attitudes. Implicit negative attitudes toward Asians (as measured by an IAT), but not explicit prejudice, predicted weaker support for hiring Asian candidates who had moderate qualifications. However, when the Asian candidate had distinctively strong qualifications (and a failure to hire the applicant was not justifiable on a factor other than race), neither explicit nor implicit prejudice predicted the hiring decision. Support for the Asian applicant was generally strong in this case.

In summary, the research we have presented in this section not only provides further general evidence for the aversive racism framework, but it also illustrates the ways that aversive racism specifically biases employment decisions. To the extent that current antidiscrimination laws in the United States require clear evidence that race was *the* determining factor (not some other factor) and bias was intentional, the subtle effect of aversive racism may be relatively immune to prosecution. As shown in our replications over time, the effects of aversive racism in employment contexts may occur largely unrecognized, and as a consequence remain largely unaddressed, over time.

Health Care

Significant and persistent disparities occur in the quality of care received by black patients compared to white patients in the United States (Geiger, 2003; Smedley, Stith, & Nelson, 2003). With respect to care for coronary heart disease, for example, blacks are less likely than whites to be seen by a coronary specialist, less likely to be prescribed appropriate preventive and emergency medications for their heart disease, and less likely to receive surgical procedures intended to remedy various types of coronary heart disease (see Dovidio et al., 2008, for a review).

Despite ample evidence of racial disparities in health and health care, controlled experimental studies investigating subtle discrimination among health care professionals are rare in the literature. Thus, in this section we consider the *implications of* the aversive racism framework for understanding health care disparities.

Consistent with the research on aversive racism in other domains, which reveals that discriminatory actions are more likely to occur when situational demands are unclear or when norms for appropriate actions are weak or ambiguous (Dovidio & Gaertner, 2004), racial disparities in treatment are greater when physicians engage in "high-discretion" procedures, such as recommending a test or making a referral for a procedure or drug, than in "low-discretion" procedures, such as emergency surgery (Geiger, 2003). For example, racial disparities in prostate cancer, for which physicians generally have considerable discretion with regard to screening and treatment, are particularly pronounced. Black men are significantly less likely than white men to receive screening tests for prostate cancer. In addition, physicians are more likely to delay active treatment of blacks than whites for prostate cancer (see Dovidio et al., 2008, for a review).

Whereas most studies in the coronary heart disease literature have used archival data, one notable exception is a study by Schulman et al. (1999) involving primary care physicians at a national conference. This experiment reveals the causal influence of patient race on medical decisions. Physicians viewed videotapes of an actor playing the role of a patient complaining about chest pain, and gender and race of the patient (black or white) were systematically manipulated. Women and blacks were significantly less likely to be referred for further testing than were men and whites, and black women were only 40 percent as likely to receive such a referral as were white men. Although this experimental study has been challenged methodologically, the results are consistent with the findings from archival data.

Recently, Green et al. (2007) extend this line of research to explore the role in which physicians' explicit and implicit racial attitudes and stereotypes might affect their medical decisions. Their findings support the basic premise of the aversive racism framework that people who appear nonprejudiced, and presumably believe they are egalitarian, may be influenced by their unconscious biases to discriminate against blacks in subtle but significant ways. In this study, physicians reported no explicit biases toward blacks relative to whites, but had more negative implicit attitudes. Moreover, the more negative these implicit attitudes were, the less likely respondents were to recommend the thrombolytic drugs for black patients.

In summary, consistent with the aversive racism framework, racial bias appears to have a systematic influence in health care delivery, particularly in high discretion contexts. This bias is also related to providers' implicit racial biases. Moreover, research on aversive racism suggests that because racial bias is subtle and can be rationalized, its operation and impact are typically underestimated among whites. Indeed, Epstein (2005) argues that the Institute of Medicine (IOM) Panel on Racial and Ethnic Disparities in Health Care (Smedley et al., 2003) overemphasized the potential role of the racial biases in accounting for disparities in health care. Epstein stated, "it is doubtful that hidden forms of discrimination are prevalent in a profession whose professional norms are set so strongly against it" (p. 26). However, as the research on aversive racism demonstrates, genuinely strong egalitarian values do not insulate people against being subtly biased.

COMBATING AVERSIVE RACISM

The social psychological literature can also help guide the development of practical interventions that can attenuate and reduce racial bias. Traditional prejudice-reduction techniques have been concerned with changing conscious attitudes—old-fashioned racism—and obvious expressions of bias, and have utilized traditional educational programs or persuasive messages to change explicit attitudes (Stephan & Stephan, 2001). However, because of its pervasiveness, subtlety, and complexity, the traditional techniques for eliminating racial bias are ineffective for combating aversive racism. Aversive racists already recognize prejudice as harmful, but they do not recognize that *they* are prejudiced. Other techniques are thus required.

Addressing Unconscious Attitudes and Beliefs

As we described earlier, aversive racism is characterized by conscious (explicit) egalitarian attitudes and negative unconscious (implicit) attitudes and beliefs. Simply because implicit attitudes are unconscious and automatically activated, however, does not mean they are immutable to change. To the extent that unconscious attitudes and stereotypes are associations learned through socialization, we propose that they can also be unlearned or inhibited by equally well-learned countervailing influences. We posit that with extensive practice, it is possible to change even implicit beliefs. For example, extended practice in associating counter-stereotypic characteristics with a group can inhibit or suppress the "automatic" activation of cultural stereotypes (Kawakami, Dovidio, Moll, Hermsen, & Russin, 2000).

The problem in practice is that whites are typically motivated to avoid seeing themselves are racially biased and often try to behave as such. Whites often adopt a colorblind orientation, particularly when they anticipate racial tension. However, efforts to be colorblind and suppress acknowledgement of race can produce a "rebound effect," in which implicit attitudes become activated even more. Furthermore, because minorities seek acknowledgement of their racial identity, attempts by whites to be colorblind may alienate minority group members and further contribute to racial distrust (Dovidio et al., 2002).

In efforts to reduce prejudice, it may be possible to capitalize on aversive racists' good intentions and induce self-motivated efforts to reduce unconscious biases by making them aware. Work by Monteith and Voils (1998) indicates that when low-prejudiced people recognize discrepancies between their behavior (i.e., what they *would* do) and their personal standards (i.e., what they *should* do) toward minorities, they feel guilt and compunction, which subsequently produces motivations to respond without prejudice in the future. With practice over time, these individuals learn to reduce prejudicial responses and respond in ways that are consistent with their nonprejudiced personal standards. This process of self-regulation may produce changes in even unconscious negative responses when extended over time (Dovidio, Kawakami, & Gaertner, 2000).

Redirecting In-group Bias

One basic argument we have made in our analysis of social biases is that the negative feelings that develop toward other groups may be rooted, in part, in fundamental, normal psychological processes. One such process is the categorization of people into in-groups and out-groups. As we noted earlier, social categorization contributes to aversive racism. Because categorization is a basic process fundamental to intergroup bias, we have targeted this process as an avenue through which we may attempt to attenuate and reduce the negative repercussions of aversive racism. To do this we have proposed the Common Ingroup Identity Model (Gaertner & Dovidio, 2000).

The Common Ingroup Identity Model is rooted in the social categorization perspective of intergroup behavior and recognizes the central role of social categorization in intergroup bias. Specifically, if members of different groups are induced to think of themselves as a single superordinate group rather than as two separate groups, attitudes toward former out-group members will become more positive through in-group bias. Thus, by changing the basis of categorization from race to an alternative dimension, one can alter who "we" is and who "they" are, undermining a contributing force to contemporary racism. Formation of a common identity, however, does not necessarily require groups to forsake their other identities. It is possible for members to conceive of themselves as holding a "dual identity" in which other identities and the superordinate group identity are salient simultaneously.

CONCLUSION

The influence of aversive racism is pervasive; it affects race relations and outcomes for blacks in a variety of ways. It persists because it remains largely unrecognized and thus unaddressed. However, we propose that it can be combated with new approaches and strategies that are uniquely targeted at critical components of aversive racism. For example, because aversive racists are truly motivated to be nonprejudiced, making them aware, in a nonthreatening way, of their unconscious biases can arouse motivations to change in fundamental ways, which can eventually reduce unconscious biases. Nevertheless, without sufficient recognition of the subtle nature of contemporary biases and without the appropriate tools for combating these particular biases, significant progress toward a truly just society will be difficult to achieve. Good intentions alone are not good enough.

NOTE

Preparation of this chapter was supported by NSF Grant # BCS-0613218 awarded to the first two authors.

REFERENCES

Blair, I. V. (2001). Implicit stereotypes and prejudice. In G. B. Moskowitz (Ed.), *Cognitive social psychology: The Princeton Symposium on the Legacy and Future of Social Cognition* (pp. 359–374). Mahwah, NJ: Erlbaum.

Bobo, L. (2001). Racial attitudes and relations at the close of the twentieth century. In N. J. Smelser, W. J. Wilson, & F. Mitchell (Eds.), *Racial trends and their consequences* (Vol. 1, pp. 264–301). Washington, DC: National Academy Press.

Dovidio, J. F. (2001). On the nature of contemporary prejudice: The third wave. *Journal of Social Issues, 57,* 829–849.

Dovidio, J. F., & Gaertner, S. L. (2000). Aversive racism and selection decisions: 1989 and 1999. *Psychological Science, 11,* 319–323.

Dovidio, J. F., & Gaertner, S. L. (2004). Aversive racism. In M. P. Zanna (Ed.), *Advances in experimental social psychology* (vol. 36, pp. 1–51). San Diego, CA: Academic Press.

Dovidio, J. F., Gaertner, S. L., Kawakami, K., & Hodson, G. (2002). Why can't we just get along? Interpersonal biases and interracial distrust. *Cultural Diversity & Ethnic Minority Psychology, 8*, 88–102.

Dovidio, J., Kawakami, K., & Beach, K. (2001). Implicit and explicit attitudes: Examination of the relationship between measures of intergroup bias. In R. Brown & S. L. Gaertner (Eds.), *Blackwell handbook of social psychology* (Vol. 4, pp. 175–197). Oxford, UK: Blackwell.

Dovidio, J. F., Kawakami, K., & Gaertner, S. L. (2000). Reducing contemporary prejudice: Combating explicit and implicit bias at the individual and intergroup level. In S. Oskamp (Ed.), *Reducing prejudice and discrimination* (pp. 137–163). Hillsdale, NJ: Erlbaum.

Dovidio, J. F., Kawakami, K., & Gaertner, S. L. (2002). Implicit and explicit prejudice and interracial interaction. *Journal of Personality and Social Psychology, 82*, 62–68.

Dovidio, J., Kawakami, K., Johnson, C., Johnson, B., & Howard, A. (1997). The nature of prejudice: Automatic and controlled processes. *Journal of Experimental Social Psychology, 33*, 510–540.

Dovidio, J. F., Penner, L. A., Albrecht, T. L., Norton, W. E., Gaertner, S. L., & Shelton, J. N. (2008). Disparities and distrust: The implications of psychological processes for understanding racial disparities in health and health care. *Social Science and Medicine, 67*, 476–487.

DuBois, W.E.B. (1903/1986). *Writings* (reprinted, W. E. Burghardt, Ed.). New York: Viking.

Epstein, R. A. (2005). Disparities and discrimination in health care coverage: A critique of the Institute of Medicine study. *Perspectives in Biology and Medicine, 48*(1, Suppl.), S26–S41.

Faranda, J., & Gaertner, S. L. (1979, March). *The effects of inadmissible evidence introduced by the prosecution and the defense, and the defendant's race on the verdicts by high and low authoritarians.* Paper presented at the annual meeting of the Eastern Psychological Association, New York.

Fazio, R. H., Jackson, J. R., Dunton, B. C., & Williams, C. J. (1995). Variability in automatic activation as an unobtrusive measure of racial attitudes: A *bona fide* pipeline? *Journal of Personality and Social Psychology, 69*, 1013–1027.

Gaertner, S. L., & Dovidio, J. F. (1977). The subtlety of White racism, arousal, and helping behavior. *Journal of Personality and Social Psychology, 35*, 691–707.

Gaertner, S. L., & Dovidio, J. F. (1986). The aversive form of racism. In J. F. Dovidio & S. L. Gaertner (Eds.), *Prejudice, discrimination, and racism* (pp. 61–89). Orlando, FL: Academic Press.

Gaertner, S. L., & Dovidio, J. F. (2000). *Reducing intergroup bias: The Common Ingroup Identity Model.* Philadelphia, PA: The Psychology Press.

Geiger, H. J. (2003). Racial and ethnic disparities in diagnosis and treatment: A review of the evidence and a consideration of causes. In B. Smedley, A. Stith, & A. Nelson (Eds.), *Unequal Treatment: Confronting racial and ethnic disparities in health care* (pp. 417–454). Washington, DC: The National Academies Press.

Green, A. R., Carney, D. R., Pallin, D. J., Ngo, L. H., Raymond, K. L., Iezzoni, L. I., et al. (2007). Implicit bias among physicians and its predictions of thrombolysis decisions for Black and White patients. *Journal of General Internal Medicine, 22*, 1231–1238.

Greenwald, A., McGhee, D., & Schwartz, J. (1998). Measuring individual differences in implicit cognition: The implicit association test. *Journal of Personality and Social Psychology, 74,* 1464–1480.

Hodson, G., Hooper, H., Dovidio, J. F., & Gaertner, S. L. (2005). Aversive racism in Britain: Legal decisions and the use of inadmissible evidence. *European Journal of Social Psychology, 35,* 437–448.

Johnson, J. D., Whitestone, E., Jackson, L. A., & Gatto, L. (1995). Justice is still not colorblind: Differential racial effects of exposure to inadmissible evidence. *Personality and Social Psychology Bulletin, 21,* 893–898.

Kawakami, K., Dovidio, J. F., Moll, J., Hermsen, S., & Russin, A. (2000). Just say no (to stereotyping): Effects of training in trait negation on stereotype activation. *Journal of Personality and Social Psychology, 78,* 871–888.

Knight, J. L., Guiliano, T. A., & Sanchez-Ross, M. G. (2001). Famous or infamous? The influence of celebrity status and race on perceptions of responsibility for rape. *Basic and Applied Social Psychology, 23,* 183–190.

Kovel, J. (1970). *White racism: A psychohistory.* New York: Pantheon.

Monteith, M. J., & Voils, C. (1998). Proneness to prejudiced responses: Toward understanding the authenticity of self-reported discrepancies. *Journal of Personality and Social Psychology, 75,* 901–916.

Otero, L., & Dovidio, J. F. (2005). Unpublished data. Department of Psychology, University of Connecticut, Storrs, CT.

Pearson, A. R., Dovidio, J. F., & Pratto, F. (2007). Racial prejudice, intergroup hate, and blatant and subtle bias of Whites toward Blacks in legal decision making in the United States. *International Journal of Psychology and Psychological Therapy, 7,* 145–158.

Saucier, D. A., Miller, C. T., & Doucet, N. (2005). Differences in helping Whites and Blacks: A meta-analysis. *Personality and Social Psychology Review, 9,* 2–16.

Schulman, K. A., Berlin, J. A., Harless, W., Kerner, J. F., Sistrunk, S., Gersh, B. J., et al. (1999). The effect of race and sex on physicians' recommendations for cardiac catheterization. *The New England Journal of Medicine, 340*(8), 618–626.

Sidanius, J., & Pratto, F. (1999). *Social dominance: An intergroup theory of social hierarchy and oppression.* New York: Cambridge University Press.

Smedley, B. D., Stith, A. Y., & Nelson, A. R. (Eds.). (2003). *Unequal treatment: Confronting racial and ethnic disparities in health care.* Washington, DC: National Academy Press.

Sommers, S. R., & Ellsworth, P. C. (2000). Race in the courtroom: Perceptions of guilt and dispositional attributions. *Personality and Social Psychology Bulletin, 26,* 1367–1379.

Sommers, S. R., & Ellsworth, P. C. (2001). White juror bias: An investigation of prejudice against Black defendants in the American courtroom. *Psychology, Public Policy, and Law, 7,* 201–229.

Son Hing, L. S., Chung-Yan, G., Hamilton, L., & Zanna, M. (2008). A two-dimensional model that employs explicit and implicit attitudes to characterize prejudice. *Journal of Personality and Social Psychology, 94,* 67–81.

Stephan, W. G., & Stephan, C. W. (2001). *Improving intergroup relations.* Thousand Oaks, CA: Sage.

U.S. Census Bureau. (2008). *The 2008 statistical abstract.* Retrieved May 15, 2008, from http://www.census.gov/compendia/statab/cats/labor_force_employ ment_earnings.html.

CHAPTER 3

The Other Diversity: The Cost of Being GLBT in America's Health Care

Terri Erbacher, Yuma Iannotti-Tomes,
Tania Czarnecki Wismar, Caitlin Gilmartin,
Deanna Marie Ryder, Narrimone Vivid Thammavongsa,
Eric Watson, and Lauren Webb

Acculturation into mainstream America is a difficult task for any individual who identifies with subcultures. A subculture can be viewed as a cultural subgroup that is differentiated by social status, ethnic background, religion, socioeconomic status, or sexual orientation that collectively unify the group outside the primary culture (Berube, 2001). American standards of beauty, wealth, happiness, or general lifestyle can create a dichotomous reality for individuals that identify with contrasting diversities. Many gay, lesbian, bisexual, and transgendered individuals (GLBTs) identify with lifestyles or belief systems that contrast with mainstream America, such as straying from traditional familial roles. It is therefore vital to develop an understanding of the impact of identifying as GLBT within the mainstream American culture.

More alarming is the dearth of research addressing health and mental health concerns of the GLBT population. In particular, mental health issues are exacerbated by socialization and marginalization from the mainstream community. As a result, GLBTs are less likely to seek health care regarding physical and mental victimization and other aspects that require medical or mental health attention. Therefore, future directives must address methods of handling GLBT issues and minimizing social marginalization while empowering GLBTs to take control of their health and mental issues in a supportive and connected medical environment.

HEALTH ISSUES OF GLBT POPULATIONS

GLBT populations are as diverse as the American culture. While not unlike the general population in terms of many health concerns and issues, these individuals face different dilemmas regarding sexual health, particularly due to increased risk related to the unique exposures of MSM (men who have sex with men, etc.) and behaviors indirectly linked to other unique exposures (e.g., sociocultural stressors, victimization, alienation, etc.).

Sexual Health of Gay Men and Lesbians

Atop the list of major health concerns among gay and bisexual men are the HIV (human immunodeficiency virus) and AIDS (acquired immune deficiency syndrome) epidemics as MSM comprised more than two-thirds (68%) of all men with HIV living in the United States in 2005 (Centers for Disease Control and Prevention, 2007b). Recent research reports numerous predictors or risk factors related to risky sexual behavior. Those risk factors include an individual's beliefs about HIV noninfection and its relation to unprotected anal intercourse (UAI). In a recent study by Halkitis, Zade, Shrem, and Marmor (2004), a sample of HIV noninfected Caucasian men were canvassed with various surveys measuring frequent sexual behaviors, substance use, HIV resistance knowledge, and beliefs and behaviors for noninfection. The findings reveal three main beliefs related to sexual risk taking in the MSM population. The first main belief refers to an optimistic bias that medical advances in the treatment of HIV would thwart the chances of the disease affecting them. The second belief pertains to the idea of having a low probability of HIV transmission, while the third highly regarded belief among MSM individuals involves the idea that a healthy immune system was capable of resisting infection.

Following concerns about HIV and AIDS, other sexually transmitted diseases (STDs) are also on the rise. Syphilis, an STD that promotes ulcerative genital lesions, is the most significant STD affecting gay and bisexual men. Heffelfinger, Swint, Berman, and Weinstock (2007) reveal a 19 percent increase between 2000 and 2003 that is attributed to MSM populations. Numerous studies suggest that the lesions produced from syphilis infection makes acquisition of HIV much easier, as the HIV infected secretions can easily penetrate open sites (Heffelfinger et al., 2007).

Though few confirmed cases of female-to-female sexual transmission of HIV are reported, it should not be discounted. Since HIV transmission can take place in the vaginal fluids, infected vaginal secretions and menstruous blood can permeate the mucus membranes of the genital area (Centers for Disease Control and Prevention, 2007a). Additionally, STDs such as Herpes, human papillomavirus (HPV), and bacterial vaginosis frequently occur among WSW (women who have sex with women). Research suggests that Herpes and HPV are common because the modes of transmission are skin-to-skin or mucous contact, which can easily occur among WSW (Marrazzo, 2004). Bacterial vaginosis, which is an infection with potential effects of promoting premature birth, low birth weight, and easier transmission of HIV, is currently the most studied STD among WSW because it occurs so frequently and its mode of transmission is unclear (Marrazzo et al., 2002). Most alarming are the potentially life-threatening consequences of STDs, especially HPV, as this virus may increase the likelihood of cervical cancer (Marrazzo et al., 2002) and Herpes, which can impact liver function.

HIV/AIDS, STDs, and Sex Work for Transgenders

When working with transgendered individuals, more research tends to focus on MTF (male to female) persons as opposed to FTM (female to male), though both are susceptible to HIV and STDs. Current research suggests rates of HIV to be highest for African American MTF transgender persons, with the Latino population rounding out second (Wilkerson, 2001). Many specific risk factors are evident for transgenders that lead to increased risk of HIV and STDs. Research by Wilkerson (2001) posits that many transgenders engage in sex work in order to decrease both the medical and psychological costs needed for sex reassignment surgery. Sex work or providing sexual favors for money is a high-risk business that may expose the individual to unprotected sex that in turn may lead to HIV or STD infections. Furthermore, sex work leaves the individual vulnerable to infection due to increases in numbers of sexual partners (Clements-Nolle, Marx, Guzman, & Katz, 2001).

RECENT RISKY SEXUAL BEHAVIORS

Bug Chasing and Gift Giving

"Bug chasing" and "gift giving" are newly discovered subcultures in the gay world that puts MSM at a higher risk of HIV and STDs because of unprotected sex and high-risk sexual behavior. However, this topic is most controversial because this subculture of behavior involves individuals who purposely seek out individuals in order to be infected with HIV (bug chasing) and those who offer their HIV-positive serostatus to those who seek it (gift givers). Though relatively new, researchers have sought explanations of these behaviors.

Researchers first needed to differentiate these behaviors from that of barebacking, or having unprotected anal sex (Moskowitz & Roloff, 2007). In doing so, the researchers utilized a Web site dedicated to MSM that regularly sought out barebacking for pleasure. The site employed profiles with varying scales regarding sexual behavior and qualities wanted in a partner. These included personal serostatus measures, drug and alcohol use, amount of partying, and whether or not they were a "bug chaser." Similarly, these questions were rated regarding the individual the user was seeking. From their study, the researchers developed two classification groups: apathetic bug chasers and ardent bug chasers. Apathetic bug chasers are found to be in search of partners with sero-ambiguous status, while ardent bug chasers actively seek out sero-discordant partners.

In another study, Grov and Parson (2006) explore the bug chasing phenomenon through examination of personal profiles of a bareback sex matching Web site. Findings suggest that many individual beliefs included those previously mentioned related to advances in medical treatment for HIV and AIDS. However, they also unveil beliefs that individuals seek infection because it is thought HIV in gay sex is inevitable. Thus, in order to control the situation and decrease health anxiety, the individual actively seeks the infection. As this phenomenon is still relatively new, more research is urgently needed to fully understand bug chasing behavior and how it affects the lives of MSM.

On the Down Low (DL)

The term *down low* predominately refers to men who identify themselves as straight, yet they have sex with other men while neglecting to tell their female partner or any other person (Millet, Malenbranche, Mason, & Spikes, 2005). This issue has come into mainstream media as a result of increased cases of HIV in women in "monogamous" relationships with men. Most research regarding individuals on the DL pertains to African Americans; however, Latinos are also reporting homosexual behavior on the DL, while Caucasians report disclosing their DL behavior more often than the previous two groups (Martinez & Hosek, 2005).

Factors identified by studies link risky sexual behavior to sensation seeking and reported ease of obtaining sex from men as opposed to women. However, these individuals may not seek health care or disclose their homosexual behavior to their female partners because they fear being labeled and thus maintain their status on the DL (Millet et al., 2005). Also related to health behaviors of African American DL individuals are the decrease in use of protection during intercourse and large numbers of partners, which increases susceptibility to acquiring HIV and passing it on to future female and male sex partners (Martinez & Hosek, 2005). As more information is uncovered regarding DL behavior, more implications may develop to adequately facilitate a decrease in the spreading of HIV and STDs. Possible interventions include learning information on safer sex, knowing one's serostatus, and disclosing one's personal sexual history to partners.

MENTAL HEALTH CONCERNS AMONG GLBT

Many GLBTs, due in part to socialization issues, such as those on the DL are often at a higher risk of experiencing mental health problems compared to heterosexuals. Other concerns such as depression, anxiety/stress, substance abuse, and harassment/victimization lead to further disparities between heterosexual and homosexual individuals (Mills et al., 2004).

Socialization and Stigmatization

Difficulties regarding socialization and subsequent mental health concerns for GLBTs begin from an extremely early age. Isay (1999) states that homosexual patients had difficulty establishing relationships as adults as many of them report that their fathers' disapproval of their feminine characteristics early on forced them to detach emotionally from their mother and reject behaviors associated with the female sex. Isay (1999) posits that this emotional detachment proved to be deleterious to future relationships as patients also report that they are not able to remain in stable relationships, demonstrate anxiety, and engage in risky behavior. Landolt, Bartholomew, Saffrey, Oram, and Perlman's (2002) studies confirm that dysfunctional familial relationships actually impair future relationships as, in these instances, the reason for familial and peer rejection and isolation was the individual's sexual orientation.

Familial rejection is not the only socialization challenge for GLBT patients/clients. According to Miller and Thoresen (2003), more than two-thirds of people in the United States identify with a church or synagogue as membership to a religious organization is seen as a means to a better lifestyle, general well-being, comfort in a time of crisis, and an innate sense of self-purpose. As GLBTs adapt to define their sexuality identity, they are faced with the challenge of finding their place in the religious community; however, they are often greeted with condemning messages, homosexual biases, and punitive stances on homosexuality (Heermann, Wiggins, & Rutter, 2007). Heermann et al. (2007) report that the Jewish religion considers same-sex partnerships a sin, while Mormons use excommunication as a punishment for homosexual relationships. Often GLBTs are forced to choose between their sexuality and religious beliefs. Overly negative homosexual attitudes, organizational judgments, and prosecutions leave GLBTs feeling like outcasts and their only salvation is to deny their sexuality or live in secret to preserve their religious identity (Heermann et al., 2007). The process to reconcile the conflict between the two identities is associated with depression, shame, guilt, low self-esteem, suicidal ideation, and even abandonment of religious beliefs (Rodriquez & Ouellette, 2000).

Heermann et al. (2007) point out that many GLBTs find strength through spirituality as opposed to a formal religious organization, despite harsh adversity. They define the term spirituality as the drive for wholeness, purpose, meaning, and self-awareness to connect with others and a higher power (i.e., God). Subsequently, spirituality encompasses the same ideas as religion (Hill & Pargament, 2003). Further, research shows that GLBTs struggling with religious identity find comfort and understanding by developing the spiritual connection of God's love for them (Yarhouse, Brooke, & Pisano, 2005).

It is without question that finding one's personal identity within one's own culture is a difficult task. As individuals begin on this journey of self exploration and cultural identification, feelings of self-doubt, uncertainty, social isolation, and confusion can emerge (Mennuti, Freeman, & Christner, 2006). Consequently, minority individuals who are also GLBT can struggle with finding their own identity with the imposed stereotypes of the mainstream. For example, within the African American community, homosexuality is taboo or perverse (Negy & Eisenman, 2005). The African American community has been noted to have extreme negative attitudes towards homosexuals even when compared to Caucasians (Negy & Eisenman, 2005). Further, there is a direct correlation between higher rates of immersion into the African American culture and negative attitudes towards homosexuality.

Depression and Anxiety

While some risk factors overlap, such as relationship status and satisfaction, dissolution of an intimate relationship, and perceived lack of or low social support, Matthews, Bartholomew, Saffrey, Oram, and Perlman (2002) hypothesize that GLBTs can be affected by additional unique risk factors, including the coming-out process, level of disclosure of sexual orientation, discrimination experiences, and chronic stress associated with being a member of a stigmatized minority group. Mills et al. (2004) report that for GLBTs, distress and depression are often associated with a history of antigay threats or violence, not identifying as gay or queer, and feeling alienated.

Cochran, Sullivan, and Mays (2003) find that gay and bisexual men are 3.0 times more likely to meet the criteria for major depression and 4.7 times more likely to meet the criteria for a panic disorder than heterosexual men. Further, nearly 20 percent of gay-bisexual men are comorbid for two or more disorders, a prevalence exceeding that of heterosexual men. Cochran and Mays (2000) reveal higher rates of panic attacks and find that homosexually active men are more likely to meet the criteria for major depression than heterosexually active men. Lesbian and bisexual women appear to experience higher rates of generalized anxiety disorders compared to heterosexual women (Cochran & Mays, 2000). Higher rates than expected are also found among homosexually active women for one-year prevalence of depression, posttraumatic stress disorders, simple phobias (Gilman et al., 2001) and suicides (Matthews et al., 2002).

Hart and Heimberg (2001) suggest that a likely mental health outcome of expectations of rejection for sexual minority group members may be social anxiety. Gilman et al. (2001) reveal that 12-month prevalence rates of social anxiety disorders are 8.8 percent in homosexual men versus 6.3 percent in heterosexual men. Sandfort, deGraaf, Bijl, and Schnabel (2001) report a 12-month prevalence of social anxiety disorders to be 3.0 percent in heterosexual men versus 7.3 percent in homosexual men, with lifetime prevalence rates to be 5.5 percent versus 14.6 percent, respectively.

Meyer (2003) states that a significant determinant of psychological problems among GLBTs is expectations of being rejected. Therefore, social interactions can be sources of distress for those with a concealable stigma as these individuals are likely to become preoccupied with thoughts concerning their hidden identity (Smart & Wegner, 1999) and with avoiding giving off clues about their sexual orientation (Pachankis & Goldfried, 2006). Pachankis and Goldfried (2006) further state that GLBTs who conceal their sexual orientation may be likely to experience greater anxiety in social situations than those who are open about their sexual orientation. In early research on the negative mental health consequences of not disclosing aspects of oneself, Jourard (1959) states that if becoming fully known to another person is seen as a source of danger, then the mere presence of another person can serve as an anxiety-evoking stimulus and that, not surprisingly, this hinders the formation of close interpersonal relationships.

As mentioned earlier, even if one does not directly experience victimization, the potential for it occurring can be enough to create a sense of threat; studies show that gay men have a greater fear of negative evaluation than heterosexual men (Pachankis & Goldfried, 2006). Thus, D'Augelli (1992) finds that 57 percent of his sample changed their lives to avoid discrimination or harassment, including avoidance of certain locations and people, and distorted or restricted self-presentation to others (e.g., lying about the sex of a dating partner).

Drug and Alcohol Use

GLBT individuals of all sexes and ages are at an increased risk of using illicit substances, though this varies depending upon the age and sex of the individual. Researchers document that GLBT adults and youth are targeted by tobacco companies and that these populations retain the highest rates of smoking (Archer, Hoff, & Snook, 2005). The current smoking rate for urban MSM is 31.4 percent (higher than men in the general population), 28.6 percent for bisexual men, 38.1 percent for lesbians, and 55.3 percent for bisexual women. Remafedi (2006) indicates that GLBT individuals aged between 13 and 24 are at a higher risk of smoking cigarettes, possibly due to stress, habitual substance abuse, socializing in particular smoky venues, and marketing. Moreover, Semple, Patterson, and Grant (2002) reveal that HIV-positive homosexual males using methamphetamine are less likely to use condoms and would partake in anonymous sex and engage in intercourse with multiple partners. Halkitis and Jerome (2008) note that gay and bisexual African American methamphetamine users are more likely to be HIV-positive, have lower educational attainment, and have lower incomes. Parsons, Kutnick, Halkitis, Punzalan, and Carbonari (2005) document that the use of several substances and risky sexual behaviors correlates with increased risk of HIV transmission.

GLBT women are also at risk. After following the activities of WSW, Bell, Ompad, and Sherman (2006) conclude that they are participating in sexual risk behaviors and drug use, and are sharing needles for intravenous drug use at a higher rate than heterosexual women. Scheer et al. (2002) reveal similar behaviors such as WSW engaging in intercourse with HIV-positive men, having multiple partners, trading sex for money, and engaging in anal sex and intravenous drug use. Hepatitis B and C are also more prevalent among this group.

Cochran, Keenan, Schober, and Mays (2000) further report that lesbians use alcohol more frequently than their heterosexual counterparts and cite incompetent treatment as a factor that exacerbates alcohol use/abuse patterns. Gruskin, Hart, Gordon, and Ackerson (2001) reveal that lesbian and bisexual women under the age of 50 participate in even more alcohol and smoking behaviors, perhaps to cope with the oppression embedded within society. Amadio (2006) examines heterosexism (bias against GLBTs by heterosexuals) in relation to alcohol-related problems and finds that there is a positive correlation for WSW. Weber (2008) documents that GLBT participants who were classified as having at least one alcohol or drug use disorder experienced more heterosexism than those who were not classified.

Suicide Does Not Discriminate

Due to varied mental health issues, numerous studies show that gay adolescents are at a higher risk of completing suicide compared to their nongay counterparts (Mills et al., 2004; Silenzio, Pena, Duberstein, Carel, & Knox, 2007). Further, a nationally representative sample of 11,940 high-school students was asked about romantic attractions, romantic relationships, and suicidality (Russell & Joyner, 2001). This study finds that youth reporting either same-sex attraction or relationships are about twice as likely as their peers to attempt suicide. A large part of the risk is mediated by other suicide risk factors: hopelessness, depression, alcohol abuse, suicidality in friends or relatives, and physical victimization. However, increased risk remains after taking such factors into account (Russell & Joyner, 2001).

Goldfried and Bell (2003) posit that GLBT adolescents are more suicidal as a result of inadequate support systems (e.g., lack of familial and community support). McAndrew and Warne (2004) hypothesize that the continued increase in suicidal GLBT youths attests to the failure of the public health agenda, and Ida (2007) emphasizes that therapists should initiate discussions with patients about mental health and the possibility of encountering discrimination.

Precipitating Factors of Suicide

One of the most prominent and heavily researched sociocultural difficulties for GLBT communities is the process of "coming out" (Kitts, 2005) or publicly identifying one's sexual orientation. On the one hand, these individuals will not only find relief in identifying with others, but also have access to support from various GLBT communities (Russell & Joyner, 2001). Conversely, quite often these individuals are faced with experiencing great family discord, rejection from peers, ostracism, harassment, violence and victimization; which all contribute to increased depression, anxiety, anger, and suicidal behavior (Kitts, 2005).

Additionally, when a gay or bisexual individual from an ethnic minority was confronted with the ordeal of coming out, homophobia, poverty and racism were all factors contributing to increased rates of stress and depression (Diaz, Ayala, Bein, Henne, & Martin, 2001).

Interestingly, GLBT suicides are inversely related to age (Leach, 2006). It is posited that this may be due, in part, to the "coming out" process as the average coming-out age has dropped to 16 years old, with studies finding that many members of the GLBT community begin identifying themselves as gay/lesbian/bisexual as early as the age of 10, if not earlier (Herdt & McClintock as reported in Ryan, Futterman, & Stine, 1998). As GLBTs become more secure in their own sexuality, deal with familial reactions, and become involved with social networks and gain support from other GLBTs, levels of depression, and in turn, suicidality decrease.

VICTIMIZATION OF GLBT INDIVIDUALS

The victimization of gays and lesbians, whether "out" or in the process of "coming out," is becoming recognized as a significant health crisis and social problem affecting males, females, various age groups and all cultures. Research continues to show that victimization of GLBTs is related to higher rates of mental health concerns, including mood instability, anxiety, high risk behaviors and substance abuse.

GLBT victimization is a broad category that includes homophobic statements, hearing others discussing gays and lesbians using derogatory statements, and harassment, whether verbal or physical in nature. Victimization can also be manifested in acts of vandalism, robbery, assault, rape and murder. Herek, Cogan, and Gillis (2002) asked 154 subjects to provide specific stories of their victimization. Many interviewees described hate crimes that were perpetrated by groups of strangers in proximity to a gay-identified venue. The severity of the attacks ranged from threats to physical assaults and in the case of one interviewee, the murder of a friend.

The prevalence rates of antigay aggression are not fully known, as stigma and fear of sexual orientation disclosure often prevent reporting. An early study by the National Gay and Lesbian Task Force (1984) indicates that 94 percent of surveyed gay men and lesbians have experienced some form of victimization during their lifetime, with nearly half of these respondents having been threatened with physical violence. These findings continue to reach concerning rates over 20 years later.

D'Augelli, Grossman, and Starks (2006) examined the prevalence rates of victimization among 528 lesbians, gay and bisexual youths, with a mean age of 17. Results indicate that approximately 80 percent of the youths experienced verbal abuse, 14 percent were physically attacked and 9 percent were sexually assaulted due to their sexual orientation.

Several studies find that lesbian and gay survivors of biased crimes display significantly more psychological distress compared to victims of similar nonbiased crimes (Herek, Gillis, & Cogan, 1999; Rose & Mechanic, 2002), including higher rates of Posttraumatic Stress Disorder (PTSD), depression, anxiety, anger and suicidality. Additionally, psychological distress related to GLBT violence may be longer lasting than that seen in gay/lesbian victims of nonbiased crimes (Herek et al., 1999). Various hypotheses exist seeking to explain this increased distress from biased violence, including the theory that victimization affects the victim's beliefs about self and the world (Noelle, 2002). The findings of Herek et al. (1999) that gay and lesbian survivors of antigay crimes were more likely to believe the world is unsafe, to view others as malevolent, to exhibit a low sense of personal mastery and to attribute personal setbacks to sexual prejudice is consistent with the hypothesis that experiencing a hate crime links the victim's post-crime feelings of vulnerability and powerlessness to their sexual identity. Kaysen and Lostutter (2005) hypothesized that in addition to negative beliefs related to victimization, antigay violence can lead to increased internalized homophobia, in which GLBTs internalize negative societal views of homosexuality.

Feeling Safe in Educational Settings

The Gay, Lesbian, Straight Education Network (GLSEN) is the largest organization working to end antigay bias in schools. From 1997 to 1998, GLSEN surveyed 42 of the largest public school districts in the nation. Its study reveals that 32 of the schools surveyed provide no training for staff on issues facing GLBT students in school (MacGillivray, 2000). Moreover, the survey reports that a typical high-school student hears antigay slurs as often as 26 times a day. Faculty will intervene in such incidents only three percent of the time. Because of this lack of intervention, 19 percent of GLBT students suffer physical attacks associated with sexual orientation, 13 percent of these students skip school at least once per month, and 26 percent drop out altogether (MacGillivray, 2000). For GLBT students, provocation and distress heighten to such a great level that, oftentimes, these students experience depression and/or attempt suicide.

The school nurse is identified as an important first point of contact as GLBTs often present to the nurse after being victimized; children of middle school age are especially vulnerable due to the social pressures and change associated with this developmental period (Davis, 2006). Professional organizations of school nurses have called for a cultural competence initiative so that school nurses may be available as support to GLBT students (Davis, 2006).

The state of Massachusetts has been used as a model for implementing school policy to create safe schools for sexual minority students. The former state governor, William F. Weld, signed an executive order on February 10, 1992, to create the nation's first Governor's Commission on Gay and Lesbian Youth (Henning-Stout, James, & Macintosh, 2000). The Commission's 1993 report, *Making Schools Safe for Gay and Lesbian Youth*, addresses several issues, such as the problems of harassment of GLBTs in school, isolation and suicide, dropout and poor school performance, the need for adult role models, and families of gay and lesbian youth. In December 1993, the Gay and Lesbian Student Rights Bill was passed in Massachusetts. Concurrently, the state amended its law pertaining to educational rights to include consideration for sexual orientation, which makes the state a leader in developing safe environments for sexual minority staff and students (Henning-Stout et al., 2000).

UTILIZATION OF HEALTH CARE SYSTEMS

Barriers to Utilizing Health Care Systems

The current models of managed care, insurance, and health care practice create systemic barriers to health care utilization. Managed care is not currently designed with sexual minorities in mind (Gay and Lesbian Medical Association [GLMA] LGBT Health Experts, 2001). Further, the denial of insurance benefits to same-sex partners may decrease the utilization of health systems and increase emergency department visits for GLBTs. Even those who report a high level of primary care doctor utilization are more likely to utilize emergency department visits than their sexual majority peers when controlled for other variables such as SES, age, educational level, etc. (Sanchez, Halipern, Lowe, & Calderon, 2007). Mental health and cigarette use are two variables strongly related to the increase of emergency department visits. Other associated variables include abuse by partner, marijuana use, and asthma. This suggests that GLBTs are not accessing appropriate preventative medical or psychological intervention.

It is not just the system that is affecting utilization rates, but the attitudes of providers themselves. Inadequate and misleading data can perpetuate negativity against GLBT populations, again providing a barrier to health care access and treatment. Makadon (2006) cites a 1999 report from the Institute of Medicine that reveals a lack of lesbian-specific research and suggests that misconceptions about risk can negatively affect the ability of lesbians to both seek health care and access treatment. Lombardi (2001), a professional with the Drug Abuse Research Center at the University of California, attests to this dilemma. He reports that helping transgender individuals obtain services is difficult because service providers do not want to work with these clients. This lack of acceptance on the part of health care providers adversely influences whether these individuals access and adhere to treatment. Further, a vast majority (88%) of respondents to a survey by the GLMA report hearing a medical colleague make a disparaging remark about a patient (Stein & Bonuck, 2001).

Confidentiality, another barrier, is an important aspect of any patient-provider relationship, but it is essential in interactions with GLBT individuals as it may affect utilization and access rates. In particular, GLBT adolescents may delay or avoid utilizing health services for fear of parental disclosure (Ryan, Futterman, & Stine, 1998) or disclosure by the physician to a health insurance company or employer (Stein & Bonuck, 2001). Due to the increased stigma associated with receiving mental health services and the discrimination associated with being identified as GLBT, confidentiality as an ethical and legal principle becomes a key factor in culturally competent practice. Creating safe environments for GLBT individuals is integral and full disclosure by GLBTs will depend upon an individual's perceived level of confidentiality.

Results show that approximately 17 percent of the GLBT community reports delayed or avoided health systems utilization due to reasons associated with their sexuality (Stein & Bonuck, 2001). Diminished primary care access reveals higher rates of negative health behaviors in this community (Sanchez et al., 2007). This is compounded by the fact that even members of the sexual minority community who have comparable rates of utilization often experience more days of poor mental health than their sexual majority counterparts (Diamant & Wold, 2003); thus, they may need additional or targeted medical care not currently offered.

A significant barrier is how many health care systems treat sexual minorities as a risk group rather than a diverse group (De Cecco & Parker, 1995, as cited in Schilder et al., 2001). GLBT persons are still a marginalized, undefined group who often do not have a voice as to their own unique health care needs (GLMA & LGBT Health Experts, 2001). In order to provide services that are culturally relevant and tailored to suit the specific needs of this population, researchers, educators, and health care professionals will need concrete and comprehensive information about this population (Meyer, 2001). Like the individuals who comprise the American population, GLBT communities are diverse. Various GLBTs live in urban as well as rural locations, and they are of diverse ethnicities and varying socioeconomic backgrounds. To reinforce the existing diversity within GLBT communities, Meyer (2001) states:

White gay men in New York City's Chelsea neighborhood share little with transgender sex workers just a few blocks away in Greenwich Village; with gay men developing a gay liberation movement in Guadalajara, Mexico; with lesbians in Northampton, Massachusetts; or with bisexual married women on Long Island, New York. (p. 856)

Conversely, the ease of communication and level of comfort with primary care providers are shown to be associated with increased levels of health care access and utilization from the lesbian community (White & Dull, 1997, as cited in Stein & Bonuck, 2001). Eighty-seven percent of gay men and lesbians who utilize health providers report that during the experience, they were given the same amount of respect as a heterosexual client.

FUTURE DIRECTIVES AND CONCLUSION

The first steps to establishing an ideal health care system for GLBT communities would mean utilizing health care providers who are committed to initiating nonjudgmental dialogues about sexual orientation and history, and training personnel to recognize the use of sensitive semantic and pragmatic language during consultations and follow-ups. They would consider how individual medical practices create a welcoming environment for GLBTs. In addition to heightening cultural competency, medical training would include formal education about sexual minority groups. As a result, medical professionals would become more familiar with the needs of GLBT individuals. Providers need to become aware of potential risk behaviors and trends in order to effectively address issues with each patient. Routine care, such as screening of and immunizing against hepatitis A and B, screening for sexually transmitted diseases and certain cancers, assessing drug, alcohol, and tobacco use, screening for psychological health and mental health disorders, domestic violence, hate crimes, post-traumatic stress, and helping patients to deal with the stigma associated with being a sexual minority and the social and psychological process of coming out are areas that health professionals need to consider when providing services to GLBT populations (Makadon et al., 2006).

REFERENCES

Amadio, D. M. (2006). Internalized heterosexism, alcohol use, and alcohol-related problems among lesbians and gay men. *Addictive Behaviors, 31,* 1153–1162.

Archer, R., Hoff, G. L., & Snook, D. W. (2005). Tobacco use and cessation among men who have sex with men. *American Journal of Public Health, 95,* 929.

Bell, A. V., Ompad, D., & Sherman, S. G. (2006). Sexual and drug risk behaviors among women who have sex with women. *American Journal of Public Health, 96,* 1066–1073.

Berube, M. S. (Ed.). (2001). *Webster's II new college dictionary.* New York: Houghton Mifflin Company.

Centers for Disease Control and Prevention. (2007a). HIV/AIDS among women who have sex with women. Retrieved January 25, 2008, from http://www.cdc.gov/hiv/topics/women/resources/factsheets/wsw.htm.

Centers for Disease Control and Prevention. (2007b). HIV and Aids in the United States: A picture of today's epidemic. Retrieved February 23, 2008, from http://www.cdc.gov/nchstp/od/General%20HIV%20Fact%20Sheet%20 FINAL%20no%20embargo%20-%20Nov%202006.pdf.

Clements-Nolle, K., Marx, R., Guzman, R., & Katz, M. (2001). HIV prevalence, risk behaviors, healthcare use, and mental health status of transgender persons: implications for public health intervention. *American Journal of Public Health, 91*, 915–921.

Cochran, S., Keenan, C., Schober, C., & Mays, V. (2000). Estimates of alcohol use and clinical treatment needs among homosexually active men and women in the U.S. population. *Journal of Consulting and Clinical Psychology, 68*, 1062–1071.

Cochran, S., Sullivan, J., & Mays, V. (2003). Prevalence of mental disorders, psychological distress, and mental services use among lesbian, gay, and bisexual adults in the United States. *Journal of Consulting and Clinical Psychology, 71*, 53–61.

Cochran, S. D., & Mays, V. M. (2000). Relation between psychiatric syndromes and behaviorally defined sexual orientation in a sample of the U.S. population. *American Journal of Epidemiology, 151*, 516–523.

D'Augelli, A. R. (1992). Lesbian and gay male undergraduates' experiences of harassment and fear on campus. *Journal of Interpersonal Violence, 7*, 383–395.

D'Augelli, A. R., Grossman, A. H., & Starks, M. T. (2006). Childhood gender atypicality, victimization and PTSD among lesbian, gay and bisexual youth. *Journal of Interpersonal Violence, 21*(11), 1462–1482.

Davis, C. (2006). School's out for bullying. *Nursing Standard, 20*, 24–25.

Diamant, A., & Wold, C. (2003). Sexual orientation and variation in physical and mental health status among women. *Journal of Women's Health, 12*, 41–50.

Diaz, R. M., Ayala, G., Bein, E., Henne, J., & Martin, B. V. (2001). The impact of homophobia, poverty, and racism on the mental health of gay and bisexual Latino men: Findings from 3 to U.S. cities. *American Journal of Public Health, 91*, 927–943.

Gay and Lesbian Medical Association (GLMA) & LGBT Health Experts. (2001). *Healthy people 2010 companion document for lesbian, gay, bisexual, and transgender (LGBT) health.* San Francisco, CA: Author.

Gilman S. E., Cochran, V. M., Mays, M., Hughes, D., Ostrow, D., & Kessler, R. C. (2001). Risk of psychiatric disorders among individuals reporting same-sex sexual partners in the NCS. *American Journal of Public Health 91*, 933–939.

Goldfried, M., & Bell, A. (2003, December). Extending the Boundaries of Research on Adolescent Development. *Journal of Clinical Child and Adolescent Psychology, 32*(4), 531–535.

Grov, C., & Parson, J. (2006). Bug chasing and gift giving: The potential for HIV transmission among barebackers on the internet. *AIDS Education and Prevention, 18*, 490–504.

Gruskin, E. P., Hart, S., Gordon, N., & Ackerson, L. (2001). Patterns of cigarette smoking and alcohol use among lesbians and bisexual women enrolled in a large health maintenance organization. *American Journal of Public Health, 91*, 976–980.

Halkitis, P. N., & Jerome, R. C. (2008). A comparative analysis of methamphetamine use: Black gay and bisexual men in relation to men of other races. *Addictive Behaviors, 33*, 83–93.

Halkitis, P. N., Zade, D. D., Shrem, M., & Marmor, M. (2004). Beliefs about HIV noninfection and risky sexual behavior among MSM. *AIDS Education and Prevention, 16,* 448–458.

Hart, T. A., & Heimberg, R. G. (2001). Presenting problems among treatment-seeking gay, lesbian and bisexual youth. *Journal of Clinical Psychology, 57,* 615–627.

Heermann, M., Wiggins, M., & Rutter, P. (2007). Creating a space for spiritual practice. Pastoral possibilities with sexual minorities. *Pastoral Psychology, 55,* 711–721.

Heffelfinger, J. D., Swint, E. B., Berman, S. M., & Weinstock, H. S. (2007). Trends in primary and secondary syphilis among men who have sex with men in the United States. *Journal of Public Health, 97,* 1076–1084.

Henning-Stout, M., James, S., & Macintosh, S. (2000). Reducing harassment of lesbian, gay, bisexual, transgender, and questioning youth in schools. *School Psychology Review, 29,* 180–191.

Herek, G., Cogan, J., & Gillis, R. (2002). Victim experiences in hate crimes based on sexual orientation. *Journal of Social Issues, 58*(2), 319–339.

Herek, G., Gillis, J., & Cogan, J. (1999). Psychological sequelae of hate-crime victimization among lesbian, gay, and bisexual adults. *Journal of Consulting and Clinical Psychology, 67,* 945–951.

Hill, P. C., & Pargament, K. I. (2003). Advances in the conceptualization and measurement of religion and spirituality. *American Psychologist, 58,* 64–74.

Ida, D. (2007, June). Cultural competency and recovery within diverse populations. *Psychiatric Rehabilitation Journal, 31,* 49–53.

Isay, R. A. (1999). Gender in homosexual boys: Some developmental and clinical considerations. *Psychiatry, 62,* 187–195.

Jourard, S. M. (1959). Healthy personality and self-disclosure. *Mental Hygiene, 43,* 499–507.

Kaysen, D., & Lostutter, M. A. (2005). Cognitive processing therapy for acute stress disorder resulting from an anti-gay assault. *Cognitive and Behavioral Practice, 12*(3), 278–289.

Kitts, R. (2005). Gay adolescents and suicide: Understanding the association. *Adolescence, 40,* 621–629.

Landolt, M. A., Bartholomew, K., Saffrey, C., Oram, D., & Perlman, D. (2002). Gender nonconformity, childhood rejection, and adult attachment: A study of gay men. *Archives of Sexual Behavior, 33,* 117–128.

Leach, M. M. (2006). *Cultural diversity and suicide.* Binghamton, NY: Haworth Press.

Lombardi, E. (2001). Enhancing gender healthcare. *American Journal of Public Health, 91,* 869–872.

MacGillivray, I. K. (2000). Educational equity for gay, lesbian, bisexual, transgendered, and queer/questioning students: the demands of democracy and social justice for America's schools. *Education and Urban Society, 32,* 303–323.

Makadon, H. J. (2006). Improving healthcare for the lesbian and gay communities. *New England Journal of Medicine, 354,* 895–897.

Makadon, H. J., Mayer, K. H., & Garofalo, R. (2006). Optimizing primary care for men who have sex with men. *The Journal of the American Medical Association, 296,* 1–7. Retrieved November 17, 2007, from http://wf2dnvr10.webfeat.org.

Marrazzo, J. M. (2004). Barriers to infectious disease care among lesbians. *Emerging Infectious Diseases*. Retrieved January 25, 2008, from http://www.cdc.gov/ncidod/EID/vol10no11/04–0467.htm.

Marrazzo, J. M., Koutsky, L. A., Eschenbach, D. A., Agnew, K., Stine, K., & Hillier, S. L. (2002). Characterization of vaginal flora and bacterial vaginosis in women who have sex with women. *Journal of Infectious Diseases, 185*, 1307–1313.

Martinez, J., & Hosek, S. G. (2005). An exploration of the down-low identity: Nongay-identified young African American men who have sex with men. *Journal of the National Medical Association, 97*, 1103–1113.

Matthews, M. A., Bartholomew, K., Saffrey, C., Oram, D., & Perlman, D. (2002). Gender nonconformity, childhood rejection, and adult attachment: A study of gay men. *Archives of Sexual Behavior, 33*, 117–128.

McAndrew, S., & Warne, T. (2004). Ignoring the evidence dictating the practice: Sexual orientation, suicidality and the dichotomy of the mental health nurse. *Journal of Psychiatric and Mental Health Nursing, 11*, 428–434.

Mennuti, R. B., Freeman, A., & Christner, R. W. (2006). *Cognitive behavioral interventions in educational settings: A handbook for practice*. New York: Routledge.

Meyer, H. (2003). Prejudice, social stress, and mental health in lesbian, gay, and bisexual populations: Conceptual issues and research evidence, *Psychological Bulletin, 129*, 674–697.

Meyer, I. H. (2001). Why lesbian, gay, bisexual, and transgender health? *American Journal of Public Health, 91*, 856–859.

Miller, W. M., & Thoresen, C. E. (2003). Spirituality, religion, and health: An emerging research field. *American Psychologist, 58*, 24–35.

Millet, G., Malebranche, D., Mason, B. & Spikes, P. (2005). Focusing "down low": Bisexual black men, HIV risk and heterosexual transmission. *Journal of the National Medical Association, 97*, S52–S60.

Mills, T. C., Paul, J., Stall, R., Pollack, L., Canchola, J., Chang, Y. J., et al. (2004). Distress and depression in men who have sex with men: The urban men's health study. *American Journal of Psychiatry, 161*(2), 278–285).

Moskowitz, D. A., & Roloff, M. E. (2007). The existence of a bug chasing subculture. *Culture, Health, and Sex, 9*, 347–357.

National Gay and Lesbian Task Force (NGLTF). (1984). *Anti-gay/lesbian victimization: A study by the National Gay Task Force in cooperation with gay and lesbian organizations in eight U.S. cities*. Washington, DC: Author.

Negy, C., & Eisenman, R. (2005). A comparison of African-American and White college students' affective and attitudinal reactions to lesbian, gay, and bi-sexual individuals: An exploratory study. *The Journal of Sex Research, 42*(4), 291–298.

Noelle, M. (2002). The ripple effect on the Matthew Shepard murder: Impact on the assumptive worlds of members of the targeted group. *American Behavioral Scientist, 46*, 27–50.

Pachankis, J. E., & Goldfried, M. (2006). Social anxiety in young gay men. *Journal of Anxiety Disorders, 20*(8), 996–1015.

Parsons, J. T., Kutnick, A. H., Halkitis, P. N., Punzalan, J. C., & Carbonari, J. P. (2005). Sexual risk behaviors and substance use among alcohol abusing HIV-positive men who have sex with men. *Journal of Psychoactive Drugs, 37*, 27–37.

Remafedi, G. (2006). Lesbian, gay, bisexual, and transgender youths: Who smokes, and why? *Journal of Adolescent Health, 38,* 151–152.

Rodriguez, E. M., & Ouellette, S. C. (2000). Gay and lesbian Christian: Homosexual and religious identity integration in the members and participants of a gay-positive church. *Journal for the Scientific Study of Religion, 39*(3), 333–347.

Rose, S., & Mechanic, M. (2002). Psychological distress, crime features, and help-seeking behaviors related to homophobic bias incidents, *American Behavioral Scientist, 46,* 14–26.

Russell, S. T., & Joyner, K. (2001). Adolescent sexual orientation and suicide risk: Evidence from a national study. *American Journal of Public Health, 91,* 1276–1282.

Ryan, C., Futterman, D., & Stine, K. (1998). Helping our hidden youth. *American Journal of Nursing, 98,* 37–41.

Sanchez, J. P., Halipern, S., Lowe, C., & Calderon, Y. (2007). Factors associated with emergency department utilization by urban gay, lesbian, & bisexual individuals. *Journal of Community Health, 32,* 149–156.

Sandfort, T.G.M., deGraaf, R., Bijl, R. V., & Schnabel, P. (2001). Same-sex sexual behavior and psychiatric disorders: Findings from NEMESIS. *Archives of General Psychiatry, 58,* 85–91.

Scheer, S., Peterson, I., Page-Shafer, K., Delgado, V., Gleghorn, A., Ruiz, J., et al. (2002). Sexual and drug use behavior among women who have sex with both women and men: Results of a population-based survey. *American Journal of Public Health, 7,* 1110–1111.

Schilder, A. J., Kennedy, C., Goldstone, I., Ogden, R. D., Hogg, R. S., & O'Shaughnessy, M. V. (2001). Being dealt with as a whole person, care seeking and adherence: The benefits of culturally competent care. *American Journal of Public Health, 91,* 895–896.

Semple, S. J., Patterson, T. L., & Grant, I. (2002). Motivations associated with methamphetamine use among HIV+ men who have sex with men, *Journal of Substance Abuse Treatment, 22,* 149–156.

Silenzio, M. B., Pena, J. B., Duberstein, P. R., Carel, J., & Knox, K. L. (2007). Sexual orientation and risk factors for suicide ideation and suicide attempts among adolescents and young adults. *American Journal of Public Health, 97,* 2071–2075.

Smart, L., & Wegner, D. M. (1999). Covering up what can't be seen: Concealable stigmas and mental control. *Journal of Personality and Social Psychology, 77,* 474–486.

Stein, G. L., & Bonuck, K. A. (2001). Physician-patient relationships among the lesbian and gay community. *Journal of the Gay and Lesbian Medical Association, 5,* 87–93.

Weber, G. N. (2008) Using to numb the pain: Substance use and abuse among lesbian, gay, and bisexual individuals. *Journal of Mental Health Counseling, 30,* 31–52.

Wilkerson, G. J. (2001). What we don't know: The unaddressed health concerns of the transgendered. Retrieved January 25, 2008, from http://www.trans-health.com/displayarticle.php?aid=7.

Yarhouse, M. A., Brooke, H. L., & Pisano, P. (2005). Project inner compass: Young adults experiencing sexual identity confusion. *Journal of Psychology and Christianity, 24*(4), 352–360.

CHAPTER 4

Immigration and Social Justice: Latinos and the Twenty-first-century Wave

Ken Martinez

The United States is a land of immigrants, or at least that is what it was meant to be. The U.S. Constitution signed in 1787 protects those seeking freedom from persecution for their religious or political beliefs because after all, the reason for the founding of the "land of the free" was to ensure these protections. The poem written by Ezra Lazarus on the Statue of Liberty proclaims, "Give me your tired, your poor, your huddled masses yearning to breathe free, the wretched refuse of your teeming shore. Send these, the homeless, tempest tossed, to me: I lift my lamp beside the golden door." Over the last 230 years, various fundamental challenges have confronted Lady Liberty's welcome in sentiment, behavior, policy and law. The new country grew and diversified with waves of immigrants during this period. With diversification came enrichment of cultures and languages, and concurrently also came conflict.

Reactions by those already in the so-called New World have been either positive or, in many cases, negative. What has caused the land of immigrants to reject each new wave once the previous wave has settled? Has it been a case of "ownership?" That is, once I am in, close the door behind me because this land belongs to me now and no one new? Has it been a case of competition and greed for what has been perceived to be limited wealth, opportunity and resources? Has it been a case of ethnocentrism or racism towards certain groups because of the color of their skin, the language they speak, their religion, or their cultural and national heritage? Has it been the primal need to keep another group down (and out) while feeling and acting superior, at least temporarily, over the other? These issues and their ramifications will be explored.

We must begin with the fundamental question, who was here first? We often forget that indigenous peoples including the Athabascans, Anastasi, Mayans, and Aztecs inhabited this continent prior to any immigrants. Their culturally and scientifically advanced civilizations are frequently forgotten because they no longer exist in the numbers they had in the pre-colonization era. Immigration, therefore, must be viewed within the context of an already conquered land. The colonization practices, persecution or abuse that many immigrants fled was being replicated in the new land on the indigenous people from whom the land was taken. As the New World was conquered in the late 1400s to the 1700s and a fledgling nation made up of new immigrants was being founded in the late 1700s, we must acknowledge the historical trauma that the original inhabitants of the continent endured. All the people who came after the "Native Americans" have been immigrants. The reality is that most of our ancestors, including our Hispanic/Latino ancestors, began as guests in a conquered land.

The English-born founders of the new United States were, for the most part, wise in their deliberation and writing of the founding documents and in developing a new paradigm of what it means to be a citizen of a free democratic nation. However, a closer look at the founding documents paints a contradictory picture. Naturalization is one of the few subjects mentioned in both the Declaration of Independence and the U.S. Constitution; therefore, its importance as a basic right was meant to prevent discrimination between a naturalized citizen and a native-born citizen. Yet, the U.S. Constitution in 1787 was signed with a provision to count all black slaves as three-fifths of one person, hence rendering them at 60 percent "value" or "worth." The Naturalization Act of 1795 restricted citizenship to "free white persons" who resided in the United States for five years and who renounced their allegiance to their country of origin. So, while naturalized citizens were valued enough to be mentioned twice, black slaves were not considered equal to white naturalized citizens according to the Constitution.

The concept of "social justice," the equal worth of all that includes equity and access to all resources, was challenged at the outset of this country's birth. Throughout the history of the United States, entitlement to fair treatment and equal rights for immigrants has vacillated depending on the political climate, economic stress, internal/external threats that were real or unreal and the immigrants' skin color. The country's social justice conscience is continually being tested with each new wave of immigrants. Hence, the colonization of American Indian land, the imperialistic attitude of the early Pilgrims toward Native Americans, and the legislation of black slaves to a "less than" equal status as fellow human beings set the stage for re-enacting the dynamic of the oppressor and the oppressed, endemic in the European world and now in the New World. While the major reason for the founding of this country was to escape religious discrimination and persecution, early Americans repeated the very discrimination, persecution and devaluing of the life they sought to escape. From the beginning of this country, the differential valuing of human beings and assignment of dignity based on race and ethnicity continues today.

AMERICAN IMMIGRATION HISTORY AND POLICY: FOR WHOSE NEEDS AND WHAT POLITICS?

As new immigrant waves crashed upon the shores of the United States, each national group was greeted with varying reactions depending on where they came from, why they came, and the color of their skin.

The first waves of immigration in the 1800s were primarily European. After the French Revolution, French and other Europeans like those that stormed the Bastille immigrated to the United States in reaction to the oppressive rule of the French monarchy. The response of Americans already in the United States was *fear* of "radicalism" by the new immigrants. In the 1840s to 1850s, the Irish immigrated in significant numbers due to famine. The response of Americans already in the United States was *fear* of the Irish Catholics who were thought to be loyal to the Pope; therefore, it was concluded that they would be disloyal to the U.S. government. Then, the Italians and Eastern European immigrants immigrated in the early twentieth century. The *fear* of these groups was based upon the "nondemocratic tendencies" they were thought to espouse (Pachon, 2007).

Immigrants came from the East as well. After the California gold rush of 1849, Chinese immigrants began arriving and quickly found work building the railroads, working the agricultural fields and mining the land. Along with manual labor employment, they also established successful businesses and commerce. Their entrepreneurial success caused concern and *fear* among Americans that had arrived before them. The legislative backlash to the *fear* of their increasing numbers and their success was the Naturalization Act of 1870, which limited American citizenship to "white persons and persons of African descent" and barred Asians from U.S. citizenship. Notice the shift from disenfranchising blacks 75 years earlier to now targeting and excluding the latest group of color. In 1882, the Chinese Exclusion Act was passed to specifically restrict Chinese immigration.

In the late 1800s, Japanese immigrants arrived in Hawaii and the mainland to work the agricultural fields; many replaced the Chinese immigrants who had been excluded from entering the country. *Fear* abounded alternating between the Chinese and the Japanese as the "yellow peril"; this heightened during and post–World War II, prompted by the military threat of the Japanese and the communist threat of the Chinese. Throughout history, however, both groups have been accused of threatening the living standard of white, U.S.-born workers and the fabric of American society, a familiar refrain today against undocumented Latinos.

In 1901, President William McKinley was assassinated by a person described as a Polish "anarchist." In response to that incident, the U.S.

Congress passed the Anarchist Exclusion Act, which allowed "political opinions" to be the basis for exclusion for entry into the United States. This was one of the first times that subjective criteria codified in law such as a person's "political opinions" could be used to prevent entry into the country. It set a precedent for the use of a narrow legal interpretation of immigration law.

In 1907, the United States and Japan agreed that Japanese were allowed to migrate to Hawaii to fill the need for farm laborers; however, they were barred by Executive Order from migrating from Hawaii to the continental United States. In 1913, California passed the Alien Land Law, which rendered "aliens ineligible from citizenship" (meaning Chinese and Japanese) from owning property in California. The Chinese Exclusion Act of 1882 was not rescinded until 1943; it was not until the end of the 1940s that all restrictions on Asians acquiring U.S. citizenship were abolished.

Yet, in response to the Japanese government's bombing of Pearl Harbor in December, 1941, the *fear* of Japanese infiltration lead to Executive Order 9066 authorizing the internment of 112,000 Japanese Americans who were U.S. citizens. In an unprecedented action, the U.S. government deprived these Americans of all their rights as citizens; they were stripped of their homes and property and dispersed all over the country in internment camps, much like prisoners of war. These citizens were considered threats to U.S. security, and were not released until World War II was over.

In 1923, the U.S. Supreme Court (*U.S. v. Bhaghat Singh Thind*) ruled that Indians from Asia could not become naturalized U.S. citizens. In 1934, the Tydings-McDuffie Act simultaneously gave independence to The Philippines, but also took away Filipinos' status as U.S. nationals and severely restricted Filipino immigration by establishing an annual immigration quota of 50. However, in 1942 at the beginning of World War II, the government reclassified Filipinos as U.S. citizens so they could register for the military and fill the need for new recruits (Mintz, 2007).

Latinos have encountered the same double standards over the decades. In 1924, the United States Border Patrol was formed and the term "illegal alien" was formally adopted by the U.S. government. (The etymology of the word "alien" is Latin from the word *alienus* meaning "not one's own." In this case, it refers to one's own country, but has the additional popular connotation of not being from this planet.) After the United States entered World War II in 1942, the U.S. *Bracero* Program was initiated to import over four million Mexican farm laborers to replace U.S.-born laborers who were serving in the U.S. military. The Mexicans were welcomed as laborers, but required to undergo dehumanizing conditions such as forced bodily fumigation with DDT before being allowed to enter the United States.

In 1954, following the end of World War II and the return of the military transitioning back to a civilian work force, the U.S. government once again reversed itself and enacted "Operation Wetback" to deport the very workforce they had proactively recruited during a time of national and economic need. The once-welcome *braceros* who sustained the economic infrastructure of the country during wartime were now summarily deported; they were no longer needed.

United States immigration policy and practice has historically been manipulated to accommodate the immediate economic or war-time needs of the government, while at the same time justifying discrimination towards immigrants of color. No doubt, each immigrant wave has been discriminated against, although immigrants of color have tolerated the largest injustices as borders open and close depending upon nationalistic needs and popular tolerance, or lack thereof, towards immigrants with different skin color. American Indians, Africans, African Americans, Asians and Latinos have suffered from social injustices and discrimination that has all too easily been justified.

LATINO DEMOGRAPHICS TODAY: FACTS AND MISCONCEPTIONS

The demographics of the United States population are changing algorithmically, especially for Latinos. As of 2007, the country's Hispanic/Latino population reached 45.5 million and constituted 15.1 percent of the U.S. population. By 2050, the U.S. Census Bureau estimates that there will be at least 102.6 million Latinos, constituting 24 percent of the U.S. population. Hispanics/Latinos are the largest and fastest growing ethnic/racial group in the country (U.S. Census Bureau, 2008). Cumulatively, the four major ethnic/racial groups currently constitute about 106 million people or 35 percent of the total U.S. population. (U.S. Census Bureau, 2008). Additionally, two out of five Latinos are immigrants and one in ten children in the U.S. lives in a family in which at least one parent is a non-U.S. citizen and one child is a U.S. citizen (Reardon-Anderson, Capps, & Fix, 2004).

Frequent misconceptions abound about Latino immigrants, including the stereotypes that they are lazy and don't work, don't pay taxes, live off welfare programs and don't contribute to society. In fact, most Latino immigrants work. Undocumented men come to the U.S. almost exclusively to work. In 2003, over 90 percent of undocumented men were employed, a rate higher than that for U.S. citizens or legal immigrants (Passel, Capps, & Fix, 2004). Undocumented immigrants also pay taxes. The U.S. Social Security Administration has estimated that three quarters of undocumented immigrants (approximately seven million) pay payroll taxes, contributing $6–7 billion conservatively in Social Security funds per year that they will be unable to claim (Porter, 2005). Undocumented immigrants pay real estate taxes, whether they own their own homes or rent, and they pay sales and other consumption taxes like everyone else. These taxes pay for schools and other essential services. *The New York Times* states that "even though differentials exist within the immigrant population by time of arrival, citizenship, and place of birth, studies show immigrants are equal to U.S.-born citizens in terms of paying taxes" (Porter, 2005). Latino immigrants pay for social services they receive through taxes they pay and the growth in the economy that they spur.

A recent study reports that for every 1 percent increase in the ratio of immigrants to natives, prices go down by about 0.5 percent (Lach, 2007). The study states that immigration acts as a brake on inflation. Immigrants spend more time comparison-shopping than natives, forcing markets to run more efficiently and thereby making cheaper prices available for all. So, there is no validity to the argument that immigrants are a drain to the national economy.

Another frequently-voiced concern is that immigrants, both legal and undocumented, raise the crime rate. Incarceration rates among young men are the lowest for immigrants, even those who are less educated. In 2000, the incarceration rate for U.S.-born men between 18 and 39 years old was 3.5 percent, five times higher than the incarceration rate of their immigrant counterparts. The large increase in illegal immigrants has not resulted in a rise in crime even though the immigrant population has doubled to around 12 million, violent crime has declined 34 percent, and property crime has fallen 26 percent since 1994 (Rumbaut & Ewing, 2007).

Crime by immigrants is not the problem, but crimes against immigrants are a problem. The Federal Bureau of Investigations (2007) Hate Crimes Statistics Report shows the sharpest increase in the number of hate crimes reported against Hispanics/Latinos based on their ethnicity or national origin since it began reporting the statistic. In 2006, Hispanics comprised 62.8 percent of hate crime victims, compared to 51.5 percent in 2004, an increase of 25 percent. This increase took place even before the wave of local and state anti-immigrant legislation in 2007.

More than 1,404 pieces of anti-immigrant legislation were introduced in state legislatures during the first half of 2007, with 182 bills becoming law in 43 states (Faiola, 2007). This is a major long-term consequence of anti-immigrant sentiment.

ACHIEVING THE AMERICAN DREAM?: BEHAVIORAL HEALTH OF LATINOS DETERIORATES WITH SUCCEEDING U.S.-BORN GENERATIONS

Latino immigrants, like most immigrants, go to the United States to find *el Sueno Americano*, the American Dream. Economic opportunities are far more plentiful in the United States than in their home countries. Unfortunately, other challenges are faced by immigrants and their succeeding generations that are more insidious, such as the threat to their mental health and well-being.

Mexican Americans have a higher proportion of two-parent families and lower divorce and separation rates compared to U.S.-born Caucasians

(Frisbie & Bean, 1995). Mexican immigrant women have better nutrient intake and their children have lower child mortality rates and higher birth weights than the children of U.S.-born mothers of Mexican descent (California Department of Health Services, 1993; Escobar, 1998; Guendelman & Abrams, 1995; Voelker, 1994).

Immigrants also generally appear to have lower rates of mental disorders than their U.S.-born counterparts, 50 percent less in some studies. Latinos, who self-reported lesser ability to speak, read and write English showed a lower overall risk for mental disorders and a reduced risk for substance use. Second and later generations of immigrants have a higher risk for mental disorders than their parents (National Survey of American Life and National Latino and Asian American Study, 2007). The prevalence of alcohol and other drug abuse was more than four times higher in U.S.-born individuals of Mexican descent than those born in Mexico (Vega et al., 1998). Eighty-eight percent of U.S.-born Latino children and youth have unmet mental health needs, highest of all ethnic/racial groups (Kataoka, Zhang & Wells, 2002). U.S.-born Latinos have high rates of depression, anxiety-related disorders and rates of suicidal ideation and attempts especially among Latina adolescents, yet Latino children and youth utilize mental health services at lowest rates compared to all other ethnic/racial groups. Latinos have the highest unmet need among all groups, yet the lowest utilization. Place of birth was more influential on the prevalence of psychiatric disorders than age, sex, or socioeconomic status, concluding that poverty is not a predictive factor for mental illness.

The conclusion is that the longer an immigrant family lives in the United States, the worse their mental health prognosis. It appears that the more exposure to American society, the less healthy Latinos become. So what are Latinos aspiring to become? Like others before them, Latinos seek good health, prosperity, safety, freedom, and limitless opportunity. Yet, in many cases, especially for those that are more recently arrived, that dream has been much harder to realize given the hostile reception they have received.

LATINO IMMIGRATION TODAY: HAS HISTORY TAUGHT US ANYTHING?

Our hope as a young and historically-maturing nation is to learn from our past. When we do not, we repeat our mistakes. The country has grown and been strengthened by the diversity of our population. The indigenous cultures that preceded us on this continent and the cultural weave of immigrants since then have nurtured the nation since its birth. Nevertheless, we find ourselves repeating past intolerant behavior towards the most current wave of immigrants: Latinos.

The United States has had a very ambivalent relationship with immigrants as evidenced by the exclusion/inclusion laws passed towards

Africans, African Americans, Chinese, Japanese, Filipinos, and others over the years. The Bracero Program and Operation Wetback are the latest examples of the contradictory relationship that the United States has had with immigrants, in this case Latinos. The American economy has always been dependent economically on inexpensive labor, hard work and ready pool of immigrants. The most recent dependency on Latinos began in the agricultural fields that Cesar Chavez and the United Farm Workers later organized. It has moved to the meat packing, manufacturing, service jobs, construction, and other manual labor jobs that have grown with economic prosperity. The white labor force, because of better education that leads to more desirable job choices with expectation of higher pay and growth in the nonmanual labor sector, has not filled those positions. Mexican and other Latin American immigrants, whose weak home country economies accelerate their workforce migration, have filled the low paying jobs by the millions.

So, what is contradictory about the American relationship with Latino immigrants today? The same ambivalence that Americans have always had towards immigrants of color; Americans have always loved cheap labor but have simultaneously felt threatened by large numbers of people who speak a different language and look different to them. Navarrette (2008) states that U.S.-born Hispanics/Latinos "condemn the hypocrisy of a society that is addicted to illegal immigrant labor but looks for others to blame for the addiction." This, he points out, despite the fact that Latinos/ Hispanics account for a higher ratio of Medal of Honor recipients than any other group.

Today, tens of thousands of documented and undocumented Latino immigrants have been arrested since 2006 under massive nationwide sweeps called "Operation Return to Sender" and "Operation Wagon Train" being conducted by the U.S. Immigration and Customs Enforcement (ICE). The raids have devastated families because they are conducted at work sites and parents are detained without any contact or planning with their remaining families and children. In some cases, the immigrants' children, many of whom are U.S.-born citizens, are placed in state custody. Given that there are approximately 5 million U.S.-born children in families with at least one undocumented parent and approximately 20 percent of school age children are immigrants or children of immigrants, the toll is significant (Hernandez, Denton, & Macartney, 2007).

The number of arrested adults, many of whom are parents, has tripled since 2001 to 311,000 so far in the first quarter of 2008 and raids continue every day. Many get sick in custody, both physically and mentally ill. Approximately 15 percent out of 33,000 detainees held on any given day, or 4,500 detainees, are mentally ill. Care is inadequate or nonexistent. In prisons for the mentally ill, the ratio of staff to patient is 1 to 10, but in the immigration detention centers, it is 1 to 1,142 despite the high percentage of people with mental illness.

Suicide is the most common cause of death among detained immigrants. Fifteen out of 83 deaths have been attributed to suicide from 2003 to the first quarter of 2008. Therefore, the human rights of arrested detainees are compromised even though they are detained only for the purposes of deportation. The prison system or immigration detention centers are unable to handle the numbers of detainees, much less in a humane manner (Priest & Goldstein, 2008).

Not only are the children traumatized by the sudden and long-term separation from their parents, the child welfare systems are overwhelmed with children who are not victims of abuse or neglect, but are in custody solely because they are forcibly abandoned. Families are torn apart, a new generation of traumatized children is produced, child welfare systems are ill-equipped, hostility is bred and local economies are devastated. At every level, the country is not well served. Many local mayors, city councils and county commissioners speak against the raids because of the decimation of their local economies and some because of the social injustice inherent in the mass deportations.

So what is today's *fear* about? Pachon (2007) states that today's *fear* of Latino immigrants is that they may harbor "dual nationalist loyalties," a familiar refrain. Unfortunately, the *fear* of Latino immigration is more complicated today. It disguises, not very successfully, an underlying ethnocentric and racist attitude that is based upon a sense of superiority by the dominant culture as well as a sense of uncertainty by the dominant culture regarding the loyalty that Latinos have to the United States. The dominant culture does not trust that acculturation and assimilation are occurring with Latinos.

Acculturation is a natural cultural phenomenon and Latinos like other immigrants are experiencing it, for better or worse. Like other ethnic immigrants in the past, Latinos are still Latinos even after immigrating and retain their cultural identity while actively participating in and acculturating to American life. Transnationalism does not hinder the bonds with the United States (Waldinger, 2007). Therefore, fostering acculturation, speaking a second language (English), and sharing another cultural heritage ought to be encouraged and validated, not punished and made illegal.

Fear by some in the dominant culture also masks their resentment over several issues: immigrants' use of public services including educational, social and health services; the perception that undocumented immigrants don't pay taxes; Latino immigrants taking lower paying jobs thought to belong to others; immigrants' who don't speak English when they arrive; their cultural "ways"; and their skin color being different, frequently darker, than the dominant culture. The truth is that Latino values such as the importance of family (*familismo*), respect of others, especially elders (*respeto*), the importance placed on relationships (*personalismo*) are as traditional, and some would say "conservative," as those espoused by those most vocally condemning them.

A 2008 study by Jacob Vigdor reveals that through an assimilation index he created, immigrants assimilate at different rates. The study used U.S. Census data between 1890 and 2006 to measure current and historical similarities between those born in the United States and immigrants. Over the last 25 years, immigrants have assimilated faster than their counterparts 100 years ago. He measured economic (employment, education, home-ownership), cultural (ability to speak English, marriage to natives, number of children) and civic (naturalization and military service) assimilation indices. Vigdor found that immigrants from developed countries do not necessarily assimilate better than others; those who arrive as children are almost indistinguishable from U.S.-born and those who speak English don't necessarily do better economically than those who don't. The study reports that Mexicans, Chinese and East Indians, according to his scale, assimilate slower than others such as Canadians, Filipinos and Koreans. Mexicans assimilate faster culturally and more slowly economically or civically (Vigdor, 2008).

Some may interpret the index to measure the degree of similarity between those born in the United States and those born outside the United States, which may falsely imply that those who are different from the U.S.-born standard must strive to become like their U.S.-born counterparts. The author cautions against this interpretation or implied goal by stating that they are not imposing a requirement that immigrants have to become more like those born in the United States but that the process can work both ways. That is, those born in the United States can be favorably influenced by what immigrants bring and offer the country.

Vigdor states that one of the things that may be preventing Mexicans from assimilating more quickly is that they are primarily economic immigrants who expect to go back home, so there is less pressure to assimilate. While some may interpret the results of this study to indicate that Mexicans are resistant to assimilation and therefore should be treated more harshly than other immigrant groups, the fact is that variations for cultural versus economic versus civic assimilation vary from immigrant group to immigrant group depending upon the receptivity of the host nation's political and legal positions. If a Mexican immigrant is not allowed to become a naturalized citizen because of the host nation's explicit and implicit immigration laws and practice, he is of course going to score low on civic assimilation since it is not legally possible to meet that indicator. If he is limited economically by not being able to find higher paying jobs and therefore unable to own a home due to the host nation's laws and practices, he is going to score lower on the economic index. Yet he is still learning English and raising a family in the United States, therefore scoring higher on the cultural index. Canadians score lower in civic assimilation because they choose not to seek U.S. citizenship and therefore do not serve in the military, yet Canadians are not viewed as resisting assimilation or being unpatriotic as are Mexicans frequently accused. So, while some U.S. citizens assume that the goal for immigrants should be assimilation, the host culture may not allow that to happen because of its laws and practices, at least according to the Vigdor index. Acculturation takes place regardless of the assimilation expectations of others or the barriers posed to prevent assimilation from happening.

THE REACTION

The result and the typical reaction to "immigration hysteria" are to "get tough." Arizona, in 2007, enacted the toughest anti-immigrant legislation in the country. It voted to suspend the business license, for up to 10 days, of any firm that knowingly hired undocumented workers and revoke the license for a second offense. The intended consequence was realized: the exodus of many immigrants (to neighboring states). The unintended consequence was the exodus of the state's much-needed labor force, but to such an extent the lawmakers did not calculate. It caused a huge negative impact to the state's economy. This quietly prompted the introduction of new legislation intended to stabilize the economy by instituting a "temporary guest worker pilot program" for a two-year work term. The message is we don't want to live with you, but we can't live without you, so let's use your essential labor temporarily and then send you back for another batch of cheap labor, regardless of the consequence to you or your family.

The inescapable truth is that the population of Latinos is growing and immigration is not the only reason. Births account for the majority of the increase in the Latino population. The United States must confront the statistical facts and the economic realities of an ever growing number of Latinos that cannot be easily solved with the stroke of an Executive Order pen or legislative or municipal mandate as has been the answer with prior immigrant waves. Latinos have become an integral thread in the cultural fabric of the country and an essential component of the economic foundation.

Unfortunately, history has taught us lessons that have gone unheeded, including the fact that our usual response to immigrants is, at minimum, reactionary. It becomes "us" against "them," that reduces a complex issue into a simplistic antagonistic battle with no winner. It usually means more anti-immigrant laws, polices and regulations. It polarizes the citizenry. It throws us back into divisive and ineffective arguments such as the "melting pot" theory and the perceived need to assimilate to the point of homogenization, instead of acculturate. It diminishes us into a world of dichotomies such as English-only versus bi- or multilingual; patriotic versus anti-American; citizen versus "alien"; high-wage earner versus low-wage earner; employer versus employee; and entitled versus unentitled.

What have we learned? Not as much as the repeated historical lessons could have taught us. We have not learned that the "fears" are unfounded; that the scare tactics are only that; that the instinctual need to exclude is not just self-preservation but overt ethnocentrism or racism; that no matter how much we know intellectually, our emotional response is stronger; that viewing the world dichotomously is easier than grappling with the implications, complications and richness of the "gray."

CHALLENGES TO TRANSFORMING THE SYSTEM TODAY

We have come a long way since the days of slavery, segregation on buses and in restaurants, and teachers washing students' mouths with soap because of the language they spoke in the classroom. The most formidable challenge we face today, though, is confronting the still existent but more refined form of racism and ethnocentrism in this country, best described as "institutional racism." Institutional racism can be defined as the manifestation of racism in social, economic, educational and political forces or policies that operate to foster discriminatory outcomes (Barker, 2003; Barndt, 1991).

We have not come very far in practicing equity for everyone, the equity that is afforded those in the dominant society, especially when it comes to immigrants. While individual racism and ethnocentrism are less obvious, yet still present, today institutional, structural racism and ethnocentrism are their twenty-first-century form. It is more insidious, more difficult to single out when it is disguised in policy and regulation, yet embedded in practice. The effect is not immediately or individually overtly obvious but the aggregate outcomes are measurable. For example, the denial rate for home mortgage loans is higher for Latinos (as well as African Americans) than for whites (Huck, 2000); loan denials are more likely and costs of borrowing are higher for low-income families and families of color; differences in credit constraints by race and ethnicity persist, indicating discrimination in the credit industry (Center for American Progress, 2007); and the perception of Americans who feel they have received poor quality medical treatment or care in the past five years because of their racial or ethnic background (whites 1%, Hispanics 21%) or because of their accent or how well they speak English (whites 2%, Hispanics 21%), (Elders, 2006). These are but a few examples of the structural or institutional racism that abound today.

CONCLUSION

Diversity in mind and in action—U.S. history and the "national mind" as reflected in legislation, policy, and practice—has not fulfilled the intent of Ezra Lazarus' poem, or the intent of the founding fathers. Instead of accepting the tired, poor, huddled masses, homeless and tempest tossed, the door is shut, especially for immigrants of color. Our rhetoric about equality and diversity must match our actions. We can do better.

Recommendations for a Socially Just Immigration Policy

The current immigration discourse has the potential for a different response, a transformational one that changes the dialogue from a divisive finger-pointing blame of others to one of mutual benefit and understanding; one not only of tolerance, but acceptance of those who add value and diversity to our collective American culture.

1. We must move the discussion from emotional hyperbole and partisan politics to indisputable facts, including economic and cultural facts about the contributions that immigrants have and still make to this country. Immigrants are value added, economically and culturally.
2. Redefine the issue historically as the latest installment in a series of immigration waves that have broadened and strengthened the shoulders of the country. While the immigration experience is difficult when it is occurring, the outcomes from each past immigrant wave have been positive and fruitful. Americans can be proud that the vastness of land and the country's wealth of opportunity are valued by those who seek to improve themselves and contribute to their adopted country.
3. Begin and/or continue an informed national dialogue on race/ethnicity as a defining American issue. It is still a relevant debate that requires national, state and community leadership to advance. We cannot rely on the fragile cover of "political correctness" to protect us from an honest dialogue about differences and similarities based only on skin color and language spoken. The dialogue of inclusion must also include a discussion about world view, historical context, insidious beliefs and practices, shared and distinct values, beliefs and traditions that are cumulatively healthy and enriching.
4. We need an informed, humane, socially just and comprehensive immigration policy (not a blind purging policy full of racist/ethnocentric overtones) that is based on humane societal, economic and political realities. Certain facts are undeniable. The number of Latino citizens and undocumented workers in the United States upon which the U.S. economy is dependent is significant and isn't going away. Specifically, an immigration policy must include:

   A reasonable pathway to citizenship for those immigrants that are in the United States already and whose families are contributing members of the nation's society and economy. The pathway could include an application with a process that lasts no more than five years, employment by at least the family bread winner using an immigrant worker identification system, paying taxes, learning English, a reasonable and nonprohibitive fee and being free from felony convictions that are not immigration-related charges brought for the sole purpose of sabotaging the naturalization process.

   For those Latino immigrants who do not reside in the United States, but who wish to become citizens, utilize a procedure that is similar to the process above and that applies to any immigrant of any nation.

As a nation that is proud of its immigrant founding fathers and mothers, we have an opportunity to foster the potential of a new group of immigrants who, like them, sought refuge and a better life free from tyranny, persecution and discrimination. The contributions of the Eastern European, Italian, Irish, Asian, and other immigrant waves have enriched the cultural and economic wealth of the country. There is no difference in the most current Latino immigrant wave other than the color of their skin.

A nation is strong as long as its leaders govern on behalf of everyone. That is accomplished through a unifying message that communicates the mutual benefit of a diverse society for everyone and the practice to back it up. If our leaders' message is to disenfranchise segments of our population because of their country of origin, the language they speak, the religion they practice or the color of their skin, then we lose. We are in desperate need of wise leadership on immigration.

REFERENCES

Barker, R. L. (2003). *The social work dictionary* (5th ed.). Washington, DC: NASW Press.

Barndt, J. R. (1991). *Dismantling racism: The continuing challenge to white America.* Minneapolis: Augsburg Fortress.

California Department of Health Services. (1993). Center for Health Statistics. California Birth Cohort File. California Department of Health Services.

Center for American Progress. (2007, August 15). *Access denied: Minorities and low-income families face barriers to credit.* Common Dreams.org News Center. Retrieved August 15, 2007, from www.commondreams.org/news2007/0815-06.htm.

Elders, J. M. (2006). The politics of health care. *Social Research, 73*, 805–818.

Escobar, J. (1998). Immigration and mental health: Why are immigrants better off? *Archives of General Psychiatry, 55*, 781–782.

Faiola, A. (2007, October 15). States' immigrant policies diverge: In differences, some see obstacles for a national law. *Washington Post,* A01.

Federal Bureau of Investigations. (2007, November 20). Hate Crimes Statistics Report. Retrieved December 12, 2007, from http://www.fbi.gov/ucr/hc2006/dowloadfiles/html.

Frisbie, W. P., & Bean F. D. (1995). The Latino family in comparative perspective: Trials and current conditions. In C. Jacobson (Ed.), *Racial and ethnic families in the United States* (pp. 29–71). New York: Garland.

Guendelman, S., & Abrams, B. (1995). Dietary intake among Mexican American women: Differences and a comparison with white non-Hispanic women. *American Journal of Public Health, 85*, 20–25.

Hernandez, D. J., Denton, N. A., & Macartney, S. E. (2007, April). Children in immigrant families—The U.S. and 50 states: National origins, language and early education. In *Children in America's newcomer families* (Research Brief Series). Albany, NY: Child Trends and The Center for Social and Demographic Analysis, University at Albany, SUNY.

Huck, P. F. (2000). *Home mortgage lending by applicants race/ethnicity: Do HMDA figures provide a distorted picture?* Chicago: Federal Reserve Bank of Chicago,

Consumer Issues Research Services, Consumer and Community Affairs Division, Policy Studies.

Kataoka, S., Zhang, L., & Wells, K. (2002). Unmet need for mental health care among U.S. children: Variation by ethnicity and insurance status. *American Journal of Psychiatry, 159*(9), 1548–1555.

Lach, S. (2007, August). Immigration and prices. *Journal of Political Economy, 115*(4), 1–49.

Mintz, S. (2007). *Back to ethnic America: Landmarks in immigration history.* Digital History. Retrieved March 22, 2008, from http://www.digitalhistory.uh.edu/historyonline/immigration_chron.cfm.

National Survey of American Life and National Latino and Asian American Study. (2007, January). *American Journal of Public Health, 97*(1), 1–98.

Navarrette, R. (2008, April 24). All Hispanics unfairly lumped together with illegals. *Albuquerque Journal.*

Pachon, H. (2007, April). Tomas Rivera Policy Institute. *Los Angeles Times* (Opinion-Editorial).

Passel, J. D., Capps, R., & Fix, M. (2004). *Undocumented immigrants: Facts and figures.* Washington, DC: The Urban Institute.

Porter, E. (2005, April 5). Illegal immigrants are bolstering social security with billions. *New York Times.*

Priest, D., & Goldstein, A. (2008, May 13). Suicides point to gaps in treatment; errors in psychiatric diagnoses and drugs plague strained immigration system. *Washington Post.*

Reardon-Anderson, J., Capps, R., & Fix, M. (2004). *The health, behavior, and well-being of children in immigrant families* (Policy Brief B-52). Washington, DC: The Urban Institute.

Rumbaut, R. G., & Ewing, W. A. (2007). *The myth of immigrant criminality and the paradox of assimilation: Incarceration rates among native and foreign born men.* Washington, DC: Immigration Policy Center.

U.S. Census Bureau. (2008). 2008 national population projections. Retrieved May 1, 2008, from http://www.census.gov/population/www/projections/2008projections.html.

Vega, W. A., Kolody, B., Aguilar-Glaxiola, S., Alderete, E., Catalana, R., & Carveo-Anduaga, J. (1998). Lifetime prevalence of DSM-II-R psychiatric disorders among urban and rural Mexican Americans in California. *Archives of General Psychiatry, 156,* 928–934.

Vigdor, J. L. (2008, March). *Measuring immigrant assimilation in the United States.* Civic Report, Manhattan Institute for Policy Research, No. 53.

Voelker, R. (1994). Born in the USA: Infant health paradox. *Journal of the American Medical Association, 272,* 1803–1804.

Waldinger, R. (2007). *Between here and there: How attached are Latino immigrants to their native country?* Washington, DC: Pew Hispanic Center.

CHAPTER 5

Gerodiversity and Social Justice: Voices of Minority Elders

Michiko Iwasaki, Yvette N. Tazeau, Douglas Kimmel,
Nancy Lynn Baker, and T. J. McCallum

Age may be a matter of chronology and biology, but aging is a culturally contextualized experience. The face of American elders in the future will be more multifaceted in terms of race, ethnicity, sexual orientation, religion, and disability status and their intersections. Minority status such as race, ethnicity, gender, age, sexual orientation, social-economic levels, religion, and disability are often studied and addressed in piecemeal fashion. In that process, psychologists have accumulated considerable information from valuable empirically-based research that has focused on one culture or issue at a time. These cultural factors, however, do not exist as isolated influences and incidences. Instead, they intersect with all the other threads that make up the tapestry of human existence.

Although the process of aging and issues related to aging are relevant to all individuals, aging is often overlooked when studying ethnic diversity or is discussed in terms of a separate minority status. The meaning of growing older is framed by culture. Both the meaning of aging and the experience of aging is shaped by one's culture and by the relationship of that culture to the dominant paradigms and practices of the society or nation in which one resides. Aging-related issues may present particular challenges and additional hardships to minority communities; they may also involve special meanings and opportunities to grow. The present status of older adults within a cultural group in the United States represents the rich and complex cumulative effect of one's life experiences as a minority individual either born in the United States or emigrated from another country.

WHAT IS GERODIVERSITY?

The term *gerodiversity* represents an approach to the issues of aging embedded within a cultural diversity framework; a framework that treats people not just as individuals but as existing within an ecological context that includes their cultural identity, cultural heritage, local social culture, family and interpersonal relationships, as well as the larger society's dominant social frameworks. While conventional approaches to aging issues may seek to address the special issues of minority group elders, *gerodiversity* is an assertion that all aging occurs in a cultural context. In this framework, the term *gerodiversity* addresses the differences in values and meanings of and about elders that exist among cultures and the special challenges of aging as part of a group that experiences discrimination or economic and social oppression.

Gerodiversity necessarily implies a social justice perspective. Various issues faced by minority elders cannot be fully understood without a social justice concept. While traditional views about social justice focus on outcomes (i.e., equal distribution of resources), the contemporary view emphasizes *the process* of decision-making and interaction that occurs at an individual and system level (Young, 1990). Moreover, Bell (1997) asserts, "the goal of social justice is full and *equal participation* of *all* groups in a society that is mutually shaped to meet their needs" (p. 3). Because the lives of today's minority elders reflect a long history of societal oppression, it is vital not only to ensure their participation, but also to treat with sensitivity how they are included or treated in any decision-making process. With these assertions, the term gerodiversity entails an action-oriented communication and decision-making process to promote equal access to societal resources for all seniors regardless of their historically marginalized group status.

DEMOGRAPHY OF GERODIVERSITY

The number of elders among racially and ethnically diverse groups is expected to increase at astonishing rates. According to the U.S. Census, older minority adults comprised 17 percent of all American seniors in 2003 and are projected to reach 39 percent in 2050 (AgingStats.Gov, 2008). Older Hispanics and older Asian Americans are the two fastest-growing populations among all racial and ethnic groups; the population growth for older Hispanics between 2003 and 2050 is projected to be 300 percent and the population growth for older Asian Americans is approximately 270 percent. While the proportion of older African Americans and other racial minorities (e.g., American Indians, Alaska Natives, Native Hawaiians, and combinations of two or more races) are also expected to continue growing, the relative proportion of non-Hispanic white elders is expected to decrease between now and 2050.

It is not currently possible to accurately report the population of older gay, lesbian, bisexual, and transgender (GLBT) persons. However, it is thought that at present there are between one and three million over the age of 65 and, by the year 2030, it is estimated that four to six million older Americans will be GLBT (Cahill, South, & Spade, 2000). These GLBT elders, of course, exist within all of the diverse cultural groups that make up the U.S. population. Many GLBT persons are in long-term relationships—64 percent of lesbians and 46 percent of gay men—and one in six unmarried households are same-sex couples in California (Swift, 2008). According to National Gay and Lesbian Task Force (NGLTF, n.d.), the percentage of same-sex cohabiting couples has increased 10 percent nationally between 2004 and 2006.

Disability status is common among older adults as 42 percent of American seniors reported having a disability (U.S. Census Bureau, 2003). For many seniors, disability is a result of illnesses correlated with aging. A longevity trend has begun to be evident among persons with various types of developmental disabilities as well. Currently, there are estimated to be 641,000 individuals over 60 years of age with developmental disabilities, and the number is projected to double by 2030 because of greater life expectancy of persons with these conditions (Heller, n.d.).

GERODIVERSITY AND SOCIAL JUSTICE: VOICES OF MINORITY ELDERS

According to the American Psychological Association Working Group on Older Adults (APA, 1998), older adults who are also ethnic/racial minority members often have numerous challenges regarding health and psychological services including delays in obtaining health-related treatments, underutilization of mental health services, higher incidences of obesity and late onset diabetes, poverty, unemployment, stereotyping, discrimination, lack of properly normed assessment tools, and frequent misdiagnosis. With minorities projected to reach 39 percent in 2050 (AgingStats.Gov, 2008), the cultural and ethnic needs of these groups take on great importance. In this section, we highlight major issues faced by the elders of various cultural minority groups.

African American Elders

African Americans experienced a forced migration by way of slave trade, enforced segregation, and social institutions that were racially discriminating in many ways, including political disenfranchisement. The elders of the African American community are historical witnesses to the social justice movements in the United States and other countries with black heritage. Many of them were in fact social activists in various historical racial struggles. Many of today's African American elders remember the time before the Civil Rights Act of 1963, which outlawed discrimination in employment and public accommodation, the Voting Rights Act of 1965 that provided a legal right to political enfranchisement, and the various U.S. Supreme Court decisions in the 1950s and 1960s that established blacks' access to formerly white only public schools.

The historical and sociodemographic disadvantage of African Americans continues to affect their lives in various ways. Among the 65 and older population, black elders have the highest rate of poverty (26.4%) among all racial groups (Administration on Aging, 2004). Poverty is more apparent among those who reside in the South and in urban areas. Among subgroups of black Americans and all other racial minority elders, unmarried black women between the ages of 65 and 74 had the highest poverty rate of 47 percent (Administration on Aging, 2004). This is not surprising given that, on average, black women both currently and historically have earned less than white women, who in turn earn less than almost any group of men. Many of today's black female elders had low-wage domestic service jobs where employers frequently did not pay Social Security on their behalf. Thus, there has not been a pension, retirement savings, or health insurance. In addition, a common phenomenon in which grandparents, especially grandmothers, raise their own grandchildren creates an even greater economic burden for black elders. Multigenerational living, particularly grandparents caring for their grandchildren, presents unique challenges to this population by further impacting socioeconomic status and health (Burton & Dilworth-Anderson, 1991).

African Americans are known to have lower life expectancy than whites. The racial difference in life expectancy becomes less with age: six years differences in life expectancy at birth versus two years at age 65 (Administration on Aging, 2004). Black elders display comparatively high rates of diabetes and hypertension in addition to other chronic health problems (Siegel, 1999). Many of the diseases afflicting older African Americans reflect a lifetime of poor access to health care and proper nutrition due to low socioeconomic status associated with limited educational opportunities, substandard housing, and poor working conditions. This litany of problems can be attributed to institutional as well as other overt and insidious forms of racism in America. Problems associated with access to and negative experiences with American health care systems further hinder various efforts to rectify racial and ethnic health disparities. Historical mistrust of health care institutions includes the infamous 40-year Tuskegee Syphilis Study of 1932 in which African American sharecroppers were not provided with penicillin for treatment once the treatment had been discovered in the 1940s. Today's research indicates that older African Americans are less satisfied than whites with the health care they receive, and that they are more likely to receive unequal treatment and inappropriate care compared to the white majority (Kelley-Moore & Ferraro, 2004).

This general portrait of African American elders overlooks the diversity within the population, as is the case with generalizations about each of the groups discussed in this chapter. Family history, cultural background, economic level and educational level affect patterns of aging in all minority groups. For example, affluent African American elders, African American immigrants from Caribbean Islands, and those from families with high levels of education are different from the general patterns of aging for this population.

Hispanic/Latino Elders

The Hispanic/Latino population is the one of the fastest growing demographic groups in the United States (U.S. Census Bureau, 2004), and like many ethnic/racial minority groups, this population is difficult to describe as a singular entity given that Latinos represent over 40 different nationality groups. Latinos in the United States have largely come by way of immigration from Mexico, Central and South America, Cuba, and Puerto Rico. However, significant portions of the Southwest, including Texas and California, were appropriated from Mexico in the middle of the nineteenth century. Many individuals of Mexican ancestry trace their "arrival" in the United States to that annexation. Adding to the lack of clarity about the definition of "Hispanic" is the fact that immigrants from Mexico, Latin American countries, and often the Caribbean are generally considered Hispanic regardless of whether they trace their heritage to Spain, other European countries, or to the Native peoples of Mexico or Latin America. In fact, some immigrants from those countries identify as Hispanic although a significant part of their ancestral heritage comes from the African slave trade.

Although not the only unifying force for this group, slated to be the largest minority group in the United States by year 2025, the Spanish language is a major common factor; so is the historical dominance of Catholicism. Customs and attitudes toward self, family and community are also strong forces. In spite of being generally protective in nature, social support mechanisms can be affected by rapid rates of acculturation and assimilation by younger family members. For example, strong familial ties dictate that *respeto* (respect) for older adults include a caregiving role for youth of their elders. However, traditional extended family ties can be altered when elderly Latinos are cared for in institutions (e.g., long-term care facilities), as opposed to being cared for by adult children in the family home. In such situations, not only can traditional extended family ties be compromised, but older Latinos who may have left their country of origin under political duress may experience significant difficulties in adapting to living circumstances due in part to their distrust of government agencies.

The degree to which Latinos are acculturated is related to the degree to which Latinos access and use health services (Aguirre-Molina, Molina, &

Zambrano, 2001; Tran, Dhooper, & McInnis-Dittrich, 1997). As with other ethnic/racial minority groups, patterns of Latino use of health services differ from that of whites. For example, Latinos have less access to preventive health care and are more apt to depend on the use of emergency room services and nontraditional sources such as clergy and folk healers (Garcia & Marotta, 1997). Lack of English proficiency also serves as a limiting factor for access to health services (Preciado & Henry, 1997). Other factors correlated with access to care that can also serve as treatment barriers include low educational levels (Vazquez & Clavijo, 1995).

Socioeconomic and sociopolitical factors also play a role in migration patterns and can influence the degree to which individuals may have negative experiences involving prejudice and discrimination. For example, not being able to speak English can lead to diminished employment opportunities, low income potential, a lack of insurance, and poverty. Fear of deportation for undocumented immigrants is also a real threat for many Latinos (Echeverry, 1997). Although it has been argued that civil rights actions have done little to improve elderly Latinos' socioeconomic position (Torres-Gil, 1986), it has also been noted that increased political participation on the part of elderly Latinos suggests an emerging politics with the potential of influencing social well-being and policy (Torres-Gil & Kuo, 1998).

Asian American/Pacific Islander (AAPI)

It is very difficult to address the aging issues of today's Asian American/Pacific Islander (AAPI) population because of the substantial in-group variability. There are at least 40 subgroups among Asian Americans alone (Sandhu, 1997) that present different languages, religions, immigration history, lifestyle, and other characteristics. As with other minority groups, there is a long history of this cultural group in the United States. The earlier settlers from Asia in America, Chinese and Japanese immigrants, experienced injustice and inhumane treatment in addition to their strenuous work and hard labor contributions to the American frontier. The Chinese Exclusion Act of 1882 was the first immigration restriction law in American history to single out an ethnic group and it lasted for more than 60 years (Le, 2008). President Roosevelt's Executive Order in 1942 forced approximately 120,000 Japanese Americans (two-thirds being U.S. citizens) to give up most of their fundamental human rights and belongings and to live in war prisons (Hayashi, 2004). In addition, Asian immigrants faced a variety of legal and social discrimination including a law preventing interracial marriage.

The proportion of seniors within these Asian and Asian Pacific Islander subgroups varies. According to the 2000 U.S. Census, 20.4 percent of Japanese Americans are over the age of 65. This is high compared to the general American population (12.4%) and other Asian American and

Pacific Islander (AAPI) groups: Chinese (9.6%), Filipinos (8.7%), Korean (6.2%), Pacific Islander (5.2%), Vietnamese (5.0%), both Cambodian and Asian Indian (3.8%), or Thai (2.5%). The differences in senior representation among different AAPI groups are largely explained by their immigration patterns. Earlier immigrants with fewer newcomers (i.e., Japanese in the United States) result in more seniors than those with more recent immigration from Southeast Asia (e.g., Cambodian, Vietnamese, and Thai) or the Pacific Islands (e.g., Samoan, Tongan, and Marshallese). Due to the pre-senior age group (aged 45–64) of these newer immigrants, the next generation of AAPI elders represents more foreign-born populations (U.S. Census Bureau, 2002), which would bring a new outlook with regard to AAPIs.

The needs of AAPI elders have not been adequately addressed. Although there are some common influences, the tremendous diversity in language, religion, and traditions makes it difficult to generalize. Additionally, the lack of accurate data on AAPI's health status (for both physical and psychological health) and service utilization (APIA Health Forum, 2006; Yee, 1997, 1999) has been a major obstacle in providing information and resources that AAPIs actually need. While more data and discussion have been recently observed and recorded for the two major racial minority groups (i.e., blacks and Latino/Hispanic), AAPIs have been left out. Many large-scale studies exclude AAPIs (and also American Indians/Alaskan Natives) from the analyses because of their relative smaller population sizes compared to other racial groups. Even if some data exist, researchers attempt to analyze the data of AAPIs as a whole. Such aggregated data analyses often exclude or minimize the effects of health disparities experienced by AAPI subgroups (APIA Health Forum, 2006).

Many AAPIs face additional deep-seated barriers to health services and publicly-sponsored programs because of the lack of insurance or under-insurance, poor English proficiency, poverty, and unfamiliarity with health care information and services (APIA Health Forum, 2006). For elders of AAPIs, these challenges seem to be even more pronounced. Those who have worked for small businesses (e.g., a family owned store, restaurant, dry cleaning, etc.) or domestic jobs often did not receive health care or retirement benefits.

Further, their cultural beliefs and indigenous health practices can interfere with early detection and intervention. AAPI family members caring for their elders often do not seek formal help because of their strong family obligation or Confucianism value of filial piety. At the same time, some family caregivers are often discouraged from using available services because of the "one fits all" practice. AAPI women, therefore, struggle with performing ongoing caregiving for their loved ones.

Although several studies have indicated the negative impact of racism on AAPI's health and well-being in younger generations (Gee, Spencer, Chen, Yip, & Takeuchi, 2007; Mossakowski, 2003; Spencer & Chen, 2004), very little is known about the lasting effects of racism and discrimination on the well-being of AAPI elders. Many elders of earlier immigrant populations sacrificed their lives in order that the next generations could be successful in America. The "model minority" myth for AAPIs hinders the real needs of AAPIs who have continuously experienced discrimination, trauma, and poverty (Yee, DeBaryshe, Yuen, Kim, & McCubbin, 2007).

American Indians and Alaska Natives

It is estimated that about 6 percent of American Indians and Alaskan Natives are 65 years of age or older (U.S. Census Bureau, 2000b). Their history is one that includes the destruction of its peoples' way of life with the arrival of Europeans to the American continent through loss of native lands, disease, and social upheaval. The U.S. government later created the displacement of the Native American people and systematic destruction of their culture as a result of reservations and Indian schools. The hundreds of culturally diverse tribes and nations were forced, through governmental policies, to integrate and assimilate. The 1950s witnessed an attempt to terminate the reservations whereby Native Americans would become "independent" and move to cities; however, approximately one-third of the population remains living on reservations.

It is argued that compared to other ethnic minority groups, Native Americans have the greatest need for social, health, and mental health services (LaFromboise, 1988). Conditions that disproportionately affect Native American elders and lead to disability and death include pneumonia, diabetes mellitus, accidents, liver disease, and cirrhosis (John, Hennessy, & Denny, 1999). A recent study also reveals that the prevalence of disabilities among older American Indians and Alaska Natives was much higher than any other racial groups (Okoro et al., 2007). These conditions reflect lives that have been affected by a history of oppression. Atchley (1988) argues that a governmental view of Native Americans as "unfortunates to be protected" has translated to "many services to older American Indians on reservations as overly paternalistic as compared to services to older Americans in general" (p. 284). Native Americans also struggle with economic hardship as they are among the poorest people in the United States.

Gender, Sexual Orientation, and Gender Identity

Gender identity adds another degree of complexity to the issues of elders, as most if not all cultural groups assign different roles and value to individuals based in part on gender. Additionally, rates of acculturation often vary by gender. For elders from outside the dominant culture, the tensions between dominant culture, American values, and their culture of origin can create tensions and confusions within the family and between the family and the larger society. Furthermore, women are more likely than men to be poor. Although some elderly women in wealthy families become owners of considerable wealth due to their living longer than their husbands, more elderly women than men live in poverty.

Sexual orientation and aging involves a double stigma: older people are presumed to be asexual, and everyone is presumed to be heterosexual. For the elders of racial and ethic minorities, sexual orientation adds the third layer of -ism that exists in our society. It is typical for psychologists and other health professionals to be surprised at the idea that some of their clients might be lesbian, gay, or bisexual—or, if they are, that this makes any difference given their age. The same-sex spouse is likely to have legal power of attorney, be the health care proxy, and expect to be treated as family, even if not allowed to marry legally. The couple might even desire a conjugal visit, in private. Likewise, a bisexual person might have a heterosexual family and a same-sex spouse or significant friend. Transgender persons may have physical bodies that do not conform to their gender identity. This incongruence can be a serious health care issue because of the expectations of staff, physical effects of hormone treatment, and a reluctance of the transgender person to seek medical help in a timely fashion.

Combining sexual minority status with ethnic minority status can provide multifaceted dilemmas for aging persons and their communities. Unlike race, ethnicity or gender, sexual orientation and gender identity may foster conflicts based on personal religious beliefs or cultural heritage for some health care professionals. In many settings today, it is still acceptable to demean and joke about gay, lesbian, bisexual, or transgender persons or groups. Professionals, however, recognize that personal bias and negative attitudes can interfere with appropriate interactions and treatments. These issues are discussed in detail elsewhere (Kimmel, Rose, & David, 2006).

Aging with Disabilities

Disabilities possibly associated with aging can further complicate the challenges and issues. Individuals with disabilities did not receive protection under the law until President G. H. Bush signed the Americans with Disabilities Act of 1990 (ADA, 1990). As a civil rights law and as outlined in Titles I through IV, discrimination is prohibited against people with disabilities in a variety of settings including employment, public services, public accommodations, and telecommunications. Prior to ADA, a series of laws was created after the Civil Rights Act of 1964 (CRA, 1964) that helped individuals with disabilities, including the Rehabilitation Act of 1973 and the Individuals with Disabilities Education Act (IDEA) of 1975; however, none with as broad a scope as ADA. The laws notwithstanding, it has been argued that being old and disabled provides a form of double jeopardy (Sheets, 2005) whereby minority older adults are hindered by both racial prejudice and age discrimination and are not served by either the aging or disability service systems.

In the past, individuals with developmental disabilities (e.g., mental retardation, cerebral palsy, autism, Down syndrome, epilepsy) had short life expectancy. Nowadays, these individuals are living longer than before. Many individuals with developmental disabilities have survived to middle age or early senior years. At the same time, newer challenges occur with living longer. The major caregivers of many individuals with developmental disabilities have been their parents. Thus, many are now cared for by aged parents who committed themselves to life-long caregiving and who now face age-related illness and conditions themselves. They often express a similar concern; "What will happen if I am no longer able to take care of my child?" Furthermore, some research evidence suggests additional vulnerability to diseases and conditions (e.g., mental health disorders, dementia) for older individuals with developmental disabilities (Davidson, Prasher, & Janicki, 2003; Schupf et al., 2007). Elder minorities with developmental disabilities face additional challenges, including lack of access to services (Kuehn & Imm-Thomas, 1993). Within ethnic/racial minority cultures, disability stereotypes include characterizations of individuals being sick, cursed, incompetent, and having a power imbalance (Mackelprang & Salsgiver, 1999). We are reminded that because "everyone with a disability will age, and everyone who is aging will acquire one or more disabilities" (Zola, 1988, p. 7), the disability and aging service systems must work in tandem.

BARRIERS AND CHALLENGES TO FOSTERING GERODIVERSITY IN PSYCHOLOGY

Cultural diversity as manifested in norms, values, rituals, symbols, and social interactions has an impact on social behavior, yet it is still merely a footnote in the training for many psychologists (Aldarondo, 2007). The challenge for psychology is in fostering gerodiversity at the individual, organizational, institutional, political, and societal levels so that the voices of minority elders are heard and appropriate actions are taken.

The major barriers to fostering gerodiversity in the field of psychology reflect the intersection of ageism, racism, sexism, and heterosexism in combination with the tendency of the profession to segment interests. The same ageism that exists in American society seems to occur within the field of psychology. Within the profession of psychology, there is an under-representation of individuals trained to work with older adults (Abeles, 2008). Only a small number of students and psychologists have chosen to work with older adults. Dealing with the aging phenomena, a fundamental process of human existence does not appear to be understood or appreciated. Even though human development and life-span development represent fundamental coursework in psychology, the majority of the time is devoted to teaching infant development, child and adolescent stages, and steps leading to early adult life. It is quite common that the latter part of adulthood is covered quickly or even left for students' own reading outside of class. This practice itself is an example of ageism among educators and conveys the idea that the experiences, processes, lives, and contributions of older adults are not as important as those of the younger generations. Similarly, for those who are interested in or devoted to work with minorities, the focus is often on youth and younger adult populations with less time allotted to the later-adulthood and aging. Therefore, the area of gerodiversity does not appear to even reach the level of surface awareness in formal educational curricula.

For students to choose work in geropsychology and related fields, it is essential that those providing the training have an understanding of those factors that limit students' interest and choices in those areas. Biases and assumptions that are held toward elders begin with a lack of one's own social identity and multicultural awareness. Ageism, the "unreasonable prejudice against persons based on chronological age" (Myers, 2007), is likely less about global negative attitudes on the part of professionals toward the aged and more about misconceptions, both positive and negative (Gatz & Pearson, 1988). Nonetheless, obvious stereotypes and prejudices toward other diversity issues remain a concern. Hinrichsen (2006) makes the point that the psychologists providing services to older adults are mostly white, serving multicultural elderly, but lacking the knowledge to do so.

As is the case with many disciplines, psychology's theories frame its applied approaches. Borrowing heavily from the biomedical framework and the hypothetic-deductive approach, psychologists have demonstrated a limited view toward the concept and issues involved in human health for many years. The majority of psychologists are only trained with quantitative research inquiries that heavily rely on probability-based inferences, categorization, and compartmentalization in an ethnocentric manner. Furthermore, much of the work research in psychology has followed a "main effects" model, looking at variables one at a time rather than seeing people in social-ecological contexts. When comparing data from minority groups against the majority, researchers typically use statistical manipulations to simply adjust several key variables (e.g., age, income, education). Laveist (2008) points out that such practices create inappropriate pictures of race disparities in health. He states that many health and behavioral sciences researchers are guilty of accumulating distorted views about minorities. The lack of culturally sensitive research training and the traditional criteria for academic tenure (i.e., "publish or perish") may help to explain the cursory examination and general oversight.

From multicultural perspectives, one's health exists in a sociocultural framework that allows for the awareness and integration of other systems such as the indigenous, ethnomedical approaches that include traditional folk healing. How psychologists conceptualize health-related behaviors has important implications for research and application to clinical practices.

An example of the lack of a culturally sensitive framework is the failure to consider the family as a unit of assessment. Such a consideration is clearly beneficial when working with many minority elders, especially for cases of dementia (Gallagher-Thompson, 2006). Furthermore, a sociocultural framework allows psychologists to recognize that health-related behaviors are also influenced by the accessibility, the systems, and the quality of care available to the individuals, all of which are problematic for minority elders.

For many years, the field of psychology focused heavily on intrapsychic phenomenon and interpersonal relationships. A number of counseling and therapy approaches were developed in order to treat psychological symptoms, and yet patients/clients were viewed as quite similar, the problems were also viewed as similar, and the professions operated as if almost all individuals had access to such care. In a new era of multiculturalism in the field of psychology, however, such practices tend to be viewed as culturally insensitive interventions that ignore many socioculturally related issues that exist beyond the individual level (e.g., Atkinson, Thompson, & Grant, 1993; Sue & Sue, 2006; Vera & Speight, 2003). However, there are also many barriers at the organizational and institutional levels that serve to block meeting of the needs of minority elders. They include (a) lack of bilingual and bicultural staff, (b) the lack of linguistically and culturally appropriate tools and materials, (c) lack of aging and diversity training, (d) inappropriate structures, guidelines, and procedures, and (e) institutional ageism, racism, heterosexism, and ableism.

Current social policy reflects inequality because, as a political process, the actions of the government and its goal-directed decisions have not sufficiently included input from gerodiverse constituencies and advisory groups, a condition for change-based leadership (Cox, 1993). Likewise, the field has not provided for a gerodiversity policy direction because it has not promulgated an integrated, life-span model that includes the influences of historical, cohort, cultural, and social context (Jackson, Antonucci, & Gibson, 1990). Such a consideration would address issues such as the lack of alternative service delivery models; inter-, intra-, and multicollaborative approaches; prevention service models; contextual models of client and service providers; and bilingual staff. The report by the America Psychological Association Presidential Task Force provides an aspirational model for this type of approach to integrated health care for an aging population (APA, 2008).

COURSES OF ACTION: STEPPING OUT OF THE BOX

Building Bridges among Sub-Disciplines toward an Interdisciplinary Approach

Given the complexity of the issues related to gerodiversity, it is critical for psychologists from various sub-disciplines to work together. Instead of working within their comfort zone, psychologists and students should be encouraged to build bridges across different disciplines to communicate and exchange their resources, knowledge, skills, and professional expertise. To date, many accomplishments in promoting aging issues in the psychology field were made by members of APA Division 12-II (clinical geropsychology) and Division 20 (adult development and aging). The APA Committee on Aging (CONA) has been promoting aging work in the field of psychology and working to reduce ageism in our society. In the area of multicultural issues and social justice, members of various sub-disciplines such as counseling, school, and community psychology have contributed to move the field forward. Because of the nature of gerodiversity, it is critical to hear voices of minority elders through other groups specialized in developmental disabilities, lesbian/gay/bisexual/transgender, gender, religion, and health. Furthermore, the inclusion of other psychologists devoted to social change will be essential (e.g., APA Division 9—psychological study of social issues) when making significant differences in the lives of minority elders through social action and policy changes. The idea of "inclusion" is the central principle for cultural diversity and should be exercised in the gerodiversity movement within the psychology profession. There are also many allies outside the field of psychology such as the fields of social work, sociology, gerontology, public health, nursing, and medicine. Collaboration within these disciplines generates a complete picture of gerodiversity-related issues.

Community Participatory Activities

Stepping out of the traditional practice in psychology is crucial to becoming a competent change agent in working with minority elders. There is an urgent need to generate and accumulate research evidence and other information about the elders of minority groups. Partnership with communities in which minority elders reside is a key element in gerodiversity. Psychologists should step out of their offices, clinics, and laboratories and engage in community-based activities such as community outreach, community-participatory research, community education, health promotion, and consultation. Roysircar (2006) states, "in the social justice orientation, the community is seen as part of a health problem and, thus, a necessary part of any solution to improve the lives of people" (p. 313). Further, we argue that the community can offer many key ideas for solutions to given problems if professionals embrace community collaboration in a respectful manner and avoid the "we know better" attitude. Thus, instead of working comfortably, psychologists need go beyond intellectual awareness and take action within the community (Fox, 2003).

Policy, Advocacy, and Social Justice Training and Practice

To accomplish gerodiversity, active engagement in advocacy and policy changes are necessary and should not be seen as extra or additional. These professional activities exist along a continuum from the work necessary to facilitate client empowerment to that activity related to advocating structural and policy changes (Toporek, 2000, 2006). Noting the general lack of rights for the elderly, some advocates have called on organizations to create an international convention for the rights of older adults, similar to that of children and women (Tang & Lee, 2006). Current health policies do not reflect the mental health care needs of older adults. For example, the Older Americans Act, which was the first step to address ageism at the national level, continues to primarily focus on social and physically-related services whereas psychological services are lacking. Therefore, psychologists have been urged to make policymakers aware of such issues (DiGilio & Levitt, 2002). Regarding Medicare part B, which covers outpatient care for seniors, a substantial number of geropsychologists have engaged in political advocacy for parity service coverage for physical and mental health care. At the present time, mental health-related services provide only 50 percent coverage while most of other services receive 80 percent coverage under Medicare part B. Thus, advocating for parity coverage is a step toward social justice for aged individuals. At the same time, much needs to be done for minority elders because many minority elders are living at poverty levels or are unable to afford the copayments of Medicare. Even if they have equal access to mental health care, a substantial shortage of culturally sensitive professionals and treatment will remain as a major obstacle for minority elders to receive appropriate care.

Gerodiversity has never been fully understood without reference to the sociocultural–sociopolitical context. Mainstream psychologists often attribute existing health disparities to a single socioeconomic factor. Such assumption and interpretation minimizes unique cultural elements held by different groups of minorities. According to a recent report on urban American Indians and Alaskan Natives, a linear effect of income on various health-related issues (e.g., access to health care, smoking, diabetes, hypertension, obesity) was applicable to the general public but was not found among these groups (Urban Indian Health Institute, 2008). In other words, many existing health disparities cannot be solely explained by low income and or poverty. Such newer findings are valuable and should be available to students and psychology professionals for active discussion and collaboration among various subdisciplines (e.g., cultural diversity, research methods, statistics, health psychology, rehabilitation psychology, and life-span development).

Gerodiversity calls for social justice perspectives. For individuals who are committed to work with minority elders, building knowledge and skills in social justice is a critical part of professional competency. Social justice in psychology has been called upon to teach, engage in clinical practice, and develop public policy and research with regard to racism, sexism, classism, heterosexism, and other divisive perspectives. Such perspectives enable professionals to fairly and competently work with and treat those who are different from themselves (Mays, 2000). At the present time, only a small number of psychology programs offer specific courses devoted to social justice and related areas such as advocacy and policy. In the field of counseling psychology, Toporek and McNally (2006) discuss multiple ways to bring social justice training into academic settings: an explicit course, a service learning component, community-based research and practice, and integration to existing cultural diversity training and coursework. In all settings, they state, "critical emphasis is placed upon trainees having a positive impact on environmental settings and assuming an active role in shaping of cultural contexts" (p. 39).

Social justice perspectives are still new in the field of psychology. Thus, many psychologists trained by the traditional school of psychology may think it is irrelevant to their profession or may feel anxious and overwhelmed by the concept. In reality, many psychologists are already engaged in core elements of social justice, multicultural training, advocacy, community-driven activity, and influencing policy changes. Those who embrace the social justice movement argue that it may be time to change the "scientist-practitioner" Boulder model to "the scientist-practitioner-advocate" model (Baker & Benjamin, 2000). As many minority elders face numerous systemic barriers to receiving appropriate mental health care (e.g., problems of access to care, lack of culturally sensitive resources and services), it is indeed critical to step beyond the Boulder model and include social justice components in training of gerodiversity.

CONCLUSION

The elders of minority groups face multiple forms of oppression because of the intersection between their advanced age and minority status. The issue is further complicated because of additional social and cultural factors that may apply such as race, ethnicity, sexual orientation, and disability. As "survivors" of historical injustice and social unfairness, these elders are also "victims" of today's unequal treatment with regard to their societal welfare and overall well-being. Many issues faced by minority elders exist at the structural level as it intersects with political levels of society. Thus, social justice perspectives and practices must be fully applied when addressing the health and quality of life of individuals from one of the most vulnerable and historically marginalized groups. The concept of social justice is the "universal language" and similar visions should be expressed by those who are working with minority individuals regarding issues related to age. As older Americans have become increasingly diverse, psychology students and the specialized professional divisions, especially those who strive for professional competency in the areas of multicultural psychology and geropsychology, should step out of their usual practice and speak to each other in terms of this "universal language." Social justice in gerodiversity is not simply about helping oppressed groups because of our social science profession. Social justice in gerodiversity is also our personal responsibility because aging is a universal process affecting all of humankind regardless of the myriad of background issues involved.

REFERENCES

Abeles, N. (2008). Public sector psychology in the wake of the 2005 White House Conference on Aging. *Psychological Services, 5*, 85–93.

Administration on Aging. (2004, September 9). *Facts and figure: Statistics on minority aging in the U.S.* Retrieved April 15, 2008, from http://www.aoa.gov/prof/Statistics/minority_aging/facts_minority_aging.asp.

AgingStats.Gov. (2008, April 29). *Population age 65 and over, by race and Hispanic Origin, 2003 and projected 2050.* In 2008 Older Americans: Key indicators of Well-Being. Retrieved March 5, 2008, from http://agingstats.gov/agingstatsdotnet/Main_Site/Data/2008_Documents/Population.pdf.

Aguirre-Molina, M., Molina, C. W., & Zambrano, R. E. (Eds.). (2001). *Health issues in the Latino community.* San Francisco, CA: Jossey-Bass.

Aldarondo, E. (Ed.). (2007). *Advancing social justice through clinical practice.* Mahwah, NJ: Lawrence Erlbaum.

American Psychological Association. (1998). What practitioners should know about working with older adults. APA Working Group on the Older Adult. *Professional Psychology: Research and Practice, 29*, 413–427.

American Psychological Association. (2008). *Blueprint for change: Achieving integrated health care for an aging population.* Presidential Task Force on Integrated Health Care for an Aging Population. Washington, DC: Author.

Americans with Disabilities Act (ADA) of 1990, Public Law No. 101–336, 104, Stat. 328. (1990). Codified at 42 U.S.C. § 12101 et seq.

APIA Health Forum. (December, 2006). *Getting a reliable pulse on Asian Americans and Pacific Islanders.* Retrieved April 15, 2008, from http://www.apiahf.org/resources/pdf/AAPI_Data_Collection_Fact_Sheet.pdf www.apiahf.org.

Atchley, R. C. (1988). *Social forces and aging* (5th ed.). Belmont, CA: Wadsworth Publishing.

Atkinson, D. R., Thompson, C. E., & Grant, S. K. (1993). A three-dimensional model for counseling racial/ethnic minorities. *The Counseling Psychologist, 21*, 257–277.

Baker, D. B., & Benjamin, L. T. (2000). The affirmation of the scientist-practitioner: A Back at Boulder. *American Psychologist, 55*, 241–247.

Bell, L. A. (1997). Theoretical foundations for social justice education. In M. Adams, L. A. Bell, & P. Griffin (Eds.), *Teaching for diversity and social justice: A sourcebook* (pp. 3–15). New York: Routledge.

Burton, L. M., & Dilworth-Anderson, P. (1991). The intergenerational roles of aged Black Americans. *Marriage and Family Review, 16*, 311–322.

Cahill, S., South, K., & Spade, J. (2000). *Outing age: Public policy issues affecting gay, lesbian, bisexual and transgender elders.* New York: Policy Institute of National Gay and Lesbian Task Force Foundation.

Civil Rights Act (CRA) of 1964. 42 U.S.C. § 2000e-2(a) (1991).

Cox, T. Jr. (1993). *Cultural diversity in organizations: Theory, research, and practice.* San Francisco, CA: Berret-Koehler.

Davidson, P. W., Prasher, V. P., & Janicki, M. P. (Eds.). (2003). *Mental health, intellectual disabilities and the aging process.* Malden, MA: Blackwell.

DiGilio, D. A., & Levitt, N. G. (2002). APA Bridging the gap on aging-related issues. *Professional Psychology: Research and Practice, 33,* 443–445.

Echeverry, J. J. (1997). Treatment barriers: Accessing and accepting professional help. In J. G. Garcia & M. C. Zea (Eds.), *Psychological interventions and research with Latino populations* (pp. 94–107). Boston: Allyn & Bacon.

Fox, D. R. (2003). Awareness is good, but action is better. *The Counseling Psychologist, 31,* 299–304.

Gallagher-Thompson, D. (2006). The family as a unit of assessment and treatment in work with ethnically diverse older adults with dementia. In G. Yeo, & D. Gallagher-Thompson (Eds.), *Ethnicity and the dementias* (2nd ed., pp. 119–124). New York: Routledge.

Garcia, J. G., & Marotta, S. (1997).Characterization of the Latino population. In J. G. Garcia & M. C. Zea (Eds.), *Psychological interventions and research with Latino populations* (pp. 1–14). Boston: Allyn & Bacon.

Gatz, M., & Pearson, C. G. (1988). Ageism revised and the provision of psychological services. *American Psychologist, 43,* 184–188.

Gee, G. C., Spencer, M., Chen, J., Yip, T., & Takeuchi, D. T. (2007). The association between self-reported racial discrimination and 12-month DSM-IV mental disorders among Asian Americans nationwide. *Social Science & Medicine, 64,* 1984–1996.

Hayashi, M. B. (2004). *Democratizing the enemy: The Japanese American Internment.* Princeton, NJ: Princeton University Press.

Heller, T. (n.d.).*Older adults with developmental disabilities and their aging family caregivers.* Retrieved March 8, 2008, from http://www.strengthforcaring.com/daily-care/caring-for-someone-with-developmental-disabilities/older-adults-with-developmental-disabilities-and-their-aging-family-caregivers/.

Hinrichsen, G. A. (2006). Why multicultural issues matter for practitioners working with older adults. *Professional Psychology: Research and Practice, 37,* 29–35.

Individuals with Disabilities Education Act (IDEA). (1975). Federal Register, August 23, 1977, Vol. 42, NO. 163. Public Law 94–142 (The Education for all Handicapped Children Act of 1975).

Jackson, J. S., Antonucci, T. C., & Gibson, R. C. (1990). Cultural, racial, and ethnic minority influences on aging. In J. E. Birren & K. W. Schaie (Eds.), *Handbook of the psychology of aging* (3rd ed., pp. 103–123). San Diego, CA: Academic Press.

John, R., Hennessy, C. H., & Denny, C. H. (1999). Preventing chronic illness and disability among Native American elders. In M. L. Wykle & A. B. Ford (Eds.), *Serving minority elders in the 21st century* (pp. 51–71). New York: Springer.

Kelley-Moore, J. A., & Ferraro, K. F. (2004). The black/white disability gap: Persistent inequality in late-life? *Journal of Gerontology: Social Sciences, 59B,* S34–S43.

Kimmel, D. C., Rose, T., & David, S. (Eds.). (2006). *Lesbian, gay, bisexual, and transgender aging: Research and clinical perspectives.* New York: Columbia University Press.

Kuehn, M. L., & Imm-Thomas, P. (1993). A multicultural context. In E. Sutton, A. R. Factor, B. A. Hawkins, T. Heller, & G. B. Seltzer (Eds.), *Older adults with developmental disabilities: Optimizing choice and change* (pp. 327–343). Baltimore, MD: Brookes.

LaFromboise, T. D. (1988). American Indian mental health policy. *American Psychologist, 43,* 388–397.

Laveist, T. A. (2008, April 9). Disentangling race and socioeconomic status: Advancing understanding of race disparities in health. Presented at Department of Psychology, University of Washington.

Le, C. N. (2008). Asian American history, demographics, and issues. *Asian Nation.* Retrieved April 15, 2008, from http://www.asian-nation.org/index.shtml.

Mackelprang, R., & Salsgiver, R. (1999). *Disability: A diversity model approach in human service practice.* Pacific Grove, CA: Brooks/Cole Publishing.

Mays, V. M. (2000). A social justice agenda. *American Psychologist, 55,* 326–327.

Mossakowski, K. N. (2003). Coping with perceived discrimination: Does ethnic identity protect Mental Health? *Journal of Health and Social Behavior, 44,* 318–331.

Myers, J. E. (2007). Combating ageism: Advocacy for older persons. In C. C. Lee (Ed.), *Counseling for social justice* (2nd ed., pp. 51–74). Alexandria, VA: American Counseling Association.

National Gay and Lesbian Task Force (NGLTF). (n.d). *The issues: Aging.* Retrieved May 30, 2008, from http://www.thetaskforce.org/issues/aging.

Okoro, C. A., Denny C. H., McGuire L. C., Balluz, L. S., Goins, R. T., & Mokdad, A. H. (2007). Disability among older American Indians and Alaska Natives: Disparities in prevalence, health-risk behaviors, obesity, and chronic conditions. *Ethnicity & Disease, 17,* 686–692.

Preciado, J., & Henry, M. (1997). Linguistic barriers in health education and services. In J. G. Garcia & M. C. Zea (Eds.), *Psychological interventions and research with Latino populations* (pp. 235–254). Boston: Allyn & Bacon.

Rehabilitation Act of 1973. (1994). 29 U.S.C. § 794.

Roysircar, G. (2006). Counseling health psychology's collaborative role in the community. In R. L. Toporek, L. G., Gerstein, N. A. Fouad, G. Roysicar, & T. Israel (Eds.), *Handbook of social justice in counseling psychology: Leadership, vision, and action* (pp. 313–317). Thousand Oaks, CA: Sage.

Sandhu, D. S. (1997). Psychocultural profiles of Asian and Pacific Islander Americans: Implications for counseling and psychotherapy. *Journal of Multicultural Counseling and Development, 25,* 7–22.

Schupf, N., Patel, B., Pang, D., Zigman, W. B., Silverman, W., & Mehta, P. D. (2007). Elevated plasma beta-amyloid peptide Abeta(42) levels, incident dementia, and mortality in Down syndrome. *Archives of Neurology, 64,* 1007–1013.

Sheets, D. J. (2005). Aging with disabilities: Ageism and more. *Generations, 29,* 37–41.

Siegel, J. S. (1999). Demographic introduction to racial/Hispanic elderly populations. In T. P. Miles (Ed.), *Full-color aging: Facts, goals, and recommendations for America's diverse elders* (pp. 1–19). Washington, DC: The Gerontological Society of America.

Spencer, M. S., & Chen, J. (2004). Effect of discrimination on mental health service utilization among Chinese Americans. *American Journal of Public Health, 94,* 809–814.

Sue, D. W., & Sue, D. (2006). *Counseling the culturally diverse: Theory and practice* (5th ed.). New York: Wiley.

Swift, M. (2008, March 2). Not single, not married; Similarities found for same-sex partners, heterosexual couples. *Mercury News.* Retrieved March 15, 2008, from http://www.mercurynews.com//ci_8427113?IADID=Search-www. mercurynews.com-www.mercurynews.com.

Tang, K., & Lee, J. (2006). Global social justice for older people: The case for an international convention on the rights of older people. *British Journal of Social Work, 36,* 1135–1150.

Toporek, R. L. (2000). Creating a common language and framework for understanding advocacy in counseling. In J. Lews & L. Bradley (Eds.), *Advocacy in counseling: Counselors, clients, and community* (pp. 5–14). Greensboro, NC: Caps Publication.

Toporek, R. L. (2006). Social action in policy and legislation: Individual and alliances. In R. L. Toporek, L. G. Gerstein, N. A. Fouad, G. Roysicar, & T. Israel (Eds.), *Handbook of social justice in counseling psychology: Leadership, vision, and action* (pp. 489–498). Thousand Oaks, CA: Sage.

Toporek, R. L., & McNally, C. J. (2006). Social justice training in counseling psychology: Needs and innovations. In R. L. Toporek, L. G. Gerstein, N. A. Fouad, G. Roysicar, & T. Israel (Eds.), *Handbook of social justice in counseling psychology: Leadership, vision, and action* (pp. 37–43). Thousand Oaks, CA: Sage.

Torres-Gil, F. (1986). An examination of factors affecting cohorts of elderly Hispanics. *The Gerontologist, 26,* 140–146.

Torres-Gil, F., & Kuo, T. (1998). Social policy and the politics of Hispanic aging. *Journal of Gerontological Social Work, 30,* 143–158.

Tran, T. V., Dhooper, S. S., & McInnis-Dittrich, K. (1997). Utilization of community-based social and health services among foreign born Hispanic American elderly. *Journal of Gerontological Social Work, 28,* 23–43.

Urban Indian Health Institute. (2008). *Reporting health and health-influencing behaviors among urban American Indians and Alaska Natives: An analysis of data collected by the Behavioral Risk Factor surveillance System.* Seattle, Washington: Seattle Indian Health Board.

U.S. Census Bureau. (2000a, December). *We the people: Asians in the United States. Census 2000.* (Special Reports CENSR-17). Retrieved March 5, 2008, from http://www.census.gov/prod/2004pubs/censr-17.pdf.

U.S. Census Bureau. (2000b). *American fact finder: Fact sheet for a race, ethnicity, or ancestry group.* Retrieved May 25, 2008, from http://factfinder.census.gov/servlet/SAFFFactsCharIteration?.

U.S. Census Bureau. (2002, September). *The older foreign-born population in the United States: 2000.* (Current Population Reports: Special Studies CENSR-17). Retrieved March 5, 2008, from http://www.census.gov/prod/2002pubs/p23–211.pdf.

U.S. Census Bureau. (2003, March). *Disability status: Census 2000 brief.* Retrieved March 20, 2008, from http://www.census.gov/prod/2003pubs/c2kbr-17. pdf.

U.S. Census Bureau. (2004, June 14). *Hispanic and Asian Americans increasing faster than overall Population.* Retrieved March 5, 2008, from http://www.census. gov/Press-Release/www/releases/archives/race/001839.html.

Vazquez, C. I., & Clavijo, A. M. (1995). The special needs of elderly minorities: A profile of Hispanics. In B. G. Knight, L. Teri, P. Wohlford, & J. Santos (Eds.), *Mental health services for older adults: Implications for training and practice in geropsychology* (pp. 93–99). Washington, DC: APA.

Vera, E. M., & Speight, S. L. (2003). Multicultural competence social justice, and counseling psychology: Expanding our roles. *The Counseling Psychologist, 31,* 253–272.

Yee, D. (1997). Issues and trends affecting Asian Americans, women, and aging. In J. M. Coyle (Ed.), *Handbook on women and aging* (pp. 316–334). Westport, CT: Greenwood Press.

Yee, D. L. (1999). Preventing chronic illness and disability: Asian Americans. In M. L. Wykle & A. B. Ford (Eds.), *Serving minority elders in the 21st Century* (pp. 37–50). Broadway, NY: Springer.

Yee, B. W. K., DeBaryshe, B. D., Yuen, S., Kim, S. U., & McCubbin, H. I. (2007). Asian American and Pacific Islander families: Resiliency and life-span socialization in a cultural context. In F.T.L. Leong, A. G. Inwan, A. Ebreo, L. H., Young, L. Kinoshita, & M. Fu (Eds.), *Handbook of Asian American psychology* (pp. 69–86). Thousand Oaks, CA: Sage.

Young, I. M. (1990). *Justice and the politics of difference.* Princeton, NJ: Princeton University Press.

Zola, I. K. (1988). Aging and disability: Toward a unifying agenda. *Educational Gerontology, 14,* 35–87.

CHAPTER 6

Ableism and Social Justice

Pamela F. Foley and Linda R. Walter

> Through the continuum of recorded social history, people with disabilities have been perceived as being primarily situated on the outside of a global society that, for the most part, has viewed them with varying degrees of contempt. They have been viewed as medical abnormalities needing to be cured, dissected, or displayed in circus freak shows. . . . They have been viewed through a psychological model where their experiences have been individualized and pathologized . . . and have not been given voice nor choice in many decisions that concern their welfare. (Williams, 2005, p. 7)

The number of individuals with disabilities in U.S. society is increasing for a variety of reasons. A significant factor in this increase is the large population of Baby Boomers who are now reaching retirement age, up to half of whom may eventually face some form of age-related disability such as heart disease (U.S. Census Bureau, 2007). Another contributing factor is an increased incidence in childhood/adolescent illnesses and conditions, such as autism, asthma, HIV/AIDS, diabetes and childhood obesity. Further, because of broad medical advances, more infants with severe disabilities such as spina bifida and cystic fibrosis are viable at birth and are entering the educational system and, in some cases, the workforce in greater numbers. Finally, the military conflicts in Afghanistan and Iraq have resulted in substantial numbers of individuals with disabilities such as traumatic brain injury and physical impairments. Ensuring that these individuals have the opportunity to fully participate in education, employment, health care, and recreational opportunities afforded all citizens—a fundamental principal of social justice—will be an increasingly critical societal challenge.

Since the Depression, and in some cases prior, U.S. citizens have been advocates of social justice in many venues, and this concern for equal rights has led to landmark legislation that benefits a wide range of individuals, such as Social Security, Medicare/Medicaid, the GI Bill, and civil rights laws. Further, some key legislation specifically benefits individuals with disabilities, including PL 94-141 and its successor the Individuals with Disabilities Education Act (IDEA), and the Americans with Disabilities Act (ADA) to name a few. These laws have created opportunities for individuals with disabilities to earn high-school diplomas, college degrees, and to enter the workforce in increasing numbers. However, as discussed below, their success has been limited.

As with all initiatives of change, including that of public policy, some are widely embraced while there is resistance to others. For example, social justice advocates are well aware that civil rights laws have not eradicated inequality with respect to race. For laws protecting individuals with disabilities, part of this resistance is rooted in *ableism*, which is a form of discrimination or prejudice against individuals with physical, mental, or developmental disabilities that is characterized by the belief that these individuals need to be fixed or cannot function as full members of society. Castañeda and Peters (2000) define ableism as "the discrimination against and the exclusion of individuals with physical and mental disabilities from full participation and opportunity within society's systems and activities" (p. 320). Because of the widespread presence of discriminatory beliefs and practices, even when these individuals have legally mandated access, they nonetheless face difficulties in gaining full access to higher education, employment, transportation, health care, and housing. Thus, particularly when individuals with disabilities have completed their K–12 education and are no longer eligible for school-based services, these laws can carry a hollow promise. As adults, individuals with disabilities are largely dependent on organizations voluntarily complying with laws and policies, or on advocates pressuring organizations or other entities to do so (Institute of Medicine [IOM], 2007). Additionally, the problems cited above are more severe for individuals from racial and ethnic minority groups, and for those from lower socioeconomic ranks. Not only is the incidence of disability higher in these groups, but these individuals often face the adverse effects of racism and classism in addition to ableism (Smith, Foley, & Chaney, 2008). Ableism goes beyond individual prejudice; it is a systemic issue because institutional policies and practices typically assume fully abled status. Because disability status has been historically viewed as a defect, rather than as a dimension of difference, individuals with disabilities are often excluded from discourse regarding diversity and cultural concerns.

This chapter will review the issues affecting individuals with disabilities, with the goal of increasing awareness of their increasing presence as well as barriers they face in society. The chapter will address the reasons for the rise in numbers of individuals with disabling conditions, the impact of poverty and racial minority status on the experience of disability, unique challenges for individuals with hidden disabilities such as learning disabilities and mental illness, and recommendations for both reducing individual prejudice and for systemic change to better support the full participation of individuals with disabilities in society.

WHY THE RISE IN THE INCIDENCE OF DISABILITY IS SIGNIFICANT

According to recent estimates, approximately 20 percent of individuals in the United States have some type of disability, and for a variety of reasons the number of individuals with disabling conditions is rising (Freedman, Martin, & Schoeni, 2004). As a result, schools, communities, and employers will be faced with the challenges of providing accommodations and needed care for these individuals. The following broad areas are discussed below: (a) the increased prevalence of age-related disabilities as a result of the aging Baby Boom generation, (b) increased prevalence of substantial disabling conditions in youth, which is partially related to increased survival rates for severe childhood illnesses, and (c) the increased number of military personnel with war-related disabilities.

THE INCREASED PREVALENCE OF DISABILITY IN AN AGING POPULATION

As the Baby Boom generation enters later life, age-related disabilities are expected to increase in prevalence. The U.S. Census Bureau estimates that by 2030, nearly 20 percent of the population will be 65 years of age or older, compared with only 12 percent in 2000 (IOM, 2007), and a predictable percentage of these individuals will face some disabling condition. Figures from the Pew Research Center (2005) indicate even greater numbers. Their study of Baby Boomers indicates that as the Baby Boomers born between 1946 and 1964 age, there will be 75 million adults over the age of 60, which equals 26 percent of the U.S. population. While not all elderly individuals will live with disabilities, the percentage of individuals over 65 who report some type of disability is significant: in 2006 the percentages by state, excluding nursing home residents, ranged from a low of 34.8 percent in Minnesota to 52.0 percent in Mississippi (U.S. Census Bureau, 2007).

As individuals are living longer and in larger numbers, age-related disabilities such as arthritis, Parkinson's disease, and various forms of dementia will increase. This is partially due to medical advances enabling people to live longer; and partially due to the sheer numbers of those who will reach retirement age in the next two decades. This trend is further compounded by the aging of individuals who, because of improvements in medicine, survived childhood disabling illnesses/conditions but have always required some type of assistance. As these individuals grow older, they will likely require increased assistance either with basic activities of daily living (ADLs), such as eating, dressing, and bathing, or with instrumental activities of daily living (IADLs), including bill paying, cleaning, or cooking.

An example of the impact of health issues on the aging population can be illustrated by considering the effects of diabetes. This is significant because while mortality and disability for older Americans due to other conditions such as heart disease and cancer have declined over the past several decades, diabetes is a troubling exception (Kramarow, Lubitz, Lentzner, & Gorina, 2007). The National Diabetes Education Program (NDEP), a division of the National Institutes of Health (NIH), reports that in the past decade, the incidence of both diabetes and obesity (a risk factor for diabetes) have risen dramatically (NDEP, 2007). The Centers for Disease Control (CDC, 2005) reports that the most common disabling conditions associated with diabetes are kidney failure, heart disease or stroke, blindness, and lower limb amputations resulting from circulatory disorders and related infections. Groups particularly at risk for developing type 2 or adult-onset diabetes are African Americans, Hispanic/Latino Americans, and Native Americans, as well as some Asian American communities, and the incidence of diabetes and related complications is substantially higher for individuals age 65 and older (NDEP, 2007). While many of the complications associated with diabetes can be managed through medication and lifestyle changes, as discussed later in this chapter, health care services are limited for those living in poverty. Thus, health care and health education are the least available to those who may have the greatest need for them.

Just as public policy responded to the needs of the Baby Boom generation in the 1950s by providing federal funding to build significantly more homes and more schools, and again in the 1960s by increasing aid and access to colleges through the passage of the Higher Education Act, so will the nation have to change in the next decade to meet the needs of this generation in late adulthood. However, ableism and ageism both become issues in light of the financial impact of the Baby Boomer generation on the already shrinking ability of established federal and state funded programs to meet the needs of the elderly population. Because of the country's inability to fund its current system under present policy, changes have already been made in Social Security by altering retirement ages for the Baby Boomer group and in Medicare by changing deductibles and coverage levels just at a time when these citizens will need these programs the most (Pew Research Center, 2005).

THE INCREASED PREVALENCE OF DISABLING CONDITIONS IN YOUTH

In December 2006, nearly 6.8 million children aged 3–21 were classified with various disabling conditions and attending pre-K–12 schools in the United States. This represents a substantial increase, which can be attributed to numerous factors. The first is the incidence of low birth weight of babies being born in the United States. Between 1992 and 2005, the rate of babies born under 5.5 pounds increased from 7.1 percent to 8.2 percent, and these babies are more likely to have substantial disabilities (Annie E. Casey Foundation, 2005). A marked increase has been seen in the numbers of students being diagnosed on the autism spectrum, from a little less than 10,000 in 1992 to approximately 65,000 in 2001 (U.S. Department of Education, Office of Special Education and Rehabilitative Services, & Office of Special Education Programs, 2005). In 2006, there were 224,594 students between the ages of 6 and 21 classified as autistic with another 35,111 students diagnosed as autistic in preschool programs. Other disability categories with significant numbers and a huge economic impact include 615,475 students with other health impairments such as asthma, diabetes, or HIV/AIDS, and with 465,326 with mental illness (U.S. Department of Education, Office of Special Education and Rehabilitative Services, & Office of Special Education Programs, 2006). Students in all of these categories are labor intensive in school districts and are costly in health care. Many of these students are not educated in general education classrooms with their nondisabled peers. Many of these students need instruction that requires small groups, intensive remediation, specialized programs, numerous related services (such as speech, occupational or physical therapy, counseling, and nursing care), transportation and placements in more restrictive environments. Such services are very labor intensive, and as a result, costly (U.S. Department of Education, Office of Special Education and Rehabilitative Services, & Office of Special Education Programs, 2006). Additionally, many of these students require a considerable amount of health care and health related services not only in childhood but throughout their lives. As an example, is it is estimated that a child with autism is likely to have approximately $3.2 million in health care costs during his or her lifetime (Ganz, 2007).

THE IMPACT OF DISABILITY IN RETURNING MEMBERS OF THE MILITARY

Because of advances in medicine, soldiers whose injuries would have been fatal in earlier wars are now returning—but at a high personal cost. Soldiers returning from Afghanistan and Iraq often face long-term disabilities, traumatic brain injuries, and psychological disabilities such as posttraumatic stress disorder (PTSD) and substance abuse disorders that may result from self-medicating psychological reactions, in addition to more visible disabilities such as amputations and paralysis. In a report to Congress, Fischer, Klarman, and Oboroceanu (2008) report that through 2007 the number of deaths related to Operation Iraqi Freedom and Operation Enduring Freedom (Afghanistan) was 4,548, while the number of wounded was 31,848. For the Iraq war, the ratio of deaths-to-wounded was 1:7.4, which is significantly different from the ratio of 1:2.6 reported for the Vietnam War, and 1:1.7 for World War II. In a study conducted in 2005 with veterans of Iraq and Afghanistan, Schneiderman, Braver, and Kang (2008) report that 12 percent reported symptoms consistent with mild traumatic brain injury, and 11 percent met screening criteria for PTSD. While the military has recently implemented programs to screen for and assist veterans diagnosed with psychological disorders, the resources available are inadequate to meet the needs of these returning soldiers. Further, because National Guard and Reserve personnel often receive services through private health insurance rather than through the Veteran's Administration, the actual need among these individuals is far greater.

THE IMPACT OF POVERTY AND RACE ON DISABILITY

The causes and costs of disability in low income and minority communities are more severe. This is a reciprocal problem; living in poverty increases exposure to many causes of disability, and those with disabilities living in poverty have access to fewer resources to cope with those disabilities. Lower income and racial minority communities are more likely to be in close proximity to hazardous waste sites (Mohal & Saha, 2007) and to other forms of "locally unwanted land uses (LULUs)" (Pellow, Weinberg, & Schnaiberg, 2001, p. 425), such as sewage treatment plants, medical waste incinerators, and chemical plants. Such exposure, particularly in childhood, has been linked to health problems throughout life (Wigle et al., 2008), including respiratory illness and some forms of cancer. Individuals in lower income communities are also at greater risk of disability resulting from violent crime. The exposure to disabling environmental factors in poor communities is compounded by the costs of health care in the United States, which are often prohibitive for individuals without health insurance. According to the U.S. Census Bureau, the percentage of individuals in the United States without health insurance was 15.8 percent in 2006, with 16.1 percent of Asians, 19.0 percent of blacks, and 34.1 percent of Hispanics/Latinos reporting a lack of coverage, in comparison to 10.7 percent of non-Hispanic whites (DeNavas-Walt, Proctor, & Smith, 2007). In all cases, poverty decreases the rate of insurance coverage, with 24.2 percent of those with a household income of less than $25,000 lacking any type of coverage, compared to 7.7 percent of those whose household income was $75,000 or more.

Once an individual is diagnosed with a disability, the likelihood of obtaining adequate health insurance drops significantly, since health insurance is based on risk of developing an illness rather than assuming the costs of a certain and expensive disorder (O'Day & Goldstein, 2005). Thus, without significant reform in U.S. health care policy, a substantial proportion of citizens will be forced to forgo needed health care services, to assume large levels of debt, or to shift the costs to an already burdened system of charity care.

Beyond the availability of insurance, the level of health care quality also varies based on demographic variables. The U.S. Department of Health and Human Services National Healthcare Disparities Report (U.S. Department of Health and Human Services & Agency for Healthcare Research and Quality, 2005) addresses disparities in access and quality of health care based on race, ethnicity, income, and education. Recent findings indicate that as a group, blacks and Native Americans (grouped as American Indians and Alaska Natives) received poorer health care than whites on about 40 percent of the areas measured, while these two groups received better care than whites on about 11 percent and 14 percent of these measures, respectively. Hispanics/Latinos received poorer care than whites on roughly half of the measures and better care on about 16 percent, while Asians received poorer care on about 21 percent of the measures and better care than whites on 38 percent. In all cases, poverty is a significant factor, with 85 percent of the measures being worse for poor people, and only 8 percent better than for those of higher income. While some of these measures do show improvement over the past 10–15 years, an equal or greater number are worsening. Similarly, differences were noted in the emergency care of illness or injury, with Hispanics/Latinos, blacks, and low income individuals more frequently reporting difficulties receiving prompt medical care. Further, Hispanics/Latinos more often reported that their health care providers did not explain or listen carefully. This may be related to language barriers, but this report also found that after controlling for income and education, racial minorities and Hispanics/Latinos are less likely to have a consistent health care provider who knows them and can act as an advocate. Across all income groups, blacks, Asians, and Hispanics/Latinos were less likely to receive mental health care than were non-Hispanic/Latino whites (U.S. Department of Health and Human Services & Agency for Healthcare Research and Quality, 2005). In summary, poverty and racial or ethnic-minority status increases the likelihood that (a) an individual will be exposed to environmental conditions leading to disability, (b) the individual will lack the necessary health insurance to effectively manage that disability, and (c) even when the individual does receive health care, it will be of lower quality.

ISSUES SPECIFIC TO HIDDEN DISABILITIES

Hidden disabilities, such as learning disabilities, mental illness, and some medical conditions, pose unique problems with regard to ableism.

This is largely due to a lack of awareness or understanding of these disabilities, and a tendency to judge individuals' behavior based on normative standards that assume fully abled status. Further, as discussed below, in many cases ableism is further compounded by racism. This section will address some of the issues arising from this lack of awareness and differential treatment of individuals from minority groups as they affect K–12 education, criminal justice involvement, and workplace discrimination.

DISPARITIES IN SPECIAL EDUCATION

Research has shown deleterious effects of race, ethnicity, and social class on diagnosis and classification of children with educational disabilities, particularly cognitive impairments (which until recently were classified under the term mental retardation, or MR) and specific learning disabilities (SLD). In particular, the types of disabilities for which black children are classified tend to be more frequently in these subjective and often stigmatized categories compared to the disability classifications of other children. The U.S. Department of Education, Office of Special Education and Rehabilitative Services, and Office of Special Education Programs (2005) reported that black children with disabilities were significantly more likely (17.4%) to be labeled with cognitive disabilities or MR than were Native Americans (8.2%), Asian/Pacific Islanders (9.4%), Hispanics/Latinos (8.1%), or whites (8.6%). Also, 11.3 percent of black children with disabilities received services for emotional disturbance (ED), compared to 7.7 percent of Native Americans, 5.0 percent of Asian/Pacific Islanders, 5.0 percent of Hispanics/Latinos, and 8.0 percent of whites. Skiba et al. (2008) reported that teachers referred African American children for special education services based on their behavior, and that disproportionate representation was more common in the more subjective categories of MR, ED, and SLD than for physical disabilities. Skiba et al. further cites data indicating that as the proportion of African American teachers in a school increased, the proportion of students labeled ED decreased.

Poverty was also reported as significantly affecting disability in the schools. While about 16 percent of the general U.S. population lives in poverty, 24 percent of children aged 6–21 with disabilities live below the poverty line. By contrast, in 2001 only 13 percent of students with disabilities lived in families earning greater than $75,000 a year, while 24 percent of the overall population reported this level of income. Having a disability also makes it more likely that when these children grow up they will remain in poverty. Not only is it more difficult for individuals with disabilities to obtain employment that will pay a living wage, but those with serious disabilities may find that they cannot afford to give up the health care benefits that come from Medicare or Medicaid (O'Day & Goldstein, 2005).

Unfortunately, classification with an educational disability does not ensure that the services a child receives in the schools will be appropriate. For example, when African American children receive special education services, research has shown that they are less likely to be in a least restrictive environment than are white children with the same disability classification (Skiba et al., 2008). Finally, while the data presented above reflect the United States as a whole, there are important variations between the states. For example, while national data tend to suggest an underrepresentation of Latino students in special education, studies in New York and California, with large Latino populations, show that these children are overrepresented in most categories (Skiba et al., 2008) For Native Americans, who represent about 1 percent of the U.S. public school population (Sable & Garofano, 2007), the national classification rate for all categories is about 1.5 percent (U.S. Department of Education, Office of Special Education and Rehabilitative Services, and Office of Special Education Programs, 2005). However, the proportions compared to state populations are much higher in states with large Native populations, such as Alaska and South Dakota, in which the school populations are 27 percent and 10 percent (Sable & Garofano, 2007), but their classification rates are 34 percent and 17 percent, respectively (U.S. Department of Education, The U.S. Department of Education, Office of Special Education and Rehabilitative Services, and Office of Special Education Programs, 2005). For Asian Americans, the percentage of classified students is similar to the overall percentage of Asian Americans in the public schools. In Hawaii, where the proportion of Asian Americans in the public schools is about 73 percent (Sable & Garofano, 2007), their proportion among classified students is slightly higher, at 77 percent (U.S. Department of Education, The U.S. Department of Education, Office of Special Education and Rehabilitative Services, and Office of Special Education Programs, 2005). In California, however, where the public schools are approximately 12 percent Asian/Pacific Islander (Sable & Garofano, 2007), the percentage of Asian/Pacific Islander students receiving services under the IDEA is only 6.17 percent (U.S. Department of Education, The U.S. Department of Education, Office of Special Education and Rehabilitative Services, and Office of Special Education Programs, 2005). While the reasons for this under-representation are not addressed, it is possible that this disparity is related to the model minority stereotype of Asian Americans.

HIDDEN DISABILITIES AND SCHOOL DISCIPLINE

Even when students are receiving services under the IDEA, their interactions with school personnel can be complicated by their disabilities, and these personnel are not always aware of the ways in which these disabilities may affect students' behavior. Students with learning disabilities, by virtue of the definition of the disability, have disabilities that are language based, often making it difficult for them to communicate with others effectively. For example, many LD students take things literally when they are spoken to. Thus, if someone said to a student in a sarcastic tone of voice, "I really like the way you are behaving," nondisabled students would quickly understand and modify their inappropriate behavior, while a student with a learning disability might say, "thank you." This would likely result in the student being disciplined for making a wise crack, when the assumption is that he surely knew what the teacher meant.

Unfortunately, current approaches to school discipline can affect children with hidden disabilities in negative ways. The actual numbers of students who are suspended and/or expelled from school vary by state and location, but nationally, in 2000 over 3 million students, about 70 percent of whom were male, were suspended from public schools, while the number of students expelled was over 97,000, of whom 77 percent were male (U.S. Department of Education, Office for Civil Rights, 2000). Many of these were children with disabilities. According to the U.S. Department of Education, The U.S. Department of Education, Office of Special Education and Rehabilitative Services, and Office of Special Education Programs (2005), 32.7 percent of parents of children with disabilities reported that their child had ever been either suspended or expelled from school. This was more frequent for black students (46%) compared with whites (30%) or Hispanics/Latinos (28%). The Southern Poverty Law Center (SPLC, 2008) reported that students with emotional disturbances are particularly at risk, being significantly more likely to be arrested while still in school, and only 35 percent likely to graduate. Of those who drop out, the SLPC reports that 73 percent will be arrested within five years.

Part of the issue with students being disciplined stems from changes in the ways behavioral problems are addressed in public schools. Since significant incidences have occurred in both K–12 settings, such as the shootings in Columbine, and in higher education, such as Virginia Tech, many new initiatives have been launched. An example is "zero tolerance" policies, which result in behavioral issues that may have previously been addressed by a trip to the principal's office or to a school counselor now often being referred to the police. Harvard University's Advancement Project identifies numerous cases in which students received criminal punishments for minor infractions; for example, a 10-year-old girl was arrested for bring a pair of scissors to school and a child was charged with battery for pouring milk over the head of a classmate (Advancement Project, 2005). There has also been an increase in police presence in the schools since the mid 1990s in order to address security concerns in response to violent incidents in the schools. While these measures are understandable in light of concerns about students' overall safety, they also serve to increase students' exposure to the criminal justice system via police officers who are readily available and thus more likely to be called upon to address behavioral infractions. Given the disproportionate rate at which students with disabilities receive disciplinary action, this tends to channel these students into the criminal justice system at higher rates. As mentioned above, this risk is higher for racial and ethnic minority students, as well as for males.

HIDDEN DISABILITIES AND THE CRIMINAL JUSTICE SYSTEM

Research has revealed that individuals with disabilities are disproportionately represented in the criminal justice system. According to a Bureau of Justice Statistics special report (Maruschak & Beck, 2001), over 326,000 (31.1%) of all State prison inmates reported some type of either physical or mental disability. Of specific interest are those disabilities that are not readily apparent to untrained individuals, including impairments in learning (9.9% of prisoners), and mental conditions (10.0%). Because only 22 states have systems to identify inmates with mental, emotional, or special health problems, it is likely that these numbers are underestimated. In 2000, the Office of Special Education Programs (OSEP) reported the prevalence of disabilities among school age children in the United States as 9 percent, compared with a conservative estimate of 32 percent within the juvenile justice system. Further, the SPLC (2008) reported that 70 percent of children involved in the criminal justice system have some form of educational disability, most often an emotional disturbance or specific learning disability. In any case, the evidence suggests that children with disabilities are more likely to become involved in the criminal justice system, for various reasons described below.

Criminal behavior can be linked to learning and behavioral disabilities, along with other factors including dropping out of school, substance abuse, weak family structure, gender, and poverty, among others (Quinn, Rutherford, & Leone, 2001). In many cases, these variables are interconnected, as school frustration can lead to behavioral difficulties and school dropout. It should be noted, however, that while an estimated 32 percent to 70 percent of children in correctional facilities have some type of disability, it would not be correct to state that most children with disabilities engage in criminal behavior or become involved in the criminal justices system. In fact, the percentage of students of school age who are classified with disabilities and are in correctional facilities is only .56 percent of all classified students in the general school-age population. Within this group, about 84 percent are males. This figure is somewhat higher than the proportion of males who are classified, which is 67.16 in the general K–12 population (U.S. Department of Education, Office of Special Education and Rehabilitative Services, & Office of Special Education Programs, 2006), but it is consistent with the significantly higher proportion of males in the criminal justice system overall.

Individuals with cognitive impairments and communication difficulties face unique challenges at all levels of the criminal justice system. Vernon and Miller (2005) note that these difficulties are compounded for individuals who are poorly educated or have low reading levels. Similarly, individuals with learning disabilities and psychiatric disabilities may have difficulties in communicating or understanding when they encounter police and other officials. In the face of rapid-fire questioning, such individuals may become frightened and confused, which may be inappropriately interpreted as disrespect. In describing the pathways of children through school failure through delinquency to arrest and incarceration for more serious crimes, Schroeder, Guin, Chaison, and Houchins (2004) state that "nowhere else is the failure of juvenile justice system policies more evident than in the cases of children with disabilities, African-American children, and children living in poverty. There is no doubt that the U.S. juvenile justice system policies failed not only these children, but also their eventual victims" (p. 466).

RECOMMENDATIONS

Ableism leads to unintended discrimination in a variety of forms, because the needs of individuals with disabilities are overlooked when services or facilities are planned. Thus, it is incumbent upon society as a whole—educators, employers, service providers, health care organizations, and members of the criminal justice system among others—to not only confront their own assumptions about individuals with disabilities but also to educate themselves about ways in which access to a fuller life can be ensured. Most people recognize the need for mobility-related accommodations for individuals with visible disabilities, such as ramps for those in wheelchairs, or Braille markers on elevators and doorways. However, the other needs of individuals with disabilities are more often overlooked. For the ideal of equal access to be realized, it is important for educators and employers to be aware of and willing to provide the support to which these individuals are legally entitled. Learning about the needs and, perhaps more importantly, the capabilities of individuals with disabilities will help ensure their fair treatment, as well as their ability to fully contribute to the work of the organizations to which they belong. Below we have provided recommendations for increasing awareness and for providing a more level playing field for citizens with disabilities.

Think about Universal Design

Fine and Asch (2000) note that many of the limitations placed on individuals with disabilities are the result of a "disabling environment" (p. 333), rather than the inherent result of their disability. For example, business and classroom presentations may rely on audiovisual materials;

meetings or social events may be scheduled in locations that are not easily accessible by public transportation, or that are not in accessible buildings. Universal Design (UD) is the design of products and environments to be usable by all people, to the greatest extent possible, without the need for adaptation or specialized design. This can include both physical and non-physical features that provide benefit to all users, such as incorporating ramps in the design of buildings (which also benefit abled individuals with wheeled briefcases); captioning features on televisions, which allow programs to be viewed by hearing individuals in noisy environments as well as by those with hearing impairments; or written materials on tape or online in accessible formats, which can be used by abled individuals as well as those with learning disabilities or visual impairments. Improvements to mass transit systems are helpful not only to individuals whose disabilities prevent them from driving, but also to the poor and abled individuals who may make use of these services. Individuals with disabilities are often reluctant to ask for special accommodations, fearing that their needs will be perceived as a burden. Appropriate design and planning would alleviate this issue and most likely would diminish the need for "special" accommodations for events and for everyday access if the majority of items and spaces were designed with "access for all" in mind. Links to universal design information are available from the Association on Higher Education and Disability Web site at http://www. AHEAD.org.

Increase Public Awareness of Disabilities, Including Hidden Disabilities

A recent report by the U.S. Equal Employment Opportunity Commission (U.S. EEOC, 2007) notes that a primary barrier to employment of individuals with disabilities was related to persistent myths about their skills and aptitudes. This arises in part from the fears of able-bodied people, who can't imagine being able to cope with loss of function (Smith et al., 2008). The EEOC report recommends increased effort within the federal government to disseminate information to dispel these myths. Addressing lack of awareness in public services may require training programs targeted at police, employers, schools and other public agencies. As mentioned previously, it is not uncommon for such people to be disciplined in school or reprimanded at work for such behavior, because teachers, professors or supervisors do not relate their behavior to a disability. Also, as discussed above, this also causes difficulties for individuals who become involved in the criminal justice system. It is often much easier to understand a disability when it is physically visible, which is why working with those with hidden disabilities is often a challenge—and why education regarding the presence of these disabilities is essential. It is also important to increase awareness and understanding that the issues facing individuals with disabilities can be compounded by racial and social class inequities that are inherent in U.S. society

Increase Awareness and Understanding of Disability Law and Accommodations

Part of the reason that existing disability law has had limited impact is a lack of awareness of the relevant laws, and the resulting requirements of employers and public facilities. The following is a discussion of possible types of accommodations, related laws, and additional resources for more information on disabilities. Prior to the 1970s there was little movement in public policy related to disabilities. During the Kennedy administration and later in the Johnson administration, the first real efforts were made to bring a discussion regarding all types of diversity into the forefront, including related to race, ethnicity, gender and disability. The landmark legislation was the Civil Rights Restoration Act, Section 504 of the Rehabilitation Act of 1973. It is from that legislation that the nation's disabled enjoyed the first mandated handicapped parking, curb cut outs and ramps. The law defined disability as a substantial limitation of a life activity, and put forth the concept of otherwise qualified and reasonable accommodations in employment and education. At the same time, the policy makers passed PL 94-142, which was the first national legislation mandating a variety of special education initiatives and regulations in public school districts, making special education mandatory.

The second influential pair of laws were passed in 1990; the Americans with Disabilities Act (ADA) and the Individuals with Disabilities Education Act (IDEA). The ADA took the accessibility notions from Section 504 and expanded them as a blueprint for the removal of architectural barriers and set the standard for physical accessibility and introduced "person first" language and concepts into the law, which considers the individual initially, and the disability is moved to a secondary position. For example, instead of saying "a deaf person," one would instead refer to "a person who is deaf." The IDEA expanded and refined PL 94-142 and included increased parental rights in the decision-making portion of the referral, identification, evaluation and implementation process. It also included early language of the Least Restrictive Environment (LRE) mandate discussed earlier in this chapter.

It is important that all individuals who are educators, employers, public officials and/or service providers are familiar with the laws as well as the case law that is related to all of them, especially Section 504 and the ADA. Further, because both of those laws have a rather nonspecific, broad definition of the terms "disability," "access," "otherwise qualified," and "reasonable accommodation," it is important to recognize that the implementation of these laws often depends on the results of court cases that are continually setting the parameters for each concept within those pieces of legislation. Thus, experts such as disability support offices may be called on to assist in interpreting an often complex maze of legal requirements.

It would also be helpful for those who are working with individuals who are no longer covered by IDEA (IDEA is applicable only until a student graduates high school or turns 21, whichever occurs first) to be aware of the differences between the two pieces of legislation. Briefly, IDEA mandates special education and related services as well as a Free Appropriate Public Education (FAPE), while Section 504 and the ADA provide access and reasonable accommodation. While students may have been entitled to modifications in their course requirements during elementary and high school, making these courses less rigorous, in college they are subject to the same standards as are all other students. Accommodations such as books on tape or extended time on exams may be provided to assist with learning or to allow an otherwise capable student to demonstrate learning, but the material learned must be the same. Similarly, in the workplace, employers must provide reasonable accommodations to employees who are otherwise qualified for their jobs, but they are not required to change the essential requirements of those jobs.

In order to receive accommodations in higher education or in an employment setting, it is important that adults, and those who advise them, know the process for receiving accommodations. Most of the burden on the part of the individual with the disability is to develop an effective set of self-advocacy skills that will serve them well when negotiating for accommodations. An essential element is being able to explain what the disability is, how it manifests itself and what accommodations are needed in order for the individual to do his or her work in school or in employment situations. For many individuals this is the most challenging aspect of their request, as some are lacking in the verbal skills that would enable them to explain their situation, leaving the support services provider or employer trying to assist the person not knowing what they need, or thinking that the person has cognitive or mental illness issues, when that may not be the case. A key point for everyone involved in disability work is to remember to empower, not enable those for whom we are providing accommodations. The DO-IT Center at the University of Washington has provided an extensive list of resources regarding legislation, universal design, materials for professional development, brochures, and numerous other items at http://www.washington.edu/doit/.

Understand and Utilize the Concepts of Empowerment and Advocacy

While developing personal awareness is important, that is not sufficient on its own to create the needed change. Advocacy can take place on both an individual level, in which individuals with disabilities are empowered to become their own advocates, and on a political and institutional level.

Ideally, political advocacy should also involve individuals with disabilities in a way that is supportive rather than paternalistic. In fact, some external limitations placed on individuals with disabilities may be a result of well-meaning individuals who believe that those with disabilities need to be protected, and as a result may be more disabling than empowering. For example, individuals may be excused from work responsibilities or class assignments that they are capable of handling with accommodations, or they may not be held to the same attendance or punctuality policies as other students or employees, when there is no disability-related reason they cannot manage these responsibilities. Although well-meaning, this leniency is also a result of ableism, and it is likely to arise from the discomfort of an able-bodied supervisor, teacher or professor who fears being viewed as insensitive. However, this denies individuals with disabilities the opportunities to develop and grow, as others do when they are required to manage serious life responsibility. In fact, a recent study (Liparini, 2008) reports that students with psychiatric disabilities appreciated teachers who held them to higher standards, because this provided a better level of preparation for their future independent lives.

Empowerment of Individuals

For individuals with disabilities to become empowered to act as their own advocates to the extent that they are able, it is necessary for their parents, teachers, and counselors to learn to act more as coaches than as rescuers. For children with disabilities, this means making them aware of their disabilities and accommodations, and involving them in child study team meetings as early as they are able to understand the process. As mentioned earlier in this chapter, individuals need to understand what their disability is and how it manifests itself. Without that knowledge it will be difficult for them to be their own advocates. The popular press is filled with many articles on helicopter parents and their hovering over their children managing or controlling every minute of their day. The millennial student has been studied more than any other generation (Howe & Strauss, 2003). It is the contention of some that current students are not ready for the world of work due to the lack of long term-thinking and the constant intervention of parents (Levine, 2005). For students with disabilities, whose parents have been known to be protective of their children all along, the situation is exacerbated and those who need these skills the most to succeed in life will not have developed them. Counselors, teachers, and child study teams can help parents understand the value in empowering their children to advocate for themselves.

For adults with disabilities, advocacy may involve assisting them in learning how to contact appropriate resources and assert their legal rights when necessary. Connections to support communities can be valuable in helping individuals with disabilities to develop a sense of empowerment, or confidence that they can self-advocate and mobilize other resources when necessary. For individuals with limited mobility, online communities can be quite helpful in this way. An example of an online community is WheelchairNet (http://www.wheelchairnet.org/WCN_TownHall/Docs/whatswcn.html), which was developed through the University of Pittsburgh and provides links to advocacy and empowerment resources, in addition to information for the press and for others who want to increase their awareness of and supportive involvement in disability related issues.

Political and Institutional Advocacy

Many of the factors that create what Fine and Asch (2000) refer to as a "disabling environment" (p. 333) are systemic, embedded in organizations and political systems. Thus, advocacy often requires action through efforts to change law and policy. Institutional advocacy can take place in local school districts, universities, corporations, or mental health settings. For example, organizations can be encouraged to review their forms and Web sites, in addition to their physical sites, to ensure that they are accessible to all employees, students and clients. Organizations can also add programs on disability awareness and ableism to programs that likely are already in place addressing other areas of diversity, such as race and gender. Political advocacy may be facilitated through education of political bodies. For example, Schroeder et al. (2004) clearly illustrate the institutional failures that contributed to the loss of three African American children to a life in the criminal justices system, and sharing these tragic stories led to legislation in Louisiana that created an early intervention system for at-risk children. Through interviews with prominent disability advocates, O'Day and Goldstein (2005) identify the following as the top five critical areas for advocacy: health care, employment, accessible technology, long-term care, and civil rights enforcement. Among the issues related to health care are the availability of affordable health insurance and the disincentives to employment because of a risk of losing public health care coverage through Medicare or Medicaid. Beyond the health care disincentives to employment, O'Day and Goldstein note that although the ADA provides legally protected access to employment, this hasn't increased the number of people with disabilities who are employed or actively seeking employment, which has remained at about 30 percent since 1970. Accessible technology, which is the third key area identified in the O'Day and Goldstein study, includes affordable medical equipment. However, increasing the availability of other technology can go a long way toward assisting individuals with disabilities to obtain both higher education and employment. This includes work-related equipment and software like screen readers, voice activated software and teletypwriters, as well as modifications to vehicles and mobility aids like motorized wheelchairs. Fourth, legislative advocacy is needed to ensure that individuals with disabilities can obtain long-term care outside of institutional settings. This is related to Medicaid rules that limit payment for community-based care, which clearly would be more supportive of independence. Finally, it is essential that existing laws be more energetically enforced. As noted throughout this chapter, simply passing a law is often not enough to ensure equal rights. When disability interacts with poverty, gender or racial minority status, the problem is magnified.

CONCLUSION

Social justice in the United States has long focused on issues of racism, sexism, and poverty. Ability status has not received the same attention, although individuals with disabilities have been provided with an increasing level of legal protection since the ADA was first passed and other laws were strengthened in the 1990s. For the laws to be fully effective, it is essential that ableism as a form of discrimination be considered in training programs for educators and health care professionals, as well as police, corrections officers, public administrators, and ideally members of the general public. Public awareness of specific disabilities may decrease misunderstandings that can escalate to inappropriate discipline for disability related behavior. Awareness programs may build empathy by increasing the recognition that every fully-abled individual is only one illness or accident away from learning the ways in which those with disabling conditions are discounted and marginalized. Further, awareness programs and resources for employers would address erroneous beliefs that providing accommodations would be too expensive or that individuals with disabilities are less qualified than are other employees, and they can assist employers, schools, and other facilities in implementing reasonable accommodations as well as strategies such as universal design that can decrease the need for special accommodations. While changes in language can sometimes appear arbitrary and may be discounted as mere political correctness, it may in fact be more accurate to refer to those who are fully abled as "temporarily abled." Further, increased exposure to those individuals who live with disabilities and yet have made extraordinary contributions to society, such as the physicist Stephen Hawking, actress Marlee Matlin, and New York governor David Paterson, can begin to chip away at the fears and irrational prejudices that cause unnecessary barriers to be added to those that individuals already face.

Finally, as addressed above, numerous laws already exist that provide the right to these accommodations, but the resources for enforcement of these and most other civil rights laws are inadequate—thus, it is essential that public attitudes change, so that voluntary compliance increases. Once those who enjoy temporary abled status begin to recognize and address their own prejudices, it is essential that they carry this recognition into advocacy and systemic change, which is the only way in which true reform can ever occur.

REFERENCES

Advancement Project. (2005). *Education on lockdown: The schoolhouse to jailhouse track.* Washington, DC: Author.

Americans with Disabilities Act of 1990, Pub.L. No. 101–336, § 2, 104 Stat. 328 (1991).

Annie E. Casey Foundation. (2005). Kids Count Data Center, Comparisons by topic; Low-birthweight babies: Percent: 2005. Retrieved May 22, 2008, from http://www.kidscount.org/datacenter/compare_results.jsp?i=50.

Castañeda, R., & Peters, M. L. (2000). Ableism: Introduction. In M. Adams, W. J. Blumenfled, R. Castañeda, H. W. Hackman, M. L. Peters, & X. Zúñiga (Eds.), *Readings for diversity and social justice: An anthology on racism, antisemitism, sexism, heterosexism, ableism, and classism* (pp. 319–323). New York: Routledge.

Centers for Disease Control. (2005). National diabetes fact sheet. Washington, DC: Author. Retrieved July 9, 2008, from http://www.cdc.gov/diabetes/pubs/estimates.htm.

DeNavas-Walt, C., Proctor, B. D., & Smith, J. (2007). *Income, poverty, and health insurance coverage in the United States: 2006* (U.S. Census Bureau, Current Population Reports, P60-233). Washington, DC: U.S. Government Printing Office.

Fine, M., & Asch, A. (2000). Disability beyond stigma: Social interaction, discrimination, and activism. In M. Adams, W. J. Blumenfled, R. Castañeda, H. W. Hackman, M. L. Peters, & X. Zúñiga (Eds.), *Readings for diversity and social justice: An anthology on racism, antisemitism, sexism, heterosexism, ableism, and classism* (pp. 330–339). New York: Routledge.

Fischer, H., Klarman, K., & Oboroceanu, M-J. (2008). CRS Report for Congress: American war and military operations casualties: Lists and statistics. Order code RL32492. Retrieved June 18, 2008, from http://www.fas.org/sgp/crs/natsec/RL32492.pdf.

Freedman, V. A., Martin, L. G., & Schoeni, R. F. (2004). Disability in America. *Population Bulletin, 59*(3), 3–33.

Ganz, M. L. (2007). The lifetime distribution of incremental societal costs of autism. *Archives of Pediatrics and Adolescent Medicine, 161,* 343–349.

Howe, N., & Strauss, W. (2003). *Millennials go to college.* Washington, DC: American Association of Collegiate Registrars and Admissions Officers.

Individuals with Disabilities Education Act (IDEA) Amendments of 1997, Pub L No. 105–17 §1400, 37 Stat. 111 (1997).

Institute of Medicine (IOM). (2007). *The future of disability in America.* Washington, DC: The National Academies Press.

Kramarow, E., Lubitz, J., Lentzner, H., & Gorina, Y. (2007). Trends in the health of older Americans, 1970–2005. *Health Affairs, 26,* 1417–1425.

Levine, M. (2005). *Ready or not, here life comes.* New York: Simon & Schuster.

Liparini, C. M. (2008). Student as active agent: A Grounded Theory of the postsecondary transition experiences of students with psychiatric disabilities. Unpublished doctoral dissertation, Seton Hall University, South Orange, NJ.

Maruschak, L. M., & Beck, A. J. (2001). Bureau of Justice Statistics Special Report: Medical problems of inmates, 1997. Washington, DC: U.S. Department of Justice, Office of Justice Programs. Retrieved May 31, 2008, from http://www.ojp.usdoj.gov/bjs/pub/pdf/mpi97.pdf.

Mohal, P., & Saha, R. (2007). Racial inequality in the distribution of hazardous waste: A national-level reassessment. *Social Problems, 54,* 343–370.

National Diabetes Education Program (NDEP). (2007). Diabetes: The numbers. Retrieved June 18, 2008, from http://ndep.nih.gov/resources/presenta tions/diabetesthenumber0107.

O'Day, B., & Goldstein, M. (2005). Advocacy issues and strategies for the 21st century: Key informant interviews. *Journal of Disability Policy Studies, 15,* 240–250.

Pellow, D. N., Weinberg, A., & Schnaiberg, A. (2001). The environmental justice movement: Equitable allocation of the costs and benefits of environmental management outcomes. *Social Justice Research, 14,* 423–439.

Pew Research Center. (2005). *Baby boomers approach 60: From the age of Aquarius to the age of responsibility.* Retrieved March 28, 2009, from http://pewsocial trends.org/assets/pdf/socialtrends-boomers120805.pdf.

Quinn, M. M., Rutherford, R. B., & Leone, P. E. (2001). Students with disabilities in correctional facilities. Arlington, VA: Eric Clearinghouse on Disabilities and Gifted Education. Retrieved May 28, 2008, from http://www.ericdi gests.org/2002–4/correctional.html.

Rehabilitation Act of 1973, 29 U.S.C. § 794 (1977).

Sable, J., & Garofano, A. (2007). Public Elementary and Secondary School Student Enrollment, High School Completions, and Staff from the Common Core of Data: School Year 2005–06 (NCES 2007–352). U.S. Department of Education. Washington, DC: National Center for Education Statistics. Retrieved July 9, 2008, from http://nces.ed.gov/pubsearch/pubsinfo.asp?pubid=2007352.

Schneiderman, A. I., Braver, E. R., & Kang, H. K. (2008). Understanding sequelae of injury mechanisms and mild traumatic brain injury incurred during the conflicts in Iraq and Afghanistan: Persistent postconcussive symptoms and Posttraumatic Stress Disorder. *American Journal of Epidemiology, 167,* 1446–1452.

Schroeder, J., Guin, C. C., Chaison, R., & Houchins, D. (2004). Pathways to death row for America's disabled youth: Three case studies driving reform. *Journal of Youth Studies, 7,* 451–472.

Skiba, R. J., Simmons, A. B., Ritter, S., Gibb, A. C., Rausch, M. K., Cuadrado, J., et al. (2008). Achieving equity in special education: History, status, and current challenges. *Exceptional Children, 74,* 264–288.

Smith, L., Foley, P. F., & Chaney, M. (2008). Addressing the interface of classism, ableism, and heterosexism in professional training programs. *Journal of Counseling and Development, 86,* 303–309.

Southern Poverty Law Center. (2008). Stopping the school-to-prison pipeline by enforcing special education law. Retrieved May 31, 2008, from http://www.splcenter.org/legal/schoolhouse.jsp.

U.S. Census Bureau. (2007). *Percent of people 65 years and over with a disability: 2006* (2006 American Community Survey, R1803). Retrieved June 17, 2008, from http://factfinder.census.gov/.

U.S. Department of Education, Office for Civil Rights. (2000). *OCR Elementary and Secondary School Survey: 2000.* Washington, DC: Author.

U.S. Department of Education, Office of Special Education and Rehabilitative Services, and Office of Special Education Programs. (2005). *25th Annual (2003) report to Congress on the implementation of the Individuals with Disabilities Education Act* (Vols. 1 & 2). Washington, DC: Author.

U.S. Department of Education, Office of Special Education and Rehabilitative Services, and Office of Special Education Programs. (2006). IDEA data. Retrieved June 14, 2008, from https://www.ideadata.org/PartBdata.asp.

U.S. Department of Health and Human Services & Agency for Healthcare Research and Quality (2005). National Healthcare Disparities Report, 2005. Rockville, MD. Retrieved May 23, 2008, from http://www.ahrq.gov/qual/nhdr05/nhdr05.htm.

U.S. Equal Employment Opportunity Commission (EEOC). (2007). Improving the participation rate of people with targeted disabilities in the federal work force. Washington, DC: Author. Retrieved July 11, 2008, from http://www.eeoc.gov/federal/report/pwtd.html.

Vernon, M., & Miller, K. (2005). Obstacles faced by deaf people in the criminal justice system. *American Annals of the Deaf, 150*, 283–291.

Wigle, D. T., Arbuckle, T. E., Turner, M. C., Berube, A., Yang, Q., Liu, S., et al. (2008). Epidemiologic evidence of relationships between reproductive and child health outcomes and environmental chemical contaminants. *Journal of Toxicology & Environmental Health: Part B, 11*(5/6), 373–517.

Williams, A. C. (2005). Promoting appropriate responses toward disabilities in juvenile justice settings: Applying disability studies' perspectives to practice. *Journal for Juvenile Justice Services, 20*, 7–23.

CHAPTER 7

Disability from Interpersonal Violence: Culturally Relevant Assessment and Treatment

Martha E. Banks and Rosalie J. Ackerman

As awareness of health and health care disparities increases, it is critical to attend to omission patterns of assessment and treatment. This chapter examines the relatively recent attention to traumatic brain injury (TBI). Major issues involve the increase in survival rates for people with these injuries and the development of rehabilitation for injuries previously assumed to be untreatable. The focus of assessment and rehabilitation for TBI has been on young men, including athletes, with most norms and programs based on European and European American populations. This chapter examines the need for attention to the TBI assessment and treatment needs for two underserved populations of victims of interpersonal violence: women victims of private intimate partner violence and women and men sustaining TBI in public war.

Interpersonal violence leads to a broad range of injuries. This is considered a public health hazard and has been documented by the World Health Organization (WHO; Krug, Dahlberg, Mercy, Zwi, & Lozano, 2002), Centers for Disease Control and Prevention (CDC; Bergen, Chen, Warner, & Fingerhut, 2008), and Rand Corporation (Tanielian & Jaycox, 2008), among others (Satcher & Higginbotham, 2008). Many of the injuries are responsive to treatment, but in order to be treated, they must first be diagnosed. Diagnosis can only take place if injured people have access to culturally relevant appropriate health care (Banks, 2007; Banks, Buki, Yee, & Gallardo, 2007; Marshall, Sanderson, Johnson, Du Bois, & Kvedar, 2006; Smedley, Stith, & Nelson, 2003).

While many injuries are readily recognized, some are particularly difficult. Some injuries heal quickly, whereas others can result in chronic disability. An example of this is traumatic brain injury (TBI). Given the broad range of symptoms and relatively recent development of treatments for TBI, many people are not diagnosed or treated. This chapter will provide an overview of the prevalence of TBI, describe violent behaviors that can result in TBI, and discuss the impact of TBI. The chapter focuses on two specific populations: (a) victims of intimate partner violence (IPV) and (b) service members returning from military conflicts in Afghanistan and Iraq who have been misdiagnosed, underdiagnosed, and undertreated. The chapter will end with suggestions for the development of culturally relevant assessment, treatment, research, and policy.

VIOLENT BEHAVIOR THAT CAUSES INJURY

Interpersonal violence can involve individuals or large groups of people attacking other people. Such violence, on an individual basis, appears to be most extreme when directed toward romantic partners under the aegis of IPV. IPV can happen to anyone regardless of race, age, sexual orientation, religion, gender, socioeconomic background, or education level (U.S. Department of Justice, n.d.). At the other extreme, interpersonal violence occurs in the context of war. Both IPV and war involve the dehumanization and demonization of people as justification for the infliction of injuries.

Causing Injury in Intimate Partner Violence

In IPV or domestic violence (DV), an abuser might hit, kick, slap, choke, throw things at his or her partner or otherwise attack her or him. He or she might abuse the partner sexually or use weapons. These incidents usually happen without witnesses, and the victim generally cannot stop the attack. Some forms of abuse leading to serious injury include being hit by a car, beaten, punched, thrown against a wall, attacked with household objects, strangled, pushed down stairs, shot, slapped, kicked, and pushed into traffic (GLBT Domestic Violence Coalition & Jane Doe Inc., 2006). Although most IPV occurs in privacy, there are special considerations that increase the danger for rural victims. Victims often have minimal or no access to phone service or public transportation, are located in areas with poor roads, long police and medical response times, limited social contact, and have partners who cannot be kept away (e.g., from the farm if it is their only source of income) (Minnesota Coalition for Battered Women, n.d.). Although both women and men are victims and perpetrators of IPV, women represent a higher proportion of victims and men a higher proportion of perpetrators. In addition, women are more likely to sustain more serious injuries (Petridou et al., 2002).

Jackson, Philip, Nuttall, and Diller (2004) looked at specific injuries experienced by women victims diagnosed with traumatic brain injury. These included being hit in the head or face (92%), being severely shaken (68%), and being both hit in the head or face and shaken (83%). Farley, Ackerman, and Banks (in press) note:

All 44 of the women we interviewed had sustained head injuries either by being hit in the head with objects (89%) or having their heads shoved into objects (74%). Fifty-five percent of our interviewees had been hit in the head with hands or fists. They also reported being hit in the head with bottles, bats, sticks, hammers, guns, telephones, canes, screwdrivers, belts, and branches. Twenty three percent of our interviewees had been shoved into walls, with others reporting having their heads slammed into the floor, against dashboards of cars, against furniture or sinks, or against another person.

Causing Injury in War

The means of attack in war have evolved from handheld weapons aimed by one person toward another to a range of weapons of mass destruction. In the Iraq War, a major concern has been concealed weapons intended to maim or kill, either as "roadside bombs" through detonation or by "suicide bombers." Military personnel are injured by improvised explosive devices (IEDs), mortars, vehicle accidents, grenades, bullets, mines, and falls (Tanielian & Jaycox, 2008).

PREVALENCE OF INJURIES IN VICTIM POPULATIONS

The Centers for Disease Control and Prevention (CDC) track fractures, contusions and superficial injuries, open wounds, sprains and strains, and fractures, as well as certain mechanisms of injury (being struck by or against an object or person, falls, being cut or pierced, and motor vehicle traffic incidents) for civilians seen in emergency departments and hospitals. The CDC's data do not reflect the difference between intentional and unintentional injuries sustained in interpersonal violence. In 2004, the CDC documented nearly 170,000 deaths, more than 31 million emergency department visits, and about 35 million outpatient hospital department and physician office visits due to injuries. During the 2004–2005 period of data collection, 10 percent of the hospital discharges for people admitted with injuries involved traumatic brain injury. The emergency department data suggest that 3 percent of the U.S. civilian population sustain injuries from falls, 1.5 percent are struck by or against and object or person; 1.3 percent are involved in motor vehicle traffic events, and slightly fewer than 1 percent are cut or pierced (Bergen et al., 2008). Although the CDC refers to demographics, such as gender and ethnicity, they do not report injury patterns as they differ among demographic groups.

How can culturally relevant prevention be developed if we do not know who is injured and how?

Prevalence of Injuries in Intimate Partner Violence

The injuries sustained by victims of IPV are often severe and life threatening:

Patients who are not screened for IPV miss opportunities for identification and intervention, as well as the great potential for primary and secondary prevention of IPV-associated illness, injury, and mortality. (Phelan, 2007, p. 199)

Several researchers have examined the differences between injuries sustained in IPV and those of accident victims, as well as gender differences in types and severity of IPV injuries.

Muelleman, Lenaghan, and Pakieser (1996) compare injuries sustained by battered women and other patients in emergency departments. Battered women had more facial (51% versus 11%), head (23% versus 6%), thorax (20% versus 12%), abdomen (12% versus 1%), and neck injuries (2% versus 0.1%) than other patients. The other emergency room patients had primarily spine (23% compared to 14%) and leg (32% compared to 18%) injuries.

Petridou et al. (2002) reveal the findings of a comparable study in Greece that included men and women. They report differences not only between unintended injuries and those inflicted during IPV, but also between the percentages of injuries sustained by men and women. Brain injuries were sustained by women at a rate that was twice that of men in IPV (18% versus 8%), but women and men's rates were comparable and considerably lower among people injured accidentally (5.5%). Men received more skull (18% versus 14%) and facial (36% versus 30%) injuries than women in both IPV and accidents; for the accidents five percent of men had skull injuries compared to four percent of women, and men had 10 percent of facial and head injuries compared to five percent of women. Accidents accounted for about the same percentages of injuries to arms and legs as IPV. It is important to note that the severity of the injuries, particularly the skull and facial injuries are not reported. However, the significant difference in brain injuries suggests that the skull and facial injuries sustained by women are much more severe than those sustained by men.

In a Kyriacou et al. (1999) sample of 256 women, 37 percent had head injuries, 49 percent had facial injuries, and 15 percent had neck injuries. Some women had more than one injury. Thirteen women had loss of consciousness, and one woman had a depressed skull fracture. Two women had ruptured eyeballs, and two had facial-nerve laceration. 14 percent of the women had chest injuries, 5 percent sustained injuries to their breasts, 8 percent had abdominal injuries, 17 percent sustained back injuries, 9 percent injuries to their buttocks, 39 percent had injuries to their arms and hands, and 25 percent had leg and foot injuries. Similar to the study in Greece, however, the severity of the injuries was not reported.

Valera and Berenbaum (2003) found that women victims of IPV received brain injuries at three times the rate of women in accidents. Most of those brain injuries fall in the *mild* range. It should be noted that the percentages of *moderate to severe* brain injuries are low; that reflects the reality that most people sustaining those levels of brain injury do not survive. Choking accounts for at least 27 percent of brain injuries in women victims of IPV and is not seen at all in accident survivors.

Patterns of injury and subsequent outcome have been noted by some researchers. While studying warning signs of death for victims of IPV, Wadman and Muelleman (1999) note, "head injuries [sustained by victims] predominated as the most common injury documented on ED visits preceding homicide" (p. 690). Therefore, it is critical to assess and treat brain injury in victims of IPV in order to save lives.

With increasing awareness of the seriousness of IPV, there has been a drop in the overall murder rate due to IPV. In the 20 years from 1980 to 2000, the IPV murder rate dropped by two-thirds for men, but only by one-fifth for women (Rennison, 2003). This disparity can be reduced, in part, if women's traumatic brain injuries are appropriately treated; with culturally relevant appropriate rehabilitation, victims would be better prepared to protect themselves.

Prevalence of Injuries in War

"Wounded soldiers who would have likely died in previous conflicts are instead saved, but with significant physical, emotional, and cognitive injuries" (Tanielian & Jaycox, 2008, p. 6). TBI is suspected in about 320,000 U.S. service members returning from military conflicts in Afghanistan and Iraq. Tanielian and Jaycox (2008) call for appropriate diagnosis of traumatic brain injury:

Sequelae may be quite diverse and difficult to link to the injury. Moreover, most of those who reported experiencing this injury have not been evaluated or reassured that they are likely to have experienced a mild injury. Given this situation, the potential exists for ordinary post-deployment adjustment problems to be misattributed to TBI. For this reason, all persons with suspected TBI should be evaluated to document a disability, or the lack of a disability, and to ensure that necessary rehabilitation services are provided. (p. 106)

They also note, "although traumatic brain injury has been deemed a 'signature' wound of the current conflicts, data on the prevalence of traumatic brain injury are lacking" (p. 58). These TBIs are often referred to as "blast" injuries (Tanielian & Jaycox, 2008).

It is difficult to determine which military personnel are most likely to have received TBI during the military conflicts in Afghanistan and Iraq:

Individuals who serve in the Army and the Marine Corps are more likely than others to have had a TBI. Similarly, males, enlisted personnel, and younger individuals are more likely to report experiencing a TBI during deployment. Finally, persons who experienced greater total deployment and more-extensive exposure to combat trauma were at greater risk of a probable TBI during deployment. After adjusting for covariates, however, we found that only the combat trauma exposures remained significant predictors of probable deployment-related TBI. In other words, differences between demographic groups were almost entirely attributable to differences in combat exposure among these groups. (p. 101)

African Americans are represented among the military personnel (17%) and the Rand survey (22%) at significantly higher levels than in the U.S. civilian population (12%) (Tanielian & Jaycox, 2008). Data are not available, however, on demographic patterns of combat exposure. With the current focus on TBI, PTSD, and depression as consequences of the Iraq and Afghanistan conflicts, information about other injuries is often difficult to obtain. Furthermore, there is no demographic disaggregation of information about injuries. However, as noted above, the extant assessment instruments were normed on European Americans.

Following a telephone survey of recently deployed military personnel who were no longer on active duty, Tanielian and Jaycox (2008) are critical of the limited availability of information from the Department of Defense, as that research was not peer-reviewed. Similar to the research of Hoge et al. (2008) with active duty postdeployment infantry personnel, determination of traumatic brain injury was based on self-report, rather than professional diagnosis.

How can military personnel be served with culturally relevant health care if information about injuries is based on self-diagnosis? How can treatments be developed if information about demography of injured people is withheld?

IMPACT ON VICTIMS: REPORTED AND OBSERVED SYMPTOMS

Jackson et al. (2004) looked at specific symptoms experienced by women victims diagnosed with traumatic brain injury. These included having dizziness, nausea, confusion, or feeling "out of it" (77%), and losing consciousness (40%). The same researchers examined symptoms experienced. They report that victims experienced trouble concentrating (64%), trouble remembering (62%), headaches (52%), dizziness (19%), easily distracted (66%), trouble paying attention to more than one thing (62%), forgetting appointments (57%), trouble doing more than one thing at a time (53%), difficulty finding the right words (47%), losing things (45%), trouble following directions (13%), and work became harder for them (40%). Their research population included 60 percent African American women, but they did not disaggregate their results by ethnicity.

Farley et al. (in press) report that victims of extreme IPV experienced trouble concentrating (64%), trouble remembering (64%), headaches (73%), dizziness (80%), constipation or diarrhea (32%), fatigue (48%), sleep disturbance (73%), ringing in ears (2%), irritability (59%), agitation (57%), and poor emotional control (57%).

Similar research on injured military survivors of combat (Hoge et al., 2008) reveal that respondents had trouble concentrating (31% with loss of consciousness [LOC], 26% with altered state of consciousness [ASC], and 18% with injuries other than TBI), trouble remembering (25% LOC, 16% ASC, 14% other injuries), headaches (32% LOC, 18% ASC, 12% other injuries), dizziness (8% LOC, 6% ASC, 3% other injuries), constipation or diarrhea (22% LOC, 12% ASC, 12% other injuries), fatigue (52% LOC, 40% ASC, 35% other injuries), sleep disturbance (54% LOC, 45% ASC, 37% other injuries), ringing in ears (24% LOC, 18% ASC, 14% other injuries), irritability (57% LOC, 48% ASC, 37% other injuries), stomach pain (12% LOC, 8% ASC, 9% other injuries), back pain (33% LOC, 31% ASC, 29% other injuries), extremity joint pain (37% LOC, 42% ASC, 40% other injuries), chest pain (14% LOC, 3% ASC, 5% other injuries), fainting spells (4% LOC, 1% ASC, 2% other injuries), heart pounding (19% LOC, 10% ASC, 5% other injuries), shortness of breath (14% LOC, 8% ASC, 7% other injuries), nausea, gas, and indigestion (18% LOC, 13% ASC, 15% other injuries), pain during sexual intercourse (8% LOC, 3% ASC, 4% other injuries), and balance problems (8% LOC, 7% ASC, 3% other injuries). Vasterling et al. (2006) reported that service personnel returning from the conflicts in Afghanistan and Iraq exhibited decreased attention, learning, and memory on neuropsychological evaluations.

Many cognitive problems, such as distraction, poor concentration, memory difficulties, inability to multitask, word finding, and handling of work-related tasks, were experienced by victims more than once a day. This has caused many researchers to question the validity of the concept of so-called mild traumatic brain injury. The difficulties are such that they interfere with the most important spheres of people's lives and are truly disabling (Sterr, Herron, Hayward, & Montaldi, 2006).

How can culturally relevant rehabilitation programs be developed when we lack information about demography of the victims and specifics about which problems are experienced by which people?

Impact on Families and Communities

Interpersonal violence not only affects those who are injured, it also has a substantial effect on family members, friends, coworkers, other witnesses, and the community at large. Children, who grow up witnessing interpersonal violence (whether in person or through mass media), are among those seriously affected by the violence. Frequent exposure to violence in the home not only predisposes children to numerous social and physical problems, but also teaches them that violence is a normal way of life—therefore, increasing their risk of becoming society's next generation of victims and abusers. One consideration of how interpersonal violence impacts the community at large is the high cost of health care; victims of violence use health care services at a higher rate than the general public and are often unable to cover their own health care expenses.

People in the social circles of victims with mild traumatic brain injury often complain that those people have "changed" or seem to have different "personalities." Repercussions and maladaptive behavioral reactions within family systems often trigger requests for professionals to help stabilize family functioning.

ASSESSMENT AND REHABILITATION RESEARCH

Victims of violence experience both psychological and physical trauma. Most treating professionals focus exclusively on either psychological or physical concerns. It is critical to consider both aspects when treating clients. There are treatable consequences of mild traumatic brain injury. Mild traumatic brain injury (mTBI) can be a life-altering experience and can be a source of chronic, sometimes hidden, disability in the absence of appropriate rehabilitation.

A major problem is that many health professionals, including many who work with victims of IPV, have not received training on brain function and treatments to heal injured brains. Misdiagnoses and omission of diagnoses are significant for victims with mTBI.

Such injuries have been studied in (mostly young and male) athletes. That research has generated specific strategies for quick assessment of mild traumatic brain injury, treatment, and preventive measures. Sustaining a second brain injury prior to the healing of an initial brain trauma has been demonstrated to result in poor memory, poor judgment, inability to perform at the prior level of achievement, and, in the most severe cases, death.

IPV victims (mostly female), in the absence of assessment and treatment, are at extremely high risk for second impact syndrome. For athletes, prevention of second impact injuries and implementation of rest, protective equipment, and rehabilitation are handled through monitoring by trainers and coaches. There are no on-site monitors for victims of IPV; similar injuries in victims of IPV, therefore, are not assessed and treated, nor are preventions implemented.

With increased awareness of TBI as a consequence of "blast" injuries, attempts have been made to make early diagnoses and quick interventions in or near the combat arena. The current assessments (Schwab et al. 2006) are similar to those used with athletes (Lovell et al., 2003; Matser, Kessels, Lezak, & Troost, 2001).

Problems arise with diagnosis of mTBI, because there is considerable symptom overlap with posttraumatic stress disorder (PTSD), dissociation, substance abuse, and cognitive problems due to HIV infection (Briere & Jordan, 2004; Hoge, Terhakopian, Castro, Messer, & Engel, 2007; Thompson & Kingree, 2006). The presence of one diagnosis does not preclude any of the others. It is critical to accurately diagnose in order to ensure that a victim receives appropriate treatment(s).

BRIEF OVERVIEW OF REHABILITATION

An ideal model of the route to rehabilitation for people who have sustained traumatic brain injury involves three stages of treatment. The first stage involves the actual injury and the immediate medical response to the physical injury. The first stage includes emergency treatment, possible intensive care, observation, and medical stabilization. The second stage involves assessment and acute rehabilitation to counteract immediate problems. The third or postacute stage involves many of the same treatments as the acute stage, but addresses more long-term problems. All three stages can be conducted on inpatient and outpatient bases, depending on the individual needs of the injured person and the availability of services. Neuropsychological assessment and monitoring should be built into all stages of treatment.

One difficulty with rehabilitation is that there are areas of omission that need to be addressed. Demographics are missing from most studies of victims. Most research excludes people with multiple diagnoses, for example, TBI and PTSD, substance abuse, criminal activity, and personality disorders. CDC data do not include homeless people. Stringent qualifiers for veterans' benefits omit treatment to people who have served but might have been in service only a short time or whose behavior led to less than honorable discharges. There need to be more culturally rehabilitation programs and more culturally sensitive neuropsychological assessment tools.

EXAMPLE OF CULTURALLY RELEVANT NEUROPSYCHOLOGICAL AND REHABILITATION ASSESSMENT TOOLS

The Ackerman-Banks Neuropsychological Rehabilitation Battery (ABNRB)[1] was developed to provide a valid, efficacious, and comprehensive screening instrument for the rehabilitation setting, with minimal assessment time (45 to 90 minutes) and cost for clients. The ABNRB is designed to measure functional strengths and weaknesses to efficiently develop individualized treatment plans, is relatively short (using multiple behavioral measurements for each task), and is normed on a diverse *clinical*[2] population. *The administrative time is critical for maximizing the clients' functioning by minimizing fatigue.* Use of a process approach (Bracy, 1986; Kaplan, 1989) allows insight into the clients' ability to benefit from rehabilitation (e.g., ability to follow instructions, flexibility in changing tasks, and ability to learn with practice).

The ABNRB limits the number of tasks that a client has to perform. Instead, the onus is on the test administrator to score, in detail, the quality of the performance. Unlike some neuropsychological batteries that simply indicate that a task was correctly completed or not, the ABNRB examines multiple facets of each task and each facet is scored along a continuum. The test is scored in a positive direction so that higher scores reflect better function. This is less confusing for clients and is consistent with a rehabilitative approach to assessment.

Each test task is also scored for awareness of deficits, socially appropriate behavior, and frustration tolerance. These behavioral items are included in the calculation of *t* scores, the interpretation spreadsheet, and the brief narrative. Hints for behaviors often exhibited by clients are provided on the protocol as a reminder to test administrators to track client behavior.

The goal of the authors was to develop a functional battery that included tasks accessible to men and women from different cultural backgrounds. The test includes items for tasks controlled by both the left and right brain hemispheres; this can reflect different cultural approaches to cognitive processing. Test items also include measurement of anxiety, depression, impulsivity, and frustration tolerance. The ABNRB was developed in English, with consideration of vocabulary that would be appropriate for members of several ethnic groups. In addition, the language is specifically geared to a reading level equivalent to fifth grade or lower to minimize difficulty for people with poor educational backgrounds.

In addition to the 85 specific neuropsychology tasks, the ABNRB includes an initial structured interview with detailed demographics, linguistic background, and neurological, medical, and psychological/psychiatric conditions. Psychologists are given the opportunity to indicate source(s) of information obtained in the interview. The test results are provided in a spreadsheet similar to an individual educational plan that can be shared with clients and treatment staff. Client strengths and weaknesses are briefly described with recommendations for further evaluation and/or treatment.

The ABNRB includes, in addition to the 85 actual neuropsychological test items and the structured interview, a 104-item Behavioral Interview and Checklist, designed to assess presence or absence of symptoms often exhibited by clients with brain dysfunction. Information about such symptoms can be obtained from professional observation by the psychologist and other treating professionals, as well as reports by the client and members of her or his social circles (Ackerman & Banks, 2003, 2007; Ackerman, Banks, Farley, & Sikora, 2003; Lezak, 2002). The domains of the Behavioral Interview and Checklist represent practical applications of the neurobehavioral domains of the ABNRB.

Most neuropsychological batteries are normed on nonclinical populations composed primarily of middle to upper SES European American men with at least 12 years of education. The ABNRB was normed on a *clinical* population that included 47 percent women and 17 percent African Americans. This approach addresses the concern of Poreh (2002) and Manly and Jacobs (2002) that test developers should provide information about the performance of ethnic minorities as part of the original material included with the test, rather than merely marketing a test normed on a homogeneous population or failing to disaggregate test results. The ethnic-gender groups were 7.0 percent African American female, 10.4 percent African American male, 40.1 percent European American female, and 42.5 percent European American male; members of other ethnic groups were not referred for assessment during the period of data collection (Asbury, Walker, Belgrave, Maholmes, & Green, 1994; Banks, 2008). Future research will focus on translations of the battery and determination of the cultural relevance of test items for other ethnic groups.

SUMMARY

Interpersonal violence is considered to be an international public health hazard that leads to a broad range of injuries with negative impact upon survivors and their families. Awareness is needed both to prevent injuries and to provide appropriate health services to those already injured. It is necessary for victims to be perceived as worthy of appropriate assessment and treatment. Health professionals working with people who have sustained TBI need to appreciate the availability of rehabilitation in order to refer for assessment. Rehabilitation personnel must be aware of culturally relevant assessments to provide appropriate treatment; that treatment must also be culturally relevant in order for people to benefit. An example of an assessment instrument that strives to meet the needs of some underserved populations has been provided, as well as a model of rehabilitation. Development of similar tools is strongly recommended for use with other populations.

NOTES

1. Portions of the descriptions of the development of the *Ackerman-Banks Neuropsychological Rehabilitation Battery* are taken from Ackerman and Banks (2002, 2006).

2. The clinical population consisted of inpatients and outpatients in rehabilitation programs. All had independently confirmed diagnoses of brain damage. The utility of this battery is demonstrated through the use of a *clinical* normative population as opposed to extrapolation from a "normal" sample. A clinical population provides a more accurate basis for generalization and prediction than an extrapolation from an unrelated population.

REFERENCES

Ackerman, R. J., & Banks, M. E. (2002). Epilogue: Looking for the threads: Commonalities and differences. In F. R. Ferrari (Ed.), *Minority and cross-cultural aspects of neuropsychological assessment* (pp. 387–415). Heereweg, Lisse, The Netherlands: Swets & Zeitlinger Publishers.

Ackerman, R. J., & Banks, M. E. (2003). Assessment, treatment, and rehabilitation for interpersonal violence victims: Women sustaining head injuries. In M. E. Banks & E. Kaschak (Eds.), *Women with visible and invisible disabilities: Multiple intersections, multiple issues, multiple therapies* (pp. 343–363). New York: Haworth Press.

Ackerman, R. J., & Banks, M. E. (2006). *Ackerman-Banks Neuropsychological Rehabilitation Battery© Professional Manual* (4th ed.). Akron, OH: ABackans DCP, Inc.

Ackerman, R. J., & Banks, M. E. (2007). Caregiving. In V. Muhlbauer & J. C. Chrisler (Eds.), *Women over 50: Psychological perspectives* (pp. 147–163). New York: Springer.

Ackerman, R. J., Banks, M. E., Farley, M., & Sikora, E. (2003, November 4). *Prostitution, dissociation, and traumatic brain injury.* Presented at the Annual International Fall Conference of the International Society for the Study of Dissociation, Chicago.

Asbury, C. A., Walker, S., Belgrave, F. Z., Maholmes, V., & Green, L. (1994). Psychosocial, cultural, and accessibility factors associated with participation of African-Americans in rehabilitation. *Rehabilitation Psychology, 39,* 113–121.

Banks, M. E. (2007). Overlooked but critical: Traumatic brain injury as a consequence of interpersonal violence. *Trauma, Violence, & Abuse, 8,* 290–298.

Banks, M. E. (2008). Women with disabilities: Cultural competence in rehabilitation psychology. *Disability and Rehabilitation, 3*(3), 184–190.

Banks, M. E., Buki, L. P., Yee, B.W.K., & Gallardo, M. E. (2007). Integrative healthcare and marginalized populations. In M. A. DiCowden (Ed.), *Whole Person Healthcare: Vol. I. Humanizing Healthcare.* (pp. 147–173). Westport, CT: Greenwood Publishing.

Bergen, G., Chen, L. H., Warner, M., & Fingerhut, L. A. (2008). *Injury in the United States: 2007 chartbook.* Hyattsville, MD: National Center for Health Statistics.

Bracy, O. L. (1986, March–April). Cognitive rehabilitation: A process approach. *Cognitive Rehabilitation, 4*(2), 10–17.

Briere, J., & Jordan, C. E. (2004). Violence against women: Outcome complexity and implications for assessment and treatment. *Journal of Interpersonal Violence, 19,* 1252–1276.

Farley, M., Ackerman, R. J., & Banks, M. E. (in press). Traumatic brain injury in prostituted women.

GLBT Domestic Violence Coalition & Jane Doe Inc. (2006). *Shelter/housing needs for gay, lesbian, bisexual and transgender (GLBT) victims of domestic violence.* Boston: Author. Retrieved February 23, 2007, from http://www.thenetworklared.org/GLBTDVPublicHearingReport2006.pdf.

Hoge, C. W., McGurk, D., Thomas, J. L., Cox, A. L., Engel, C. C., & Castro, C. A. (2008). Mild traumatic brain injury in U.S. soldiers returning from Iraq. *New England Journal of Medicine, 358,* 453–463.

Hoge, C. W., Terhakopian, A., Castro, C. A., Messer, S. C., & Engel, C. C. (2007). Association of posttraumatic stress disorder with somatic symptoms, health care visits, and absenteeism among Iraq war veterans. *American Journal of Psychiatry, 164,*150–153.

Jackson, H., Philip, E., Nuttall, R. L., & Diller, L. (2004). Battered women and traumatic brain injury. In K. A. Kendall-Tackett (Ed.), *Health consequences of abuse in the family: A clinical guide for evidence-based practice* (pp. 233–246). Washington, DC: American Psychological Association.

Kaplan, E. (1989). A process approach to neuropsychological assessment. In T. Boll & B. K. Bryant (Eds.), *Clinical neuropsychology and brain function: Research, measurement, and practice.* Washington, DC: American Psychological Association.

Krug, E. G., Dahlberg, L. L., Mercy, J. A., Zwi, A. B., & Lozano, R. (Eds.). (2002). *World report on violence and health.* Geneva: World Health Organization.

Kyriacou, D. N., Angelin, D., Taliaferro, E., Stone, S., Tubb, T., Linden, J. A., et al. (1999). Risk factors for injury to women from domestic violence. *New England Journal of Medicine, 341,* 1892–1898.

Lezak, M. D. (2002). Responsive assessment and the freedom to think for ourselves. *Rehabilitation Psychology, 47,* 339–353.

Lovell, M. R., Collins, M. W., Iverson, G. L., Field. M., Maroon, J. C., Cantu, R., et al. (2003). Recovery from mild concussion in high school athletes. *Journal of Neurosurgery, 98,* 296–301.

Manly, J. J., & Jacobs, D. M. (2002). Future directions in neuropsychological assessment with African Americans. In F. R. Ferraro (Ed.), *Minority and cross-cultural aspects of neuropsychological assessment* (pp. 79–96). Heereweg, Lisse, The Netherlands: Swets & Zeitlinger Publishers.

Marshall, C. A., Sanderson, P. R., Johnson, S. R., Du Bois, B., & Kvedar, J. C. (2006). Considering class, culture, and access in rehabilitation intervention and research. In K. J. Hagglund & A. W. Heinemann (Eds.), *Handbook of applied disability and rehabilitation research* (pp. 25–44). New York: Springer.

Matser, J. T., Kessels, A.G.H., Lezak, M. D., & Troost, J. (2001). A dose-response relation of headers and concussions with cognitive impairment in professional soccer players. *Journal of Clinical and Experimental Neuropsychology, 23,* 770–774.

Minnesota Coalition for Battered Women. (n.d.). Rural battered women. Retrieved May 26, 2008, from http://www.mcbw.org/files/u1/rural.pdf.

Muelleman, R. L., Lenaghan, P. A., & Pakieser, R. A. (1996). Battered women: Injury locations and types. *Annals of Emergency Medicine, 28,* 486–492.

Petridou, E., Browne, A., Lichter, E., Dedoukou, X., Alexe, D., & Dessypris, N. (2002). What distinguishes unintentional injuries from injuries due to intimate partner violence: A study in Greek ambulatory care settings. *Injury Prevention, 8,* 197–201.

Phelan, M. B. (2007). Screening for intimate partner violence in medical settings. *Trauma, Violence, & Abuse, 8,* 199–213.

Poreh, A. M. (2002). Guidelines for neuropsychological assessment of culturally diverse populations. In F. R. Ferraro (Ed.), *Minority and cross-cultural aspects of neuropsychological assessment* (pp. 329–343). Heereweg, Lisse, The Netherlands: Swets & Zeitlinger Publishers.

Rennison, C. M. (2003). *Intimate partner violence, 1993–2001* (NCJ–197838). Washington, DC: U.S. Department of Justice, Bureau of Justice Statistics.

Satcher, D., & Higginbotham, E. J. (2008). The public health approach to eliminating disparities in health. *American Journal of Public Health, 98*, 400–403.

Schwab, K. A., Baker, G., Ivins, B., Sluss-Tiller, M., Lux, W., & Warden, D. (2006). The Brief Traumatic Brain Injury Screen (BTBIS): Investigating the validity of a self-report instrument for detecting traumatic brain injury (TBI) in troops returning from deployment in Afghanistan and Iraq. *Neurology, 66*(5, Supp. 2), A235.

Smedley, B. D., Stith, A. Y., & Nelson, A. R. (Eds.). (2003). *Unequal treatment: Confronting racial and ethnic disparities in health care.* Washington, DC: National Academies Press.

Sterr, A., Herron, K. A., Hayward, C., & Montaldi, D. (2006). Are mild head injuries as mild as we think? Neurobehavioral concomitants of chronic post-concussion syndrome. *BMC Neurology, 6*(7). Retrieved May 20, 2008, from http://www.pubmedcentral.nih.gov/articlerender.fcgi?tool=pubmed&pubmedid=16460567

Tanielian, T., & Jaycox, L. H. (Eds.). (2008). *Invisible wounds of war: Psychological and cognitive injuries, their consequences, and services to assist recovery.* Santa Monica, CA: RAND Corporation.

Thompson, M. P., & Kingree, J. B. (2006). The roles of victim and perpetrator alcohol use in intimate partner violence outcomes. *Journal of Interpersonal Violence, 21*, 163–177.

U.S. Department of Justice. (n.d.). About domestic violence. Retrieved February 22, 2007, from http://www.usdoj.gov/ovw/domviolence.htm.

Valera, E. M., & Berenbaum, H. (2003). Brain injury in battered women. *Journal of Consulting and Clinical Psychology, 71*, 797–804.

Vasterling, J. J., Proctor, S. P., Amoroso, P., Kane, R., Heeren, T., & White, R. F. (2006). Neuropsychological outcomes of Army personnel following deployment to the Iraq War. *JAMA: Journal of the American Medical Association, 296*, 519–529.

Wadman, M. C., & Muelleman, R. L. (1999). Domestic violence homicides: ED use before victimization. *American Journal of Emergency Medicine, 17*, 689–691.

CHAPTER 8

The Cultural Context of Trauma Recovery: The Experiences of Ethnic Minority Women

*Thema Bryant-Davis, Annie Belcourt-Dittloff,
Heewoon Chung, and Shaquita Tillman*

The prevalence and severity of violence against women in the United States should be a cause of grave concern. Given the prevalence of victimization of ethnic minority women in particular, there has been growing recognition of the need to examine the cultural context of trauma recovery (Klevens, 2007). Researchers and practitioners recognize that culture can influence one's perception of and response to traumatic experiences (Bryant-Davis, 2005). Culture is also multifaceted in the sense that culture can be a protective factor and resource for coping, while inversely cultural oppression can be a source of micro aggressions, daily hassles, stress, and traumatic stress. To fully understand how to intervene in cases of interpersonal trauma, it is critical that one examines the cultural context in which the trauma occurred and in which the recovery process will transpire.

This chapter will examine the experiences of selected ethnic minority women in the United States, namely African American, Native American/Alaska Native, Asian American, and Latina American. It is important, however, to remember that people have multiple identities. In addition to research and clinical work that attends to ethnicity, it is also necessary to recognize the intersecting identities of gender, race, socioeconomic status, disability, migration status, sexual orientation, age, and religion (Bryant-Davis, 2005). It is at the intersection of these identities that trauma survivors confront the recovery process (Crenshaw, 1994).

AFRICAN AMERICAN WOMEN
AND TRAUMA RECOVERY

Coping Strategies

Coping strategies are used to minimize stress as well as reduce the emotional, physical, and psychological turmoil an individual experiences as a result of experiencing adverse events (Mitchell et al., 2006). African American women utilize various coping strategies when faced with traumatic experiences such as child sexual abuse (CSA), sexual assault, intimate partner violence (IPV), and community violence. Mitchell et al. (2006) identify several coping methods used by low-income, African American women who were survivors of IPV, that is, distancing (e.g., not allowing oneself to think about the abuse), accepting responsibility (blaming or criticizing oneself for the abuse), escape avoidance (e.g., overeating), and self-controlling (attempting to solve problems without the assistance of others). As the authors note these coping methods may have dire consequences for the IPV survivor, for example, the woman may develop negative views of herself, may doubt her ability to maintain a healthy relationships, and the abuse in the relationship may escalate if her partner feels threatened by her actions.

Additionally, traumatized individuals may engage in self-destructive behaviors to cope with the aftermath of traumatic experiences. One example of a self-harming behavior is the use and misuse of substances. In several studies conducted with multiple populations in which the primary drug of choice varied, researchers consistently found a high rate of sexually traumatic experiences among substance abusing women, including women in chemical dependency treatment programs (Teets, 1995), women in alcohol treatment programs (Weinsheimer, Schermer, Malcoe, Balduf, & Bloomfield, 2005), and undergraduate women with alcohol and drug problems (Braband, Forsyth, & LeBlanc, 1997). In Young and Boyd's (2000) study of African American women crack cocaine users they reveal that women with a history of sexual trauma reported being addicted to more substances and being admitted to the hospital and emergency room more often for substance-related issues. Although substance use is a maladaptive form of coping that needs to be replaced, initially using substances may enable some women to contain their inner experiences so that they are able to function as well as they do in daily life (Chiavaroli, 1992).

Protective Factors

Decades of research demonstrate that self-esteem is one of the central and most important aspects of well-being and self-concept (Baumeister, 1993). Further, research suggests that one potential negative outcome of both IPV and child maltreatment (CM) is lowered self-esteem (Orava, McLeod, & Sharpe, 1996). However, viewed from another perspective, self-esteem and related constructs (e.g., self-efficacy) may serve as resilience factors and protect women with a history of IPV or CM from negative mental health effects such as PTSD or depressed mood (e.g., Stein, Burden, & Nyamathi, 2002).

Among African American women trauma survivors, religious involvement/spirituality appears to serve as a source of strength and resilience (Newlin, Knafl, & Melkus, 2002). Religious involvement/spirituality functions as both coping strategies employed by trauma survivors as well as factors that can protect against the deleterious outcomes of traumatic experiences. Religious coping is defined as the use of religious beliefs or behaviors (e.g., prayer, seeking strength from God) to promote problem solving and prevent or alleviate the negative emotional consequences of stressful life circumstances (Koenig, Pargament, & Nielsen, 1998). Examples of religious coping behaviors described as positive include perception of God as benevolent, collaboration with God, seeking a connection with God, seeking support from church members, and giving religious help to others. Prayer is a preferred active coping strategy for African Americans (Mattis, 2002) and for African American women in particular, prayer, spiritual beliefs, and relationship with God are central coping strategies (Mattis, 2002; Shorter-Gooden, 2004). Moreover, although organized religious institutions serve as sources of formal and informal support, many African American women are more likely to use their relationship with God and prayer to cope with stressors. For example, African American women with a history of abuse may rely on prayer because it is a culturally validated private method of coping that may be perceived as safer than direct or public forms of coping aimed at changing the balance of power, the abuser's behavior, and/or leaving the relationship (Waldrop & Resick, 2004). Furthermore, research indicates that positive religious coping strategies relate to better mental health, e.g., less depression, anxiety and hostility (Koenig & Larson, 2001; Schnittker, 2001).

Social support is a critical resource for women trying to stop the violence in their lives. Moreover, social support is a risk/resiliency factor for developing PTSD (Ozer, Best, Lipsey, & Weiss, 2003) and other adverse outcomes among women with a history of IPV and CM (Bender, Cook, & Kaslow, 2003). Thompson et al.'s (2000) reveal that social support improves the coping capacity of women survivors of partner abuse. Furthermore, social support can make the difference toward the likelihood that women survivors sustain mental health and reduce the likelihood of future revictimization (Tan, Basta, Sullivan, & Davidson, 1995). African American women who seek social support may feel empowered; thus, they may use more active support strategies in their attempt to change the current situation.

Treatment

The psychological sequelae of trauma have been widely studied. In a review of the literature West (2002) states that African American women are more likely to experience lowered self-esteem, depression, PTSD, substance abuse and suicidal ideation and attempts following traumatic experiences. Various treatment modalities have been used when working with trauma survivors, namely, cognitive behavioral therapy (CBT), feminist therapy, group therapy, and incorporation of religious/spiritual interventions with the primary goal to reduce and/or alleviate these mental health effects. Although there is a paucity of literature on culturally-sensitive and efficacious treatments for African American women trauma survivors specifically, the treatment interventions discussed below are promising.

Women with histories of physical assault and sexual victimization are the most likely to report PTSD (Breslau, Kessler, Chilcoat, Peterson, & Lucia, 1999). The most studied treatments for PTSD have used cognitive behavioral techniques (Foa & Meadows, 1997) implemented in the context of an empathic and supportive therapeutic relationship. Cognitive-behavioral therapy (CBT) usually includes components of having the client expose themselves to memories of the trauma (imaginal exposure) and to real-life situations (real-life exposure), as well as cognitive restructuring (Jaycox, Zoellner, & Foa, 2002). More specifically, components of CBT for trauma include: breathing training, education about PTSD symptoms, imaginal exposure to trauma itself and confrontation of feared situations and cognitive restructuring (examining and challenging dysfunctional thoughts). The goal of CBT is to reduce the client's anxiety and stress initially brought on by the traumatic experience.

Group therapies for adults with posttraumatic stress disorder (PTSD) may be sorted into three approaches: supportive, psychodynamic, or cognitive-behavioral. Supportive group therapy places little attention on the details of traumatic events; instead, the focus is on group validation of the impact of the trauma experience. In a psychodynamic perspective, the focus is on internalized model of self and relationships to others surrounding the experience and aftermath of the trauma. Cognitive-behavioral focus group therapy uses systematic prolonged exposure and cognitive restructuring techniques to process each group member's trauma experience (Foy, Ruzek, Glynn, Riney, & Gusman, 1997). These treatment methods differ in their theoretical explanations of symptom development and therapeutic intervention, but they share a set of key features that build a therapeutic, safe, and respectful environment. These features include the following: (a) group membership determined by shared type of trauma (e.g., adult survivors of child abuse), (b) disclosure and validation of the traumatic experience, (c) normalization of trauma related responses, (d) validation of behaviors required for survival during the time of the trauma, and (e) challenge to the idea that the nontraumatized therapist cannot be helpful through the presence of fellow survivors in the group.

Feminist therapy is an integrative and eclectic approach to treatment. The overarching goal of feminist treatment is for the clients to develop *feminist consciousness* (Brown, 1994). Feminist consciousness is defined as recognition that one's own distress emerges not from individual impairments but rather from the ways in which one has been systemically invalidated, excluded, and silenced because of one's status as a minority in dominant culture (Lerner, 1993). Feminist trauma treatment in particular explicitly focuses on the empowerment of the client (Brown, 1994; Worell & Remer, 2002). Empowerment takes many forms in feminist practice, but with trauma survivors, the emphasis is on identifying how the trauma was disempowering and on developing effective strategies for responding to it.

Additionally, when working with the African American population, religious/spiritual issues are likely to be important components of intervention. Specific interventions might entail working with clients to foster the growth of effective invocation of spirituality and religion in coping with psychological sequelae and developing relationships with spiritual and religious leaders to encourage their involvement in the treatment and recovery process (e.g., Abrums, 2000; Banks-Wallace & Parks, 2004). An example of incorporating a spiritual/religious approach would be to use a "spirituality-focused genogram" (Dunn & Dawes, 1999), in which the intervention might be to use writing based/narrative approaches that can be formulated to address specific issues, including the relationship of traumatic experiences and religious beliefs (Sloan & Marx, 2004).

In conclusion, service providers working with African American women trauma survivors should always identify and assess how the intersection of their race, gender and social class impacts their vulnerability to experiencing trauma, perceptions of the traumatic experience, coping strategies, and willingness to seek services. Moreover, therapists should draw on the client's strengths. For example, service providers should acknowledge the clients' need to rely on prayer or social support systems (Mohr, Fantuzzo, & Abdul-Kabir, 2001) as a means to buffer against the negative sequelae associated with trauma.

AMERICAN INDIAN AND ALASKA NATIVE WOMEN

Trauma is a frequent antecedent to suffering observed within American Indian and Alaska Native (AI/AN) communities. Manson, Beals, Klein, and Croy (2005) examine exposure to 16 forms of clinically significant trauma within two population-based samples of American Indians residing in reservation communities (N = 3,098). American Indians sampled reported lifetime exposure rates are significantly higher than their white counterparts in the United States (average 64.8 percent of AI men and

68.0 percent of AI women reported having been physically attacked, witnessing a traumatic event, or having a close relative experience a significant traumatic event compared to 60.7 percent of men in the general population and 51.2 percent of women in the general population. American Indians are twice more likely to be victimized than all other U.S. citizens (Greenfield & Smith, 1999). American Indians are also more likely to be victimized by members of other racial backgrounds and inadequately funded Tribal Law Enforcement is well documented (Aarons, Brown, Hough, Garland, & Wood, 2001). American Indians are also incarcerated at a higher rate than other ethnic groups and are estimated to have an incarceration rate that is 38 percent higher than the national rate (Greenfield & Smith, 1999).

The most vulnerable among AI/AN populations appear to be women. In 2007, Amnesty International published a report documenting the high prevalence of sexual violence among AI/AN women (Amnesty International, 2007). AI/AN women are 2.5 times more likely to experience rape or sexual assault than women in the United States general population (Perry, 2004) and more than one in three AIAN women will be raped during their lifetime compared to one in five women in the general population (Tjaden & Thoennes, 2000). Nationwide, AI/AN women are 50 percent more likely to be the victim of a violent crime than the next highest ethnic group, African American men (U.S. Commission on Civil Rights, 2003). Duran et al. (2004) report that 77–73 percent of American Indian respondents surveyed reported having had a history of abuse or neglect and, of those respondents, nearly 90 percent were also physically and/or sexually abused. Deters, Novins, Fickenscher, and Beals (2005) examine PTSD symptoms in a sample of 89 American Indian adolescents in a substance abuse program. They report that repeated exposure to trauma was pervasive within this sample; 98 percent of participants reported at least one significant traumatic event and on average 4.1 events were reported. Respondents also reported high rates of PTSD symptoms within this study with sexual trauma exposure found as the most common predictor of PTSD symptoms.

Health Care Needs

Despite the clear need for effective health care services for American Indian communities and families, the U.S. Commission on Civil Rights (2003) reports access to health care as a primary barrier and the commission also highlights the current inadequacies in available health care, mental health care, educational, personal safety, and economic opportunities. Only 23 percent of American Indians have private insurance and 55 percent rely upon Indian Health Services for all health care needs (U.S. Commission on Civil Rights, 2003). Indian Health Services is one among several federal agencies identified to have federal funding that is insufficient to meet the multiple unmet basic needs identified as health care, education, housing, rural development, and public safety (U.S. Commission on Civil Rights, 2003). American Indians made significantly fewer visits to physician's offices (54 visits per 100,000 American Indians compared with 293 visits per 100,000 whites) and more visits to emergency rooms than other groups (U.S. Department of Commerce & Bureau of the Census, 2002). In a review of Indian Health Services, the Commission of Civil Rights concluded that, "the unmet health care needs for American Indians remain among the most severe of any group in the United States" (U.S. Commission on Civil Rights, 2003, p. 42). In fact, of any group receiving health care funding from the government, (e.g., prisoners, Medicaid recipients, and veterans), AI/ANs receive the fewest dollars per capita, with the Indian Health Service receiving only 56.8 percent of the funding necessary to match the level of services provided by the Federal Employees Health Plan (Indian Health Service, 2002).

The need for effective and accessible health care for American Indian women, families, children, and communities is easily apparent. However, despite the need, continued disparities exist with regard to available services for American Indian women encountering trauma. To date, no clinical trials aimed at evaluating the effectiveness of mental health interventions have been undertaken with an AI/AN population. An additional limiting factor lies within the nature of Western health care systems and the empirical basis for so called "Evidence Based Practices." Gone and Alcantara (2007) review some of the factors possibly confounding the identification of best practices for American Indian health care. In the area of psychopathology and psychotherapy, the amount of scientific knowledge of cross-cultural differences in pathology, definitions of illness and wellness, definitions healers, expectancies, preferences in therapy, treatment application, and treatment outcome is unknown given the serious lack of empirical research within these realms. However, despite these potential biases, many AI/ANs do have access to health care. Beals et al. (2005) report that the majority of AI individuals with a lifetime history of mental health problems sought help from either mental health professionals, medical providers, or culturally traditional sources.

Interventions

Currently, attempts are beginning to be made at the individual and community levels to advance the integration of biomedical and traditional healing methods to improve mental health among AI/AN communities. Recent authors have delineated the clinical importance of traditional health practices (Buchwald, Beals, & Manson, 2000) and some have even argued for the development of stress-coping models based directly upon cultural beliefs, traditional healing practices, and spirituality (Walters & Simoni, 2002). This resurgence has also taken the form of revitalization of traditional Native American languages, ceremonial practices, religions, cultural practices, healing strategies, and mentorship programs, and these have occurred throughout Indian Country. Numerous applied projects have emerged aiming to promote health and wellness within American Indian Communities (Andersen, Belcourt, & Langwell, 2007). These developments demonstrate progressive efforts aimed at increasing the capacity of tribal communities and collaborations between tribal community-based organizations and academic institutions.

Language immersion schools have emerged in many tribes, including the Blackfeet and Arapaho. Such schools have increased interest in Native Languages and helped to fuel resurgences of interest in Native American traditional culture. In addition, the Navajo Healing Project is a collaborative effort between Navajo and non-Navajo researchers to improve health care by understanding the nature of the therapeutic processes in Navajo religious healing (Csordas, 2004).

A recent curriculum developed to prevent AI suicide and promote psychosocial resilience is currently being implemented within multiple American Indian communities and appears to be a promising psychological intervention (LaFromboise, Hoyt, Oliver, & Whitbeck, 2006). The Circles of Care Initiative (Freeman, Iron Cloud-Two Dogs, Novins, & LeMaster, 2004; Novins, LeMaster, Jumper Thurman, & Plested, 2004), funded by the Center for Mental Health Services, is designed to research culturally appropriate mental health services models for children with emotional disturbances. Each of these clinical approaches collaborates closely with tribal communities to develop, research, and assess psychological interventions for American Indians.

Collaborations such as these open up important new avenues for the development of a more effective mental health care system for Native Americans. Thus, the journey has begun toward a better understanding of Native Americans and human kind in general. This journey will hold challenges, in that it will cause the field of psychology to question underlying assumptions that have been held for years about American Indians and American Indian communities as well as challenging some Western views about psychological reality. Native Americans do deserve to be accorded the fullest respect as human beings in research, practice, and throughout psychology in general. This process has only just begun and will likely be led by the American Indian communities themselves. Providing scientific, clinical, and professional voices to the narratives of American Indian resiliency and hope will provide a psychological science that is more representative and inclusive of all peoples.

ASIAN AMERICAN WOMEN
AND TRAUMA RECOVERY

As do women from other cultural backgrounds, Asian American women suffer from all forms of interpersonal trauma, including sexual assault, intimate partner violence, and child abuse. Even though they experience negative symptoms related to PTSD, they have the lowest rates of utilization of mental health services among American ethnic populations (Department of Health and Human Services [DHHS], 2001). However, this group has its own unique coping strategies, and it might be beneficial for mental health practitioners to become cognizant of these strategies and incorporate them in treatment settings.

Coping Strategies

In general, Asian Americans have a negative attitude toward seeking help from mental health practitioners because their community looks down on individuals who disclose personal problems to others, especially to strangers, because of the fear of dishonoring their own families (Sue, 1994). The current research on Asian Americans focuses more on these barriers to seeking help, and suggests recommendations for culturally sensitive treatment, rather than on coping strategies. By examining their own alternative coping strategies in the community, the practitioners can develop a better treatment plan for Asian American clients.

Despite the intercultural variability within this group, many studies show that Asian-American ethnic subgroups use religion as a crucial source of coping skills. For example, some Vietnamese survivors of partner violence have identified religious leaders who speak against domestic violence as significant sources of prevention and intervention (Shiu-Thorton, Santuria, & Sullivan, 2005). Since churches and ministers have a great influence in the Korean American community, Korean American immigrants often use the church as a support group to modify their partner's abusive behavior (Moon, 2005). In a similar vein, a study of Cambodian Americans reported that the local Buddhist monks are the main source of support for discouraging domestic violence (McKenzie-Pollack, 2005).

Asian American women often utilize alternative medicine to address PTSD symptoms. Some Chinese Americans utilize Traditional Chinese Medicine to treat symptoms related to PTSD. Since this form of treatment is rooted in biology, as opposed to emotions or psychology, many clients feel more comfortable with traditional medicine because they can receive treatment without having to disclose too much personal information. Furthermore, research has shown that acupuncture may be helpful in treating psychosomatization that results from PTSD (Kober, Scheck, Schuber, et al. [2003], as cited in Sinclaire-Lian et al. [2006]).

Indonesian American women often experience marital conflict as a result of the newly discovered equal opportunity between men and women that exists in American culture. These women use coping strategies that empower them. They wait until their daughters acquire more resources through social standing or education to be able to mediate the domestic violence. They also wear Western clothing and take advantage of the education and socioeconomic opportunities available to them in the United States.

Treatment Strategies

Overall, in spite of this wide range of coping strategies, most Asian American women look to their family network for assistance; therefore, enhancement of family support is an important aspect of treatment and intervention. It is especially important for mental health practitioners to remember to include all members of the Asian American client's extended family, including the in-laws, in the intervention. One reason for this is because, in some South Asian families, in-laws often reside with the victim and can be a part of the client's support group. Another more grave reason is that in-laws are often direct perpetrators of the abuse. It is important that interventions focus not only on promoting the victim's safety from her husband, but also to assess the possibility that the in-laws may be abusing the client as well (Livramento, Santana, Gupta, & Silverman, 2006).

It is also important for mental health practitioners to be respectful of the cultural values placed on family bonding when working with this population. Most Asian American women want to end the abuse, but still keep their families intact. Rather than striving for Western ideals of independence and individualism, a therapist should be mindful of the Asian ideal of interdependence and group harmony. Regrettably, most family violence services are not designed with an Eastern values system in mind (Yoshioka, Gilbert, El-Bassel, & Baig-Amin, 2003). Alternative interventions include assistance for the entire family, education in parenting skills and nonviolent discipline alternatives, and encouraging women clients to learn English (Weil & Lee, 2004). It has also been suggested that educating all men in the community, not only perpetrators, about domestic violence may be an effective intervention strategy for Asian American communities (Shiu-Thorton, Santuria, & Sullivan, 2005). Along with incorporating the family in treatment planning, it is also important for the therapist to incorporate the local community. It has been reported that community-based agencies provide more culturally sensitive services to the Asian community and are sought out before Eurocentric agencies (Iglehart & Becerra, 1995; Merchant, 2000). Community involvement is especially important given the unique background of different Asian American subgroups. For instance, trust in a therapeutic relationship is crucial for Cambodian immigrants who tend to be distrustful of formal administrations due to the historical trauma imposed by the Khmer Rouge regime in their homeland. In order to gain the trust of the community, it is important to incorporate key community agencies and institutions, as well as to gain the support of the local social service groups that are highly regarded by the community (McKenzie-Pollack, 2005).

Even though Asian Americans rely on their community for support, many Asian American victims of interpersonal violence still feel uncomfortable talking about sensitive subjects to people in their own communities because they are fearful of gossip (Weil & Lee, 2004). However, other research has shown that some Asian American victims of interpersonal violence report that they had a more positive experience working with mental health providers who shared their language, culture, or gender (Shiu-Thorton, Santuria, & Sullivan, 2005). Regardless of whether or not the practitioner shares some or all of these qualities in common with the client, it is important that the practitioner is familiar with the client's culture and can either speak her language or engage the services of an interpreter. When one uses an interpreter it is important to use the same person for each encounter, rather than using multiple people, in order to build trust and reduce the fear of gossip (Weil & Lee, 2004).

In terms of theoretical orientation, therapists who have worked with this particular population have suggested that Chinese American women who have experienced abuse tend to benefit most from a cognitive-behavioral approach (Yu, 2005), but this area of research is limited because of the wide range of within-group differences. Regardless of theoretical orientation, Asian American women who have been abused should always be equipped with referrals for services, such as English language classes, job training, housing, and legal assistance (Faulkner & Faulkner, 2005; Weil & Lee, 2004). This is especially important given that a high percentage of these victims lack resources due to their immigration status.

LATINAS AND TRAUMA RECOVERY

Latinos compose 13.4 percent of the U.S. population and are currently its largest minority group (U.S. Census Bureau, 2004). Gender-based violence is a significant health issue for Latinas in the United States; they face unique challenges in coping with trauma that may include stressors related to immigration, acculturation, language, and economic pressures (Newcomb & Carmona, 2004). As is the case for other ethnic minority women, the additional stressors of societal traumas such as racism, sexism, and poverty can exacerbate the recovery process for Latinas (Bryant-Davis, 2005).

Risk Factors

Similar to other women's experiences, risk factors for interpersonal trauma among Latinas include unemployment, poverty, substance abuse, and childhood victimization (Frye, El-Bassel, Gilbert, Raja, & Christie, 2001; Gilbert, El-Bassel, & Rajah, 2001). Latinas have similar rates to non-Latinas in terms of intimate partner abuse. Specifically the National Violence against Women Survey (NVAWS) reports a lifetime prevalence rate of exposure to IPV among Latinos of 23.4 percent (Tjaden & Thoennes, 2000). In a more recent study, Ingram (2007) finds that half of the population of Latinos report being exposed to some type of IPV. The rates from these studies are similar to the rates of non-Latinos. In terms of specific types of partner abuse, some researchers report sexual abuse by an intimate partner occurring more frequently for Latinas (Perilla, Bakerman, & Norris, 1994).

Effects of Trauma

Although the rates and characteristics of victimization may be similar to other women, the level of violence and its effects may in some cases be more severe. In one study, researchers reveal that more than half the Latina participants reported suicidal thoughts or suicide attempts as compared to 35 percent of other respondents (Krishnan, Hilbert, & VanLeeuwen, 2001). Additionally and similar to non-Latina abuse survivors, abused Latinas report poorer physical and mental health than their nonabused counterparts on a range of scales, including substance abuse, PTSD, depression, and headaches (Golding, 1999; Lown & Vega, 2001a; Newcomb & Carmona, 2004).

Protective Factors

With regard to the recovery process, social support and religiosity appear to be protective factors among Latinos (Denham et al., 2007; Lown & Vega, 2001b). Many Latinas engage in spiritual and religious practices such as Catholicism, creation and use of altars, and folk healing beliefs (Bermúdez & Bermúdez, 2002). In terms of Latina survivors of childhood sexual abuse, Hinson, Koverola, and Morahan (2002) reveal that perceived social support was inversely related to depression, so the Latinas with the highest perceived social support were the least depressed. Recognizing that many trauma survivors develop unhealthy eating habits, it is significant to note that in a study that was not focused on trauma recovery, Latinas who reported high social support also reported healthier eating behaviors (Sanders-Phillips, 1994).

Interventions

Very few publications have been released on interventions with Latina trauma survivors. Given the fact that Latinas receive inadequate health services, it is critical for mental health professionals to put forth concerted efforts in developing interventions for diverse trauma survivors. More scholarship is needed on Empirically Supported Therapies and their efficacy with U.S. ethnic minorities, particularly in the realm of trauma therapies. However, a few examples of empirical exploration provide an

examination of Latina trauma survivors. One study reports that the addition of telephone sessions was advantageous to Latina survivors of violence. In this randomized controlled trial among women recruited from
a family violence unit in an urban district attorney's office, 41 percent of
the women were Spanish-speaking women. The researchers compared
standard services offered by the District Attorney's office to standard services plus six telephone sessions on safety behaviors. This trial found that
these additional telephone sessions improved safety behavior compared
with the standard district attorney intervention (McFarlane, Malecha, &
Gist, 2004).

In another small pilot study, yoga was utilized as an intervention with
battered women, the majority of whom were Latina (Dixon-Peters, 2007).
The pre- and postmeasures indicated that the six-week yoga intervention
significantly reduced the women's self reported depression. The women
qualitatively also reported that the intervention was useful, helpful, and
effective in creating a change in them and their relationships. An additional study examined the use of mentors/advocates, counseling sessions,
and a resource card. In this controlled trial among Latinas, researchers
compared counseling plus a mentor/advocate to counseling only and to a
wallet-sized resource card. They found a decrease in levels of violence and
threats of violence at follow-up 2, 6, 12, and 18 months postintervention in
all three groups (McFarlane, Soeken, & Wiist, 2000).

Both of the previous interventions were not specifically adapted (aside
from bilingual services) for Latinos.

Trauma interventions that have been designed especially for Latinas
are less common. A few of these make note of the importance of cultural
competence training, language resource availability, and community outreach. Whitaker, Baker, and Pratt (2007) describe how cultural competence
networking among agencies may provide a more culturally appropriate
intervention for Latino communities. The agencies in the network share
expertise on cultural competence and are able to utilize the linguistic capacity of other organizations to communicate with non-English-speaking
clients; this leads to improved services for the Latino community as a
whole, and Latinas in particular. In a qualitative study with Latina immigrant abuse survivors, Perez-Neira (2006) report the women wanted
mental health services that take into account their stigmatization, financial
difficulties, difficulties with differences of culture and language, fear of
immigration authorities if they have undocumented immigration status,
and fear of discrimination.

Some practitioners and researchers have reported on cultural modifications of a number of therapeutic approaches, although not always
specifically cited in the literature as focusing on interpersonal trauma;
these interventions include feminist therapy, cognitive behavioral therapy
(including dialectical behavior therapy), expressive art therapy, narrative therapy, home-based family therapy, and psychodynamic therapy

(Comas-Diaz, 2006; Crespo, 2006; Fuentes, 1999; Organista, 2006; Recinos, 2004; Sabol, 2007). According to these scholars, cultural adaption should address socioeconomic status, gender roles, health beliefs, spirituality, and acculturation (Comas-Diaz, 2006; Falicov, 1999; Organista, 2006). Themes should be considered and therapeutic approaches should also be culturally informed. Crespo (2006) states that culturally informed psychodynamic art therapy is more effective in reducing depression among Latinas than dynamically oriented group therapy or dynamically oriented art group therapy. Culturally-informed art therapy for Latinas can include making murals or altars (Bermúdez & Bermúdez, 2002; Crespo, 2006).

Another culturally informed tool with Latinas is the use of metaphors and symbols. Specifically, Zuñiga (1992) explores the therapeutic uses of *dichos*, idioms, or sayings in the Spanish language. These sayings offer the clinician culturally-informed tools for addressing resistance, improving motivation, reframing problems, and promoting a collaborative relationship. Regarding another culturally informed modification, Perez (1999) recommends integration of cognitive behavioral therapy with interpersonal therapy with Latinas as a way of addressing the value of relationships. On another note, it is recommended that Latinas be empowered to critique the image that society holds of them and the image they hold of themselves (Sanchez & Garriga, 1995).

In conclusion Latinas face interpersonal trauma at rates comparable to non-Latinas yet they face multiple additional challenges during the recovery process. Culturally congruent interventions with Latinas must be relevant in content and approach. In content, it is important to address such issues as migration, acculturation, language, socioeconomic status, religion, discrimination, and gender roles. In approach, practitioners should consider staff training, community outreach, home-based interventions, and use of cultural forms of expressions. As with all groups, it is important to remember, however, that Latinas are diverse and the entire identity of the survivor must be taken into account.

DISCUSSION

Ethnic minority women potentially face multiple traumas, including interpersonal trauma and societal traumas such as racism, sexism, heterosexism, and poverty. African American, Native American, Asian American, and Latina American women are confronted with the challenge of coping with acute traumas, while often living in a context of chronic traumas, yet there is a dearth of scholarship on their trauma recovery process. A number of barriers are confronted by many ethnic minority trauma survivors including poverty, low resource access, a strained social network, cultural values promoting self sacrifice for the community, prior victimization, ongoing stigma, and culturally neglectful mental health agencies. Yet, ethnic minority women continue to push forward on the path to recovery, attempting to survive and for some even to thrive (Bryant-Davis, 2005).

Their coping strategies include religion and social support on the healthy side, and substance abuse and self harm on the unhealthy side. Protective factors can include education, positive cultural identity, and positive disclosure response within their social network. Effective interventions with ethnic minority women must take into account their social, economic, and cultural context, values, and beliefs. It must also be sensitive to language barriers and the impact of intergenerational trauma in terms of the sociohistorical oppression of entire communities.

Further research is needed on both prevailing treatment modalities with ethnic minority women as well as cultural modifications of these treatments. There is also need to attend to other ethnic minority women such as Arab American women and Jewish American women. One of the largest gaps is around the intersecting identities of ethnic minorities; specifically, there is need to look at the intragroup variations among ethnic minority women taking into account such factors as sexual orientation, disability status, and socioeconomic status. To reverse the trends of ethnic health disparities and to honor the ways ethnic minority women have survived, mental health researchers and practitioners must actively explore the cultural context and multifaceted voices of ethnic minority women.

REFERENCES

Aarons, G. A., Brown, S. A., Hough, R. L., Garland, A. F., & Wood, P. A. (2001). Prevalence of adolescent substance use disorders across five sectors of care. *Journal of the American Academy of Child and Adolescent Psychiatry, 40*(4), 419–426.

Abrums, M. (2000). "Jesus will fix it after awhile": Meanings and health. *Social Science & Medicine, 50*, 89–105.

Amnesty International. (2007). *Maze of Injustice: The failure to protect indigenous women from sexual violence in the U.S.* New York: Author.

Andersen, S. R., Belcourt, G. M., & Langwell, K. M. (2007). Building healthy tribal nations in Montana and Wyoming through collaborative research and development. *American Journal of Public Health, 95*(5), 784–789.

Banks-Wallace, J., & Parks, L. (2004). It's all sacred: African American women's perspectives on spirituality. *Issues in Mental Health Nursing, 25*, 25–45.

Baumeister, R. F. (1993). *Self-esteem: The puzzle of low self-regard.* New York: Plenum Press.

Beals, J., Manson, S. M., Whitesell, N. R., Spicer, P., Novins, D. K., & Mitchell, C. M. (2005). Prevalence of DSM-IV disorders and attendant help-seeking in two American Indian reservation populations. *Archives of General Psychiatry, 62*, 99–108.

Bender, M., Cook, S., & Kaslow, N. (2003). Social support as a mediator of revictimization of low-income African American women. *Violence & Victims, 18*, 419–431.

Bermúdez, J., & Bermúdez, S. (2002). Altar-making with Latino families: A narrative therapy perspective. *Journal of Family Psychotherapy, 13*(3–4), 329–347.

Braband, S., Forsyth, C., & LeBlanc, J. (1997). Childhood sexual trauma and substance misuse: A pilot study. *Substance Use & Misuse, 32*(10), 1417–1431.

Breslau, N., Kessler, R., Chilcoat, H., Peterson, E., & Lucia, V. (1999). Vulnerability to assaultive violence: Further specification of sex differences in posttraumatic stress disorder. *Psychological Medicine, 29,* 813–821.

Brown, L. (1994). *Subversive dialogues: Theory in feminist therapy.* New York: Basic Books.

Bryant-Davis, T. (2005). *Thriving in the wake of trauma: A multicultural guide.* Westport, CT: Praeger Publishers.

Buchwald, D., Beals, J., & Manson, S. M. (2000). Use of traditional health practices among Native Americans in a primary care setting. *Medical Care, 38*(12), 1191–1199.

Chiavaroli, T. (1992). Rehabilitation from substance abuse in individuals with a history of sexual abuse. *Journal of Substance Abuse Treatment, 9,* 349–354.

Comas-Diaz, L. (2006). Latino healing: The integration of ethnic psychology into psychotherapy. *Psychotherapy: Theory, Research, Practice, Training, 43*(4), 436–453.

Crenshaw, K. (1994). Mapping the margins: Intersectionality, identity politics, and violence against women of color. In M. Fineman & R. Mykitiuk (Eds.), *The public nature of private violence* (pp. 93–118). New York: Routledge.

Crespo, M. (2006). Effects of culturally specific dynamically oriented group art therapy with immigrant Latinas. *Dissertation Abstracts International: Section B: The Sciences and Engineering, 67*(5-B), 2828.

Csordas, T. J. (2004). Healing and the human condition: Scenes from the present moment in Navajoland. *Culture, Medicine and Psychiatry, 28,* 1–14.

Denham, A., Frasier, P., Hooten, E., Belton, L., Newton, W., Gonzalez, P., et al. (2007). Intimate partner violence among Latinas in eastern North Carolina. *Violence Against Women, 13*(2), 123–140.

Department of Health and Human Services (DHHS). (2001). *Mental health: Culture, race, and ethnicity-A supplement to mental health: A report of the surgeon general.* Rockville, MD: Public Health Service, Office of the Surgeon General.

Deters, P. B., Novins, D. K., Fickenscher, A., & Beals, J. (2005, July). *Trauma and PTSD symptomatology: patterns among American Indian adolescents in substance abuse treatment* Paper presented at the 9th International Family Violence Research Conference, Portsmouth, NH.

Dixon-Peters, C. (2007). The psychological effects of Hatha yoga on low-income women who are survivors of domestic violence. *Dissertation Abstracts International: Section B: The Sciences and Engineering, 68*(1-B), 619.

Dunn, A., & Dawes, S. (1999). Spirituality-focused genograms: Keys to uncovering spiritual resources in African American families. *Journal of Multicultural Counseling & Development, 27,* 240–254.

Duran, B., Sanders, M., Skipper, B., Waitzkin, H., Malcoe, L. H., Paine, S., et al. (2004). Prevalence and correlates of mental disorders among Native American women in primary care. *American Journal of Public Health, 94*(1), 71–77.

Falicov, C. (1999). Religion and spiritual folk traditions in immigrant families: Therapeutic resources with Latinos. In F. Walsh (Ed.), *Spiritual resources in family therapy* (pp. 104–120). New York: Guilford Publications.

Faulkner, C., & Faulkner, S. (2005). Domestic violence in the Indonesian American community. In D. Nguyen (Ed.), *Domestic violence in Asian American communities* (pp. 4–57). Lanham, MD: Lexington Book.

Foa, E. B., & Meadows, E. A. (1997). Psychosocial treatments for posttraumatic stress disorder: A critical review. *Annual Review of Psychology, 48,* 449–480.

Foy, D., Ruzek, J., Glynn, S., Riney, S., & Gusman, F. (1997). Trauma focus group therapy for combat-related PTSD. *In Session: Psychotherapy in Practice, 3,* 59–73.

Freeman, B., Iron Cloud-Two Dogs, E., Novins, D. K., & LeMaster, P. L. (2004). Contextual issues for strategic planning and evaluation of systems of care for American Indian and Alaska Native communities: An introduction to Circles of Care. *American Indian and Alaska Native Mental Health Research, 11*(2), 1–29.

Frye, V., El-Bassel, N., Gilbert, L., Raja, V., & Christie, N. (2001). Intimate partner sexual abuse among women on methadone. *Violence and Victims, 16*(5), 553–564.

Fuentes, M. (1999). A program evaluation of a home-based family therapy pilot program for Latino families in northern New Jersey. *Dissertation Abstracts International: Section B: The Sciences and Engineering, 60*(2-B), 0827.

Gilbert, L., El-Bassel, N., & Rajah, V. (2001). Linking drug-related activities with experiences of partner violence: A focus group study of women in methadone treatment. *Violence and Victims, 16*(5), 517–536.

Golding, J. (1999). Sexual assault history and headache: Five general population studies. *Journal of Nervous and Mental Disease, 187*(10), 624–629.

Gone, J. P., & Alcantara, C. (2007). Identifying effective mental health interventions for American Indians and Alaska Natives: A review of the literature. *Cultural Diversity and Ethnic Minority Psychology, 13*(4), 256–363.

Greenfield, L. A., & Smith, S. K. (1999). *American Indians and crime* (No. NCJ 173386). Washington, DC: US Department of Justice Office of Programs.

Hinson, J., Koverola, C., & Morahan, M. (2002). An empirical investigation of the psychological sequelae of childhood sexual abuse in an adult Latina population. *Violence Against Women, 8*(7), 816–844

Iglehart, A., & Becerra, R. (1995). *Social services and the ethnic community.* Boston: Allyn and Bacon.

Indian Health Service. (2002). *Final report of the Restructuring Initiative Workgroup, 2002.* Rockville, MD: Indian Health Service.

Ingram, E. (2007). A Comparison of Help Seeking Between Latino and Non-Latino Victims of Intimate Partner Violence. *Violence Against Women, 13*(2), 159–171.

Jaycox, L., Zoellner, L., & Foa, E. (2002). Cognitive behavior therapy for PTSD in rape survivors. *Journal of Clinical Psychology, 58,* 891–906.

Klevens, J. (2007). An overview of intimate partner violence among Latinos. *Violence Against Women, 13*(2), 111–122.

Koenig, H., & Larson, D. (2001). Religion and mental health: Evidence for an association. *International Review of Psychiatry, 13,* 67–78.

Koenig, H., Pargament, K., & Nielsen, J. (1998). Religious coping and health status in medically ill hospitalized older adults. *Journal of Nervous & Mental Disease, 186,* 513–521.

Krishnan, S., Hilbert, J., & VanLeeuwen, D. (2001). Domestic violence and help-seeking behaviors among rural women: Results from a shelter-based study. *Family & Community Health, 24*(1), 28–38.

LaFromboise, T. D., Hoyt, D. R., Oliver, L., & Whitbeck, L. B. (2006). Family, community, and school influences on resilience among American Indian adolescents in the upper Midwest. *Journal of Community Psychology, 34*(2), 193–209.

Lerner, G. (1993). *The creation of feminist consciousness.* New York: Oxford University Press.

Livramento, K., Santana, C., Gupta, J., & Silverman, J. (2006). Victims of intimate partner violence more likely to report abuse from in-laws. *Violence Against Women, 12,* 936–949.

Lown, E., & Vega, W. (2001a). Alcohol abuse or dependence among Mexican American women who report violence. *Alcoholism: Clinical and Experimental Research, 25*(10), 1479–1486.

Lown, E., & Vega, W. (2001b). Prevalence and predictors of physical partner abuse among Mexican American women. *American Journal of Public Health, 91*(3), 441–445.

Manson, S. M., Beals, J., Klein, S. A., & Croy, C. D. (2005). Social epidemiology of trauma among American Indian reservation populations. *American Journal of Public Health, 95*(5), 851–859.

Mattis, J. (2002). Religion and spirituality in the meaning making and coping experiences of African American women: A qualitative analysis. *Psychology of Women Quarterly, 26,* 309–321.

McFarlane, J., Malecha, A., & Gist, J. (2004). Protection orders and intimate partner violence: An 18-month study of 150 black, Hispanic, and white women. *American Journal of Public Health, 94*(4), 613–618.

McFarlane, J., Soeken, K., & Wiist, W. (2000). An evaluation of interventions to decrease intimate partner violence to pregnant women. *Public Health Nursing, 17*(6), 443–451.

McKenzie-Pollock, L. (2005). Domestic violence in the Cambodian American community. In D. Nguyen (Ed.), *Domestic violence in Asian American communities* (pp. 13–26). Lanham, MD: Lexington Book.

Merchant, M. (2000). A comparative study of agencies assisting domestic violence victims: Does the South Asian community have special needs? *Journal of Social Distress and the Homeless, 9,* 249–259.

Mitchell, M., Hargrove, G., Collins, M., Thompson, M., Reddick, T., & Kaslow, N. (2006). Coping variables that mediate the relation between intimate partner violence and mental health outcomes among low-income, African American women. *Journal of Clinical Psychology, 62*(12), 1503–1520.

Mohr, W., Fantuzzo, J., & Abdul-Kabir, S. (2001). Safeguarding themselves and their children: Mothers share their strategies. *Journal of Family Violence, 16,* 75–92.

Moon, S. (2005). Domestic violence in Korean community: A multicultural, multimodal, multisystems approach. In D. Nguyen (Ed.), *Domestic violence in Asian American communities* (pp. 71–88). Lanham, MD: Lexington Book.

Newcomb, M., & Carmona, J. (2004). Adult trauma and HIV status among Latinas: Effects upon psychological adjustment and substance use. *AIDS and Behavior, 8*(4), 417–428.

Newlin, K., Knafl, K., & Melkus, G. (2002). African-American spirituality: A concept analysis. *Advances in Nursing Science, 25,* 57–70.

Novins, D. K., LeMaster, P. L., Jumper Thurman, P., & Plested, B. (2004). Describing community needs: Examples from the Circles of Care initiative. *American Indian and Alaska Native Mental Health Research, 11*(2), 42–58.

Orava, T., McLeod, P., & Sharpe, D. (1996). Perceptions of control, depressive symptomatology and self-esteem of women in transition from abusive relationships. *Journal of Family Violence, 11,* 167–186.

Organista, K. (2006). Cognitive-behavioral therapy with Latinos and Latinas. In P. A. Hays & G. Y. Iwamasa (Eds.), *Culturally responsive cognitive-behavioral therapy: Assessment, practice, and supervision* (pp. 73–96). Washington, DC: American Psychological Association.

Ozer, E., Best, S., Lipsey, T., & Weiss, D. (2003). Predictors of posttraumatic stress disorder and symptoms in adults: A metaanalysis. *Psychological Bulletin, 129,* 52–73.

Perez, J. (1999). Integration of cognitive-behavioral and interpersonal therapies for Latinos: An argument for technical eclecticism. *Journal of Contemporary Psychotherapy, 29*(3), 169–183.

Perez-Neira, D. (2006). Abused immigrant Latina women's perspectives on mental health services: A phenomenological study. *Dissertation Abstracts International: Section B: The Sciences and Engineering, 67*(6-B), 3462.

Perilla, J., Bakerman, R., & Norris, F. (1994). Culture and domestic violence: The ecology of abused Latinas. *Violence and Victims, 9*(4), 325–339.

Perry, S. (2004). American Indians and crime: A BJS statistical profile, 1992–2002. *U.S. Department of Justice,* 1–56.

Recinos, D. (2004). Adaptation of dialectical behavior therapy for Latina clients. *Dissertation Abstracts International: Section B: The Sciences and Engineering, 64*(10-B), 5231.

Sabol, P. (2007). Narrative therapy: Perceptions and attitudes regarding the use of this paradigm with Latino and Filipino clients. *Dissertation Abstracts International: Section B: The Sciences and Engineering, 67*(11-B), 6746.

Sanchez, W., & Garriga, O. (1995). Reality therapy, control theory and Latino activism: Towards empowerment and social change. *Journal of Reality Therapy, 15*(1), 3–14.

Sanders-Phillips, K. (1994). Correlates of healthy eating habits in low-income Black women and Latinas. *Preventive Medicine: An International Journal Devoted to Practice and Theory, 23*(6), 781–787.

Schnittker, J. (2001). When is faith enough? The effects of religious involvement on depression. *Journal of the Scientific Study of Religion, 3,* 393–412.

Shiu-Thorton, S., Santuria K., & Sullivan M. (2005). "Like a bird in a cage": Vietnamese women survivors talk about domestic violence. *Journal of Interpersonal Violence, 20,* 959–976.

Shorter-Gooden, K. (2004). Multiple resistance strategies: How African American women cope with racism and sexism. *Journal of Black Psychology, 30,* 406–425.

Sinclaire-Lian, N., Hollifield, M., Menache, M., Warner, T., Viscaya, J., Hammer-schlag, R., et al. (2006). Developing a traditional Chinese medicine diag-nositic structure for post-traumatic stress disorder. *The Journal of Alternative and Complimentary Medicine, 12,* 45–57.

Sloan, D., & Marx, B. (2004). Taking pen to hand: Evaluating theories underlying the written disclosure paradigm. *Clinical Psychology: Science and Practice, 11,* 121–137.

Stein, J., Burden, L., & Nyamathi, A. (2002). Relative contributions of parent sub-stance use and childhood maltreatment to chronic homelessness, depres-sion, and substance abuse problems among homeless women: Mediating roles of self-esteem and abuse in adulthood. *Child Abuse & Neglect, 26,* 1011–1027.

Sue, D. (1994). Asian American mental health and help-seeking behavior: Com-ment on Solberg et al. (1994), and Tata and Leong (1994). *Journal of Counsel-ing Psychology, 41,* 292–295.

Tan, C., Basta, J., Sullivan, C., & Davidson, W. (1995). The role of social support in the lives of women exiting domestic violence shelters. *Journal of Interper-sonal Violence, 10,* 437–451.

Teets, J. (1995). Childhood sexual trauma of chemically dependent women. *Journal of Psychoactive Drugs, 27,* 231–238.

Thompson, M., Kaslow, N., Kingree, J., Rashid, A., Puett, R., & Jacobs, D. (2000). Partner violence, social support, and distress among inner-city African American women. *American Journal of Community Psychology, 28,* 127–143.

Tjaden, P., & Thoennes, N. (2000). Full report of the prevalence, incidence, and consequences of violence against women: Findings from the National Violence Against Women Survey. Retrieved March 18, 2005, from http://www.ojp.usdoj.gov.

U.S. Census Bureau. (2008). Annual Estimates of the Population by Sex, Race, and Hispanic Origin for the United States: April 1, 2000 to July 1, 2007 (NC-EST2007-03). Retrieved on April 1, 2009, from http://www.census.gov/popest/national/asrh/NC-EST2007-srh.html.

U.S. Commission on Civil Rights. (2003). *A quiet crisis: Federal funding and unmet needs in Indian country.* Washington, DC: U.S. Commission on Civil Rights.

U.S. Department of Commerce & Bureau of the Census. (2002). *The American Indian and Alaska Native population: 2000.* Washington, DC: U.S. Census Bureau.

Waldrop, A., & Resick, P. (2004). Coping among adult female victims of domestic violence. *Journal of Family Violence, 19,* 291–302.

Walters, K. L., & Simoni, J. M. (2002). Reconceptualizing native women's health: An "indigenist" stress-coping model. *American Journal of Public Health, 92,* 520–524.

Weil, J., & Lee, H. (2004). Cultural considerations in understanding family vio-lence among Asian American Pacific Islander families. *Journal of Community Health Nursing, 21,* 217–277.

Weinsheimer, R., Schermer, C., Malcoe, L., Balduf, L., & Bloomfield, L. (2005). Severe intimate partner violence and alcohol use among female trauma patients. *Journal of Trauma, 58,* 22–29.

West, C. (2002). Battered black and blue: An overview of the violence in the lives of black women. *Women & Therapy, 25*(3/4), 5–27.

Whitaker, D., Baker, C., & Pratt, C. (2007). A network model for providing culturally competent services for intimate partner violence and sexual violence.
Violence Against Women, 13(2), 190–209.

Worell, J., & Remer, P. (2002). *Feminist perspectives in therapy: Empowering diverse
women.* New York: Wiley.

Yoshioka, M., Gilbert, L., El-Bassel, N., & Baig-Amin, M. (2003). Social support
and disclosure of abuse: Comparing South Asian, African American, and
Hispanic battered women. *Journal of Family Violence, 18,* 171–180.

Young, A., & Boyd, C. (2000). Sexual trauma, substance abuse, and treatment success in a sample of African-American women who smoke crack cocaine.
Substance Abuse, 21, 9–19.

Yu, M. (2005). Domestic violence in the Chinese American community. In
D. Nguyen (Ed.), *Domestic violence in Asian American communities* (pp. 71–88).
Lanham, MD: Lexington Book.

Zuñiga, M. (1992). Using metaphors in therapy: Dichos and Latino clients. *Social
Work, 37*(1), 55–60.

CHAPTER 9

Optimal Aging in Women: A Biopsychosocial-Cultural Perspective

Laura Palmer, Masami Tokumo, and Enmanuel Mercedes

Erik Erikson, while providing perhaps the only developmental theory that extends into old age, provides the most parsimonious and most elegantly-stated developmental task for adults aged 60 and older. Erikson (1902–1994) suggests, simply, that the last stage in life is to develop a sense of ego integrity rather than to exit with a sense of despair (Erikson, 1994). While this might sound simple, it's not easy. Erikson would suggest that the sense of ego integrity is achieved when there has been sufficient task resolution at each of the previous seven stages. Erikson would further suggest, and anecdotal evidence would seem to support his suggestion, that there are several indicators of adequate task resolution of the eighth stage and several key indicators of poor task resolution, including a deep seated fear of death, a sense of despair and panic over not having sufficient time to live out one's life in a fulfilling manner, and a pervasive sense of disgust that tends to mask or minimize despair. Recalling that Erikson used a comprehensive recognition of the various factors and structures that affect and facilitate development, this chapter will address a number of biopsychosocial and cultural factors that facilitate and inhibit optimal aging in women.

DEMOGRAPHICS OF OLDER WOMEN IN THE UNITED STATES

The 65 and over population is currently experiencing a tremendous growth spurt. The United States had about 31.2 million people 65 and over in 1990 and currently has about 35.5 million, roughly 12.1 percent of the entire population. However, by 2030 this number is expected to increase to 72 million, becoming 20 percent of the population, making this the fastest growing age segment in the nation (He, Sengupta, Velkoff, & DeBarros, 2005). In addition, the 85 and older population was 34 percent larger in 2000 than it was in 1900, and life expectancy jumped from 47.3 years to 76.9 years. This change in the demographic raises the urgency to better understand this population, particularly the women who represent 57 percent of this segment.

Older women in particular face a number of unique social challenges. They are currently almost twice more likely to be below the poverty line, have a significantly less income than their male counterparts, more likely to live alone, and more likely to experience some form of disability, while outliving their partners. In 2000, the life expectancy for white and black females is 80 years and 74.9 respectively (versus 74.8 for white males and 68.2 for black males (He et al., 2005). Though the majority of women age 65 and older are non-Hispanic white (roughly 83%), there is significant representation of other ethnic groups. Of the women age 65 and older, blacks represent 8.1 percent, Hispanics represent 6.4 percent, Asians represent 3.2 percent, and American Indians represent less than 1 percent. These figures do not include mix race/ethnic group women (U.S. Census Bureau, 2006). Also, 88.8 percent of women age 65 and older women are native born, 7.7 percent are naturalized foreign, and 3.5 percent are not citizens.

While older women are more likely to live below the poverty line than older men (13% versus 7%), the figures fluctuate by age, race, and living arrangement. Women between 65 to 74 years of age had a poverty rate of 9 percent versus those age 75 and older, with a 12 percent poverty rate. Also, Hispanics and black women living alone have a poverty rate more than two times higher than non-Hispanic women white living alone (40% versus 17%). In general, the poverty rate for those who live alone is higher than those with a different living arrangement (He et al., 2005). This distribution is projected to change, with Hispanics, blacks, and Asians increasing to 11 percent, 10 percent, and 5 percent respectively, while whites are expected to decrease to 72 percent.

In terms of location and living arrangements, the distribution of where women age 65 and older live is about the same in the northeast, Midwest, and west of the United States, ranging from 4.09 to 4.46 million. However, there are about 7.51 million women age 65 and older living in the south (U.S. Census Bureau, 2006). In 2000, 5.7 percent lived in group quarters, with the majority being nursing homes, 22.1 percent lived alone, and 66.2 percent lived with others. There were some cultural differences in living arrangements as Asian, black, and Hispanic women are more likely to live with their relatives. In addition, with about 40 percent living alone, black and non-Hispanic white women are two times more likely to live alone than Asian and Hispanic women (about 20%) (He et al., 2005).

In terms of marital status, women age 65 and older are less likely to be married than men age 65 and older (43.8% versus 73.7%) and more likely to be widowed (42.5% versus 13.1%) (U.S. Census Bureau, 2006). Educational attainment appears to be increasing. Of these women, 25.4 percent have less than a high school diploma, 74 percent are high-school graduates or more, with 14.9 percent with a bachelor's degree or higher. When looking at bachelor's degree attainment of women by group age, 27.4 percent of those age 55–59 have a bachelor's degree, 22.7 percent of those age 60–64, 16.9 percent of those age 65–74, 13.2 percent of those age 75–84, and 12.6 percent of those age 85 and older (U.S. Census Bureau, 2006). Blacks and Hispanics trail behind Asians and non-Hispanic whites in terms of bachelor's attainment: 10 percent and 6 percent versus 29 percent and 19 percent, respectively (He et al., 2005).

There is an exponential change in relational status of older women as they progress from young old (65–74), the old old (74–84), and the oldest old (85 and over). In women age 65–74, 55 percent are married, 29 percent widowed and 11 percent divorced. Compare this to the women age 75–84, where 35 percent are married, 53 percent widowed and 6.9 percent divorced. For those women who are 85 years old or older, 14 percent are married, 78 percent widowed and 4 percent divorced. By comparison, 76 percent of men age 65–74 are married, 72 percent of men age 75–84 are married, and 59 percent of men age 85 and older are married (U.S. Census Bureau Data, 2003). A certain trajectory appears from we-to-me for aging, heterosexual women at a rate that is much more accelerated than for their same age male cohort members. Similar data about relationship changes and aging are not readily available for lesbian and bisexual women. Clear social as well as psychological implications are evident for the older and oldest old women in the United States. We know for instance, that there is an acute, negative impact on physical and mental health of older women across the first three years of widowhood (Wilcox et al., 2003). Another area of potential concern voiced by many older women is outliving their resources. A burgeoning retirement community and assisted living industry is seen in our country that is filling a niche for upper middle and well invested middle class seniors across the nation, and particularly in urban and suburban neighborhoods. A significant diversification across these communities is anticipated over the next 10–15 years as the Baby Boomers downsize and enter retirement. Each year, Genworth Financial—a leading global financial services provider—conducts its benchmark Cost of Care survey. It looks at the cost of long-term care across the country, along with corresponding market trends. It analyzes data from more than 10,000 nursing homes, assisted living facilities, home care providers and adult day health care facilities in all 50 states and the District of Columbia, including a comparative evaluation of 90 urban and rural regions in the United States (Genworth Financial, 2008). These facilities report a national average annual cost of $36,090 per resident, and a range of average monthly fees from the minimum of $550 to an average maximum of $8,850, an increasing life span to upward of 84 years, and a median retirement income of women 65 and older is $11,816. When there are complicating medical conditions, the cost of a nursing home is almost double that of assisted living, with a median cost of $68,408 for a semi-private room and $76,460 for a private room. While long-term care, Medicare/Medicaid and Long Term Care Insurance serve to reduce a portion or fraction of these costs, there is a substantial cost realized by the older woman or her family. Many seniors do not have a viable means of earning additional income, particularly the older and oldest old. Many of our current seniors in these age groups had limited education, and many more of these women were home makers and did not work outside of the home—thus, relying solely on their husband's pensions and Social Security. All women 65 and older fall below their male cohort members when compared on rate of Social Security, pension income, interest and dividends and income from work. Women of color participate in these sources of income at a lower rate than white women. Overall, the median income of women 65 and older, irrespective of race, falls only $3,000 above the poverty level based on the 2003 census data. This 2003 AARP report suggests, based on the 2003 Census Bureau data, that for "all women age 65 and older, the poverty rate is 12.5 percent. For African American and Hispanic women, the poverty rates are almost double that. More than one-quarter of African American women over age 65 and just under one-quarter of older Latinas (27.5% and 22%, respectively) fall below the poverty level" (Beedon, 2005). One can easily validate the concerns many older women share about not being able to afford to live much longer.

PSYCHOSOCIAL AND BIOLOGICAL FACTORS AFFECTING OPTIMAL AGING IN WOMEN

In this section, a review of the neurobiological and physical aspects of aging in women and the possible psychological impact will be provided. Limited numbers of studies are currently available that focus specifically on women's health in late life. Yee and Chiriboga (2007) attribute this phenomenon to a lack of theoretical frameworks and empirical research related to gender development after the reproductive phase of the life cycle. Aging, in general, increases vulnerability to chronic debilitating conditions and illnesses, such as osteoporosis, rheumatoid arthritis, heart disease, cancer, diabetes, dementia, and Alzheimer's disease. Considering the sex differences in longevity, women in later life are faced with higher rates of disability as well as the prevalence of some medical or mental conditions (i.e., heart disease and Alzheimer's disease).

In 2005, life expectancy was 80.4 years for women and 75.2 years for men, while life expectancy in 1900 was 50.7 for women and 47.9 years for men (Kung, Hoyert, Xu, & Murphy, 2008). From 1900 to the late 1970s, the sex gap in life expectancy increased from 2.0 years to 7.8 years; however, this number has been decreasing since 1970s. The difference in life expectancy between the sexes was 5.2 years in 2005. Today's longevity can likely be explained by the following: a decrease in infant mortality, advancement in medicine and medical technology, and better public health practices (i.e., sanitation, drinking water, nutrition). As the life expectancy at birth increases, more deaths are happening in later life. This means the cause of death is more likely chronic rather than acute illnesses (Aldwin, Park, & Spiro, 2007).

Spar and La Rue (2006) state that "most people aged 65 and older have at least one chronic medical illness, and many have multiple conditions" (p. 3), and listed arthritis, hypertension, heart conditions, and sensory impairments as the most common illnesses among elderly Americans. In 2005, heart disease, cancer, and stroke were the top three causes of death among people age 65 and older. Among women age 65 and older, with the exception of Asian American women, heart disease is the number one cause of death, followed by cancer as the second cause of death (Yee & Chiriboga, 2007). Yee and Chiriboga also note lung cancer as one of the leading subcategories among women. For Asian American women, cancer is the number one cause of death and breast cancer is the most commonly diagnosed cancer.

While the number of deaths due to these top three causes has decreased from 2004 to 2005, the number of deaths due to diabetes and chronic lower respiratory disease has increased (Kung, Hoyert, Xu, & Murphy, 2008). According to Diabetes and Women's Health Across Life Stages (Vinicor, 2001), diabetes is one of the underlying causes of death among women age 65 and older, and death rates for diabetes increases with age. The study indicates that black women's death rates are twice that of white women, and Mexican American women's death rates are almost four times that of white women. Thirty-three percent of black or Mexican American women (60 to 74 years old) are known to have type 2 diabetes compared to 16 percent of white women. Approximately 32 percent of American Indian women ages 65 and older are known to have diabetes. The alarming fact here is that diabetes in older women could bring up diabetic complications, including heart disease, stoke, kidney disease, and loss of eyesight. Having physical illnesses would decrease these women's functioning level, and as a result, it could negatively affect their psychological state.

Another increasing cause of death in recent years is Alzheimer's disease. Cognitive impairments, memory loss, and deterioration in intellectual functioning are common among both men and women in later life. Alzheimer's disease is one of the most common causes of dementia. As much as 70 percent of all causes of dementia were due to Alzheimer's disease among people age 71 and older (Plassman et al., 2007). The same data indicates that 17 percent were due to cerebrovascular disease, while other diseases (Lewy body disease, frontal or frontotemporal lobe disease, and subcortical disease) accounted for 13 percent. The prevalence of Alzheimer becomes more significant as people age. In 2008, 5.2 million Americans age 65 and older (one in eight elderly Americans) are estimated to have Alzheimer's disease (Alzheimer's Association, 2008). Rates of Alzheimer's disease in women are higher than in men (Katzman, 1993), because women live longer, on average, than men. The longer the individual lives, the greater the chance of developing Alzheimer's. According to a recent study, the percentage of women who will develop Alzheimer's disease in their remaining lifetime if they live to be at least age 55 is 17 percent where as, it is only 9 percent for men (Beiser, Seshadri, Au, & Wolf, 2008).

In addition to physical disability and medical condition, the aging process can affect the body image of older women. Physical changes including weight gain, thickening of waistline, widening of hips, hair loss and/or graying hair, and wrinkles may affect the way women view their own attractiveness, and as a result, it could influence their self-esteem. Although some women are reported to be happy with their bodies as they age, many women experience some sort of reaction toward the changes. Furthermore, concern about looking good continues into old age especially if a woman had the same issue at a younger age (Crose, 1999). Using a developmental perspective, Crose explains that women who have not successfully matured into old age and developed a healthy attitude toward their bodies would despair over the loss of their youthful appearance. She then adds, "this may be expressed by using heavy makeup and inappropriately revealing clothing or by turning to cosmetic surgery to alter their aging appearance" (p. 64). Aging does not happen overnight, it comes gradually. The key for optimal aging in women suggests coming to terms with one's expectations and understanding reality.

PSYCHOLOGICAL FACTORS, MENTAL HEALTH ISSUES AND AGING

In addition to the specific medical concerns cited in the previous section, there are some increased mental health risks for older women. There is an increased risk of suicide in the elderly, particularly when they are coping with a debilitating illness or chronic pain. Individuals 65 and over account for 14.3 suicides per 100,000 (Center for Disease Control [CDC], 2007). White men age 75 and over have the highest suicide rate of any group, with a reported rate 37.4 per 100,000 population (CDC, 2007). Older women appear to have a lower rate of suicide but a higher rate of late life depressive symptoms, minor depression and anxiety. Reports are mixed about the exact prevalence of depressive and anxious symptoms in older women. The 1999 Surgeon General's report on Mental Health documents that depressive symptoms and syndromes have been identified in 8 percent to 20 percent of older community residents (Alexopoulos, 1997; Gallo & Lebowitz, 1999) and 17 percent to 35 percent of older primary care patients (Gurland, Cross, & Katz, 1996). The 2005 White House Conference on Aging identified the recognition, assessment, and treatment of mental illness and depression among older Americans as one of the top 10 resolutions to address. While there is research to indicate that older women represent one of the lower categories of suicide risk and demonstrate a relatively lower incidence of initial presentation of major depression, salient risk factors still need to be understood and identified. Gatz and Fiske (2003) provide epidemiological evidence that supports three caveats on aging and depression specific to women:

Rates of major depressive disorder are lower in older women than in younger women; Rates of depressive symptoms are lower in midlife and become elevated among the oldest old; and, gender differences commonly observed in depression and depressive symptoms at younger ages become lessened in older adults. (p. 3)

These authors also warn researchers and practitioners to be mindful of differences between age and cohort effects, in that those women who represent the future, the Baby Boomers, will present a much higher rate for mental health services due to sheers numbers produced by increased longevity and the fact that this particular cohort is more psychologically minded and more experienced in seeking services.

Anxiety also presents with some degree of specificity in older women. Older women report a lifetime diagnosis of anxiety more often than older men (16.1% compared to 9.2%) (Center for Disease Control and Prevention [CDC] & National Association of Chronic Disease Directors, 2008). Weissman and Levine (2007) suggest that the prevalence of anxiety disorders is higher in older women than older men, due to some gender specific medical and psychological factors. Among the occurrence of multiple, simultaneous medical conditions that occur with greater frequency in women, including, but not limited to Parkinson's, chronic obstructive pulmonary disorder, urinary incontinence and thyroid disorders, is associated with an increase in anxiety. A primary psychosocial factor is the change in living arrangements, also associated as a related factor in anxiety disorders in women, which occurs with greater frequency in women due to the fact that they often outlive their spouse. A third, and perhaps less obvious factor related to the higher incidence of anxiety disorders in women than men, is that they tend to have larger social networks. While this can be a protective factor, it can also increase the likelihood and frequency of the experience of loss and a chronic reminder of one's own mortality.

Related to the incidence and experience of anxiety disorders in older women is the prevalence of posttraumatic stress disorder (PTSD) in this population. Franco (2007) suggests that the prevalence for trauma and PTSD across the lifetime for women is greater than for men, and the actual frequency and etiology is poorly understood. We know for instance, that while most Americans will experience at least one traumatic event in their lives, most go on to recover. However, the development of PTSD appears to be gender sensitive. For instance, women develop PTSD following some experience of trauma at an estimated rate of 20 percent of the population as compared to 8 percent of the U.S. population of men who experience a traumatic event (Franco, 2007).

While we have data on the prevalence of depressive and anxious symptomatology, there are few epidemiological studies on the psychological manifestations of poor task resolution of Erikson's eighth stage as discussed earlier—the increased sense of uselessness, the increased wish to die, and sense of despair in elderly women, particularly the older, and very old women in our society. One of the key factors related to despair in older women is bereavement and subsequent loneliness. In many cases, it is not only the situation that women have outlived their partners, but they have also outlived their siblings, friends and too often, their own children. Life can become void of meaning and result in a sense of resignation, hopelessness and a deep, pervasive sense of despair. On the other hand, many of this age cohort experience what we've come to refer to as a type of death anxiety. It is not solely a fear of being dead, but rather, of how that final act will present. The questions explored in our practice include "Will I die alone?" "Will I be alone?" "How long will it be before someone knows I'm dead?"

While the incidence of anxiety, depression, substance abuse, personality disorders and other mental health disorders are known to some degree, the availability of geropsychologists, particularly those who have a specific understanding of the issues of older women, is limited.

The current lack of sound theory and evidence based practice specific to the mental health and wellness needs of older women likely have several, responsible explanations. First, Sigmund Freud (1856–1939) argued that analysis is pointless with individuals 50 and older. There are likely holdouts in the analytic community that would persist in arguing that the older psyche is fixed and beyond the benefits of analysis. While Carl Jung (1875–1961) would have disagreed, the strength of Freud's position has permeated most theory and practice until recently. Even with the emergence of gerospecialities in medicine, psychology and psychiatry, the special needs of the older adult, and more specifically, older women, remain at risk of going undiagnosed and unmet. If this is true of older women who have access to privilege (white, Protestant, higher SES), then there is grossly inadequate access for ability, ethnic, racial, religious, sexual or socioeconomic minorities.

CULTURAL POSITIONS ON AGING

Our experiences are perceived, evaluated, labeled, defined by, owned or disowned, shared, or repressed—within a psychological frame of culture. Cultural similarities and differences color our day to day interactions giving them meaning and significance. In the United States, multiple cultures co-exist and provide the opportunity for rich interaction between ethnicity and race. So, given the sizeable and increasing presence of the age 65 and older community, and the inevitability of our own aging experience, it is important to understand how our multicultural experiences shape our perception and values of this group in the United States.

While there are some references to the elderly population in the multi-cultural research, there still much ground to cover. As previously cited, many significant differences exist across different aging ethnic/racial groups. These differences may not be explained by using race and ethnicity alone, but the multicultural dynamic can be utilized to inform these differences. It is important to understand that multiculturalism does not refer to minorities alone, but the interaction of all cultures, including whites.

According to the *Guidelines on Multicultural Education, Training, Research, Practice, and Organizational Change for Psychologists,* published by the American Psychological Association in 2003, culture can be defined as "the belief systems and value orientations that influence customs, norms, practices, and social institutions, including psychological processes . . . and organizations" (American Psychological Association, 2003, p. 8). In the United States we experience more of a multicultural system, as there are many cultures constantly interacting (directly or indirectly) with each other. So, to understand aging in this context, we need to understand how each of the dominant cultures views aging and what changes occur as a result of the interaction of the various cultures in the United States. Currently the white race is the largest racial group in this age segment, but we understand that there are various cultural experiences within whites, just as there are within black, Latinos, and Asians.

The increasing diversification of our aging female populations requires a responsible consideration of some key cultural considerations. For example, individualistic versus collectivistic worldviews place different values on the individual, creating different experiences for the aging group. Collectivistic cultures (such as Asians and Latinos) are more likely to have their elderly living at home with family members versus individualistic cultures. In addition, in the United States there is a high value placed on youthfulness (especially for women), which is associated with ability, productivity, strength, beauty and independence. Women potentially experience a broader range of negative psychological experiences with aging than men do as they have to deal with a specific form of gender based ageism (Hatch, 2005). While in some instances older women are revered as pillars of the family (i.e., African American women; Jones [2004], Logan [2001], and White [2004], as cited by Hines & Boyd-Franklin, 2005), many are still affected by internalized ageist and sexist norms (Hatch, 2005). Daily experiences of ageism might take the form of a physician speaking to the older woman's accompanying adult child instead of directly addressing the patient; lack of representation of older women's voices in decision-making processes; absence of representation of older women in advertising of various product lines; aging out of leading roles in film and television—to name just a few obvious examples. The impact of internalized ageism can look similar to internalized racism—a negative sense of self worth, a high sense of inadequacy, a sense of being invisible, internalized rage, depression. Hatch (2005) recognizes the parallels of sexism and ageism in the lives of older women, and how this can be a double assault to the individual's sense of self.

Yang and Levkoff (2005) explore the "double jeopardy" of internalized racism and ageism in ethnic minority elders. They suggest that internalized "ageism among older minorities is pernicious, undermining both their self-worth and the importance of their existence" (p. 43). These authors provide a synthesis of prior research that suggest the complications from this psychological double jeopardy can result in better or worse outcomes along four primary dimensions—depending on the valence of internalized perceptions of aging. Specifically, Yang and Levkoff identify the following four perceptions of aging: life expectancy, physiological markers, frailty, and defense mechanisms. The direction along a continuum of possible impact across these four perceptions is directly affected by the individual's positive or negative self attributions with clear behavioral or attitudinal correlates. For example, the ethnic minorities with a more positive sense of internalized attitudes towards aging are reported to have a lower systolic blood pressure, lower body mass index, lower cholesterol, no history of smoking and endorse more frequent exercise when assessed on the physiological markers compared to individuals with a more negative attitude toward aging, who were at the other end on the continuum across these indicators.

Older lesbians experience a unique set of factors that need to be addressed as we highlight those most vulnerable to the encounter of invisibility and disenfranchisement. While there is a starkly limited literature base addressing the specific and unique needs of this group, there are some important and relevant findings. Specifically, Goldberg, Sickler, and Dibbler (2005), review a survey conducted in 1984 by Dr. Monica Kehoe (1989) of older lesbians, with consideration of the relevance of more recent research finding. They conclude that recent studies confirm Kehoe's original observations "that older lesbians have: (1) often created a variety of social, sexual, and domestic experiences during their lives; (2) focused their social lives around a network of friends; (3) often not maintained close familial ties; and (4) avoided using conventional senior services often due to perceived discrimination" (p. 196). These authors close by emphasizing that *there* is a significant diversity across older lesbians and that we need to create an appropriate array of services to meet the diversity of needs across this varied community of women. Hughes (2007) finds a similarity in the poor access of health care services by older lesbians and gay men in Australia. This research documents that the invisibility of this particular groups of elders is a major obstacle in access and utilization of necessary medical services. Hughes concludes that "the complexity of older gay and lesbian people's sexual identities, obstacles to their expression when in contact with health and aged-care providers, and opportunities for better take-up of services in the future" (p. 207).

PROTECTIVE/RESILIENCY FACTORS IN OPTIMAL AGING IN WOMEN

Felton's (2000) study of resiliency in older women of color started with her expectation that she would find similar indicators in a qualitative study of older women as had been found previously by Wagnild and Young (1990), who define resilience in older women as a unique human phenomenon distinguished by the lived experience of rebound in health after loss late in life, as well as the ability to adjust successfully to major life losses. They further identified five specific themes thought to contribute to resilience in older women: equanimity, perseverance, self-reliance, meaningfulness, and existential aloneness (Felton, 2000, p. 105). However, Felton's findings were somewhat different in her sample of older, urban dwelling, women of color. Specifically, she found that, "participants spoke of issues related to frailty, determination, previous experience with hardship in learning how to cope, access to care, culturally based health beliefs, family support, and self-care activities. They also spoke of caring for others and functioning like efficient working machines that enabled them to experience resilience after devastating illness. . . . Participants identified very practical strategies resulting in resilience after devastating illness late in life. Resilience, for these women, occurred as a result of a plan, a strategy, not by chance or coincidence" (pp. 116–117). Thus, resiliency might take different forms, depending on the matrix of salient factors of their personal and shared histories. What appears to be a key factor in resiliency, along with good role models and inherit hardiness, is an internalized set of beliefs about aging that have been delineated by Yang and Levkoff (2005) and can be correlated with physical and psychological outcomes that are either life sustaining or critically limiting. Furthermore, internalized attributions can be effectively addressed through positive role models and psychotherapy—so there is reason for optimism.

RECOMMENDATIONS FOR FUTURE DIRECTION IN RESEARCH, PREVENTION, AND PSYCHOLOGICAL PRACTICE

A number of issues have been addressed across this chapter that highlights the need to prioritize the psychological well being of older women. We are experiencing a rapidly growing cohort of elders. These individuals present with a unique yet inherently diverse set of developmental challenges. While there is a developing research base that will inform prevention and practice with older women, what we know is inadequate. Older women, particularly ethnic, racial, and sexual minorities, remain to a significant degree, invisible. Future research agendas should include studies of optimal development and psychological well-being in older women. We will hopefully come to better understand protective and resiliency factors as well as specific risk factors that make our elders prone to multiple disease and disability patterns. Scientific investigations of the role of hormones—estrogen, progesterone, thyroid hormones—are needed for the purpose of better understanding and potential intervention and prevention of late onset disease process, depression and cognitive dysfunction that disproportionately affect older women. Particular attention is needed in the area of interpersonal violence against older women and the unique issues of older lesbian and ethnic minority women. We also need to invest in developing more widespread socioeconomic security for older women, many of whom exist below, at, or just above the poverty line. Finally, the psychological needs of an aging cohort of women are about to be placed at our doorsteps, and we are not sufficiently prepared with efficacious models of assessment, diagnosis or intervention. The initial task is to address the pervasive and pernicious ageist attitudes that blind our profession and society to the needs and strengths of older women in our society. Eventually, if we're lucky enough, we will assume the paths of aging that our mothers and grandmothers have traveled—and we have an opportunity to make that process more welcoming and rewarding.

REFERENCES

Aldwin, C. M., Park, C. L., & Spiro III, A. (2007). Health psychology and aging. In C. M. Aldwin, C. L. Park, & A. Spiro III (Eds.), *Handbook of health psychology and aging* (pp. 3–8). New York: Guildford.

Alexopoulos, G. S. (1997, November 6). *Epidemiology, nosology and treatment of geriatric depression.* Paper presented at Exploring Opportunities to Advance Mental Health Care for an Aging Population meeting sponsored by the John A. Hartford Foundation, Rockville, MD.

Alzheimer's Association. (2008). *2008 Alzheimer's disease fact and figures.* Chicago: Alzheimer's Association.

American Psychological Association. (2003). Guidelines on multicultural education, training, research, practice, and organizational change for psychologists. *American Psychologist, 58*(5), 377–402.

Beedon, L., & Wu, K. B. (2005). *Women age 65 and older: Their sources of income.* Retrieved July 13, 2008, from AARP Public Policy Institute website: http://assets.aarp.org/rgcenter/econ/dd126_women.pdf.

Beiser, A., Seshadri, S., Au, R., & Wolf, P. A. (2008). 2008 Alzheimer's disease facts and figures. Unpublished data from the Framingham heart study.

Center for Disease Control (CDC). (2007). Suicide: Facts at a glance. Retrieved July 13, 2008, from http://www.cdc.gov/ncipc/dvp/Suicide/SuicideData Sheet.pdf.

Center for Disease Control and Prevention (CDC) & National Association of Chronic Disease Directors. (2008). *The state of mental health and aging in America issue brief 1: What do the data tell us?* Atlanta, GA: National Association of Chronic Disease Directors.

Crose, R. G. (1999). Addressing late life developmental issues for women: Body image, sexuality, and Intimacy. In M. Duffy (Ed.), *Handbook of counseling and psychotherapy with older adults* (pp. 57–76). New York: Wiley & Sons.

Erikson, E. H. (1994). *Identity and the life cycle.* New York: Norton.

Felton, B. S. (2000). Resilience in a multicultural sample of community-dwelling women older than age 85. *Clinical Nursing Research, 9*(2), 102–123.

Franco, M. (2007). Posttraumatic stress disorder and older women. *Journal of Women and Aging, 19,* 103–117.

Gallo, J. J., & Lebowitz, B. D. (1999). The epidemiology of common late-life mental disorders in the community: Themes for the new century. *Psychiatric Services, 50,* 1158–1166.

Gatz, M., & Fiske, A. (2003). Aging women and depression. *Professional Psychology: Research and Practice, 34*(1), 3–9.

Genworth Financial.(2008, April). *Genworth Financial 2008 cost of care survey.* Retrieved July 13, 2008, from http://www.genworth.com/content/etc/medialib/genworth/us/en/Long_Term_Care.Par.14291.File.dat/37522%20CoC%20Brochure.pdf.

Goldberg, S., Sickler, J., & Dibble, S. L. (2005). Lesbian over sixty: The consistency of findings from twenty years of survey data. *Journal of Lesbian Studies, 9,* 195–213.

Gurland, B. J., Cross, P. S., & Katz, S. (1996). Epidemiological perspectives on opportunities for treatment of depression. *American Journal of Geriatric Psychiatry, 4*(Suppl. 1), S7–S13.

Hatch, R. L. (2005). Gender and ageism. *Generations, 29,* 19–25.

He, W., Sengupta, M., Velkoff, V. A., & DeBarros, K. A. (2005, December). 65+ in the United States: 2005. Washington, DC: U.S. Government Printing Office, U.S. Census Bureau.

Hines, P. M., & Boyd-Franklin, N. (2005). Overview: African American families. In M. McGoldrick, J. Giodano, & N. Garcia-Petro (Eds.), *Ethnicity and family therapy* (3rd ed., pp. 87–100). New York: Guildford.

Hughes, M. (2007). Older lesbians and gays accessing health and aged-care services. *Australian Social Work, 60*(2), 197–209.

Katzman, R. (1993). Education and the prevalence of dementia and Alzheimer's disease. *Neurology, 43,* 13–20.

Kehoe, M. (1989). *Lesbians over 60 speak for themselves.* New York: Harrington Park Press.

Kung, H. D., Hoyert, D. L., Xu, J. Q., & Murphy, S. L. (2008). *Deaths: Final data for 2005. National vital statistics reports* (Vol. 56, No. 10). Hyattsville, MD: National Center for Health Statistics.

Plassman, B. L., Langa, K. M., Fisher, G. G., Heeringa, S. G., Weir, D. R., & Ofstedal, M. B. (2007). Prevalence of dementia in the United States: The aging, demographics, and memory study. *Neuroepidemiology, 29,* 125–132.

Spar, J. E., & La Rue, A. (2006). *Clinical manual of geriatric practice.* Washington, DC: American Psychiatric Publishing.

U.S. Administration on Aging. (2008). *A statistical profile of older Americans 65+.* Washington, DC: Author.

U.S. Census Bureau. (2003). *The older population in the United States: 2003* (Table 2). Retrieved July 11, 2008, from http://www.census.gov/population/soc demo/age/2003older_table2.xls.

U.S. Census Bureau. (2006). *Current population survey: Annual social and economic supplement* (Tables 1.1, 1.4, 1.6, 1.8, 1.8, 2, 4 and 19). Retrieved July 11, 2008, from http://www.census.gov/population/www/socdemo/age/age_2006.html.

Vinicor, F. (2001). *Diabetes and women's health across life stages.* Atlanta, GA: Center for Disease Control and Prevention.

Wagnild, G., & Young, H. M. (1990). Resilience among older women. *Image: The Journal of Nursing Scholarship, 22*(4), 252–255.

Weissman, J., & Levine, S. (2007). Anxiety disorders and older women. *Journal of Women and Aging, 19,* 79–101.

Wilcox, S., Evenson, K. R., Aragaki, A., Wassertheil-Smoller, S., Mouton, C. P., & Loevinger, B. L. (2003). The effects of widowhood on physical and mental health, health behaviors, and health outcomes: The women's health initiative. *Health Psychology, 22*(5), 513–522.

Yang, F. M., & Levkoff, S. E. (2005). Ageism and minority populations: Strengths in the face of challenge. *Generations* (Fall), 42–48.

Yee, B.W.K., & Chiriboga, D. A. (2007). Issues of diversity in health psychology and aging. In C. M. Aldwin, C. L. Park, & A. Spiro III (Eds.), *Handbook of health psychology and aging* (pp. 286–312). New York: Guildford.

CHAPTER 10

Racial and Ethnic Disparities in Incarceration: Criminal Justice or Economic Servitude?

Natalie Porter

Glen Edward Chapman was released from death row in 2008 after being sentenced to death in 1994 for the murders of two women in North Carolina. Prosecutors dropped all charges after a Superior Court Judge granted Chapman a new trial, "citing withheld evidence, 'lost, misplaced or destroyed' documents, the use of weak, circumstantial evidence, false testimony by the lead investigator, and ineffective assistance of defense counsel, one of whom admitted drinking 12 shots of alcohol per day while on another death penalty trial (that defendant was executed). New information was also provided by a forensic pathologist that raised doubts as to whether the death of one of the women was a homicide or caused by an overdose of drugs." Chapman's lawyers, recognizing that justice had not been served on his behalf, went on to state: "Justice has not been served for the families of Ms. Ramseur and Ms. Conley, and we hope their deaths will be reinvestigated" (Death Penalty Information Center, 2008a).

Chapman is one of 129 men sentenced to death since 1973 whose cases have been overturned for reasons usually related to "mistaken eyewitness testimony, the false testimony of informants and 'incentivized witnesses,' incompetent lawyers, defective or fraudulent scientific evidence, prosecutorial and police misconduct, and false confessions. In recent years, DNA has played a role in overturning 12 of these wrongful death row convictions" (Information Please, 2007).

Chapman is African American; nearly 75 percent of the men found to have been falsely convicted and subsequently released from death row have been black or Hispanic (Information Please, 2007). People of color comprise 43 percent of the defendants who have been executed since 1975 and almost 55 percent of the current death row population (Death Penalty

Information Center, 2008b). People of color, particularly men, are also disproportionately represented at all levels of the criminal justice system, from juvenile facilities to jails to state and federal correctional institutions. The rates of incarceration of African American men have been described as reaching crisis proportions and decimating their communities. Incarceration has been called the new slavery:

Metaphorically, the criminal justice pipeline is like a slave ship, transporting human cargo along interstate triangular trade routes from Black and Brown communities; through the middle passage of police precincts, holding pens, detention centers and courtrooms; to downstate jails or upstate prisons; back to communities as unrehabilitated escapees; and back to prison or jail in a vicious recidivist cycle. (Flateau, as cited in Drug Policy Alliance Network, 2001)

The costs associated with the prison-industrial complex have replaced funding for education, mental health, and substance abuse services in many communities. Rates of incarceration are increasing in spite of crime rates that have been decreasing for more than 15 years.

In spite of the glaring inequities of the U.S. criminal justice system and the looming crisis in communities of color, incarceration has not become the rallying point for social justice groups within psychology that one would anticipate. As a white feminist, I hear little about this issue in the psychology activist circles that I frequent in spite of the diversity of many of those groups. In psychology programs, forensic programs are mushrooming, yet little attention seems to be given to questioning the criminal justice system in its current form. These programs concentrate almost solely on teaching psychologists to work within prison systems rather than to question the broader social issues feeding them. As members of the public, we may be shocked to attention by the surfacing of a profoundly racist incident such as the "Jena 6,"(described further on in this chapter) but these events do not result in scrutiny of the entire system or in coalition building across activist groups. Persistent attention to the racial and ethnic inequities in the criminal justice system has not occurred outside of a few human rights groups such as Amnesty International and Human Rights Watch. More sustained outrage has been elicited by the locking up of "unlawful combatants" at Guantanamo than by the unremitting locking up of young adult men, particularly men of color, within the United States. My intent is not to minimize the legitimate social justice work on behalf of the "unlawfully held prisoners" of Guantánamo but to make a plea for the same energy and commitment to be directed on behalf of men of color in the United States who have been facing this problem for decades. Activist groups have not coalesced around this "new slavery" (Drug Policy Alliance Network, 2001) any more than they did around the old slavery. Advocating for prisoners is often associated with being "soft on crime," which remains a so-called third rail for any aspiring office holder, a lesson learned from the Willie Horton adverts used against presidential candidate Michael Dukakis in 1988. Willie Horton became the archetype of a criminal—black became synonymous with "cold blooded murderer" and with being incapable of rehabilitation.

In this chapter, I will use a feminist and multiculturally informed ecological framework to address the inequities of the criminal justice system. My intention is to challenge social justice groups within psychology to form coalitions that cut across their specific priorities, identities, and standpoints. Through understanding the serious threat to communities of color posed by the current prison movement, we may make a sustained effort across interest and activist groups to stop the inequities for men of color, for communities of color, and for the broader U.S. society. Angela Davis (2003) calls for the abolition of prisons and the concomitant transformation of societies that would occur when human services and restorative justice replaces incarceration and punishment.

INCARCERATION IS ON THE MARCH, ESPECIALLY FOR PEOPLE OF COLOR

The Pew Center on the States Report "One in 100: Behind Bars in America 2008" (Warren, Gelb, Horowitz, & Riordan, 2008) states that more than one in 100 adults is locked up in America. The total adult inmate count at the beginning of 2008 stood at 2,319,258. The report shows that the U.S. prison population has been steadily increasing for 30 years. Over the past 2 years, the prison population increased by 3.1 percent in 2006 and by 1.6 percent (or by 25,000 new inmates) in 2007.

These statistics show that the U.S. locks up more people than any country in the world, including the far more populous nation of China. At the start of the new year, the American penal system held more than 2.3 million adults. China was second, with 1.5 million people behind bars, and Russia was a distant third with 890,000 inmates, according to the latest available figures. Beyond the sheer number of inmates, America also is the global leader in the rate at which it incarcerates its citizenry, outpacing nations like South Africa and Iran. In Germany, 93 people are in prison for every 100,000 adults and children. In the U.S, the rate is roughly eight times that, or 750 per 100,000. (Warren et al., 2008, p. 5)

In other words, with only 5 percent of the world's population the United States has a quarter of the world's 8 million prisoners (Whyte & Baker, 2000).

Incarceration rates break down in the following way: for men over the age of 18, one out of every 54 is locked up. For white men the rate is one out of 106, for Hispanic men, one out of every 36 men, and for black men, one out of 15. For black men between the ages of 20 and 34, one in nine black men are incarcerated. For women, rates of incarceration are much lower; nonetheless women of color are disproportionately incarcerated with one in 100 black females aged 35 to 39 incarcerated.

RACIAL INEQUITIES IN DEATH PENALTY SENTENCES

The race of the victim affects who goes to prison and whether one receives the death penalty. In a 1990 review of death penalty sentencing studies, the U.S. General Accounting Office reported substantial racial disparities: in 82% of the studies, individuals who murdered whites were more likely to be sentenced to death than were individuals who murdered blacks (Death Penalty Information Center, 2008b) even though whites and blacks are murdered in about equal numbers (because blacks are six to seven times more likely to be murdered than whites) (New Yorkers Against the Death Penalty, 2008). Statistics are similar for Native Americans. Since 1961, of the 15 American Indians who have been executed, 13 were executed for killing whites. Between 1979 and1999, whites were responsible for 32 percent of the 2,469 Indians murdered, whereas Native Americans killed one percent of the 164,377 whites murdered (Death Penalty Information Center, 2008c). Several studies show that the race of the victim is the strongest predictor of when a prosecutor will seek the death penalty in a case. Amnesty International's report on racism in capital cases states that "although only 32 percent of first-degree murder cases from 1995 to 2001 involved a white victim, 60 percent of the cases in which a prosecutor sought the death penalty involved a white victim. In contrast, while 43 percent of the first-degree murder cases involved a black victim, only 36 percent of the cases in which a prosecutor sought the death penalty involved a black victim. Twenty-four percent of cases involved a Hispanic victim, yet only 14 percent of the cases where the death penalty was sought involved a Hispanic victim" (New Yorkers Against the Death Penalty, 2008). The Amnesty International report summarizes the following studies:

- A report sponsored by the American Bar Association in 2007 concludes that one-third of African American death-row inmates in Philadelphia would have received sentences of life imprisonment if they had not been African American.
- A January 2003 study released by the University of Maryland concludes that race and geography are major factors in death penalty decisions. Specifically, prosecutors are more likely to seek a death sentence when the race of the victim is white and are less likely to seek a death sentence when the victim is African American.
- A 2007 study of death sentences in Connecticut conducted by Yale University School of Law reveals that African American defendants receive the death penalty at three times the rate of white defendants in cases where the victims are white. In addition, killers of white victims are treated more severely than people who kill minorities, when it comes to deciding what charges to bring (Amnesty International, 2003).

Women of color are also disproportionately represented. As of 2007, 51 women are on death row, and 39 percent of them are women of color (Death Penalty Information Center, 2008d).

RACIAL INEQUITIES IN INCARCERATION

Incarceration statistics are no better than the death penalty statistics, as demonstrated by the Pew Report cited previously. Statistics from the U.S. Department of Justice (2008) show that between 1990 and 2007, blacks were five times more likely than whites and three times more likely than Latinos to be put in jail. Put more graphically, for men born in 1991, white men have a 4 percent chance of spending some time locked up during their lifetime; Hispanics have a 16 percent chance, and African American men have a 29 percent of being locked up during their lifetime (Mauer, 1999). In an address to the American Psychological Association, Jesse Jackson (2000) pointed out that although in rural areas whites constitute 79 percent of the arrests and in urban areas whites constitute 64 percent of the arrests, 48 of those in jail or prison are black. Human Rights Watch (2000) estimates that although blacks constitute 13 percent of the U.S. population, they comprise 30 percent of the people arrested, 41 percent of the people in jail, and 49 percent of the people in prison, in spite of the fact that they account for a significantly lower proportion of crimes committed. They argue that the War on Drugs in being waged against men of color despite the statistics from several sources that show that whites use, buy, and sell drugs in substantially greater numbers than African Americans or Latinos. The rates of incarceration imply that one in every 20 black men over the age of 18 is in a state or federal prison, compared to one in every 180 whites. The proportion is even higher in some states: in Oklahoma and Iowa one in every 13 black men is in state prison; in Rhode Island, Texas, and Wisconsin one in every 14 black men is in prison. Furthermore, between 1985 and 1995, incarceration rates of black men in federal and state jail and prison populations increased at 10 times the rate of white men. In 10 states, Latino men are incarcerated at rates between five and nine times greater than those of white men (Human Rights Watch, 2000).

Racial disparities in incarceration exist for women and youth as well:

In fifteen states, black women are incarcerated at rates between ten and thirty-five times greater than those of white women. In eight states, Latina women are incarcerated at rates that are between four and seven times greater than those of white women. In six states, black youth under age eighteen are incarcerated in adult facilities at rates between twelve and twenty-five times greater than those of white youth. In four states, Hispanic youth under age eighteen are incarcerated in adult facilities at rates between seven and seventeen times greater than those of white youth. (Human Rights Watch, 2000)

LOCATING INCARCERATION WITH A FEMINIST MULTICULTURAL ECOLOGICAL FRAMEWORK

Proponents of global community psychology (Marsella, 1998) and feminist, multicultural, ecological theories (Ballou, Matsumoto, & Wagner, 2002) have offered frameworks for social action based on understanding and "addressing the individual and collective psychological consequences of global events and forces by incorporating multicultural, multidisciplinary, and multinational knowledge, methods, and interventions" (Porter, 1995; Vargas, Porter, & Falender, 2008, p. 122). Ballou et al.'s (2002) feminist multicultural ecological framework was derived from Ballou's (1996) synthesis of contextual feminist multicultural psychology, liberation psychology, and ecological theory. The framework is intended to represent "multiple dimensions of human existence, of real-world complexity, of multiple models of living and ways of knowing, of multidirectional interactions between the person and her or his contexts, and of direct, contiguous, and distal influences" (Ballou et al., 2002, p. 118). This type of analysis is needed in psychology, where we typically seek explanations and solutions at one level, whether that be the individual, familial, community, or group level. Rarely do we seek explanations that involve the interactions of these levels (with social-contextual theories such as feminist and multicultural theories being the exception) or look beyond these proximal levels to fully understand an issue.

The framework is comprised of four levels (individual, microsystem, exosystem, and macrosystem) and two meta-levels (historical and planetary/climatic), with each level intersected by four contextual/demographic "coordinates" (sex/gender, race/ethnicity, age, and class). The various levels will be discussed in the context of understanding the impact of racial and ethnic disparities in incarceration.

THE FINANCIAL IMPACT OF INCARCERATION ON INDIVIDUALS, FAMILIES, AND COMMUNITIES

One way to understand the impact of incarceration and racial/ethnic economic inequities at the individual and microsystem levels is by reviewing the financial costs of incarceration. The Pew Report (Warren et al., 2008) reveals that costs associated with prisons for all states has increased 315 percent in 20 years, from $10.6 billion in 1987 to $44 billion in 2007. Adjusted for inflation, this figure represents a 127 percent increase; funding of higher education increased 21 percent during the same period. The report explains that prison funding is now taking, on average, $1 of every $15 of states' discretionary budgets, making it the fifth largest budget category for most states. The report details how funding for pre-kindergarten programs, known to be one of the most powerful crime prevention tools, are at risk, sacrificed along with higher education for prisons.

BAD EDUCATIONAL SYSTEMS: BOTH A CAUSE
AND EFFECT OF INCARCERATION TRENDS

Psychologists and sociologists have addressed for decades how poverty, poor educational institutions, lack of employment, and racism and discrimination have been intertwined with substance abuse, mental health issues, and crime. The HBO series, *The Wire* (Simon & Nobles, 2002) and the film, *Boyz in the Hood* (Nicolaides & Singleton, 1991) depict the individual, family, community, educational, social, criminal justice, media, and institutional factors (and corruption within institutions), and their intersections with race, gender, age, and class, more graphically and with more complexity than I could do in this chapter.

The inequities in the educational system have been widely documented. The portrayal of the Baltimore city schools in *The Wire* (written by Simon, a former Baltimore police office and teacher) and an episode on the Oprah show (Winfrey, 2007), which underscores the economic and racial/ethnic disparities in U.S. schools, document the inequities. One segment of this Oprah program portrays the swapping of students between inner city Chicago and suburban Naperville high schools:

Located in a low-income community in Chicago, Harper High School graduates just 40 percent of its 1,500 students. Meanwhile, about 35 miles away in suburban Naperville, Illinois, Neuqua Valley High School—a $65 million facility—graduates 99 percent of its students. In an experiment Oprah says was inspired by Rev. Jesse Jackson, students from these two Chicago-area high schools switched classrooms.

When the Harper students arrived at Neuqua Valley, they were stunned to see what the suburban school offered—an Olympic-size swimming pool, a gym and fitness center, an award-winning music department, a huge computer lab, and a rigorous course curriculum. At Neuqua Valley, students can enroll in more than two dozen advanced placement courses, compared to the two offered at Harper.

The difference between the two schools can also be seen in their scores on state exams. At Neuqua Valley, 78 percent of students meet Illinois' reading standards, 76 percent meet the science standards, and 77 percent meet the math standards. At Harper, 16 percent meet the reading standards, 1.5 percent meet the science standards and just .5 percent meet the math standards. . . . the Harper pool hasn't been filled with water in a decade. The Neuqua Valley students have an award-winning music department, while Harper doesn't have enough instruments for a music class and relies on improvised instruments—like banging on desks.

The differences portrayed above are not unique. Jonathon Kozol (2005) in *The Shame of the Nation,* argues that the U.S. school system is more segregated than at any time since the death of Martin Luther King. He likened it to South Africa apartheid and provides data that shows that Latino and African American students are graduating from high school about five years behind white students, that is, at a seventh-grade level.

The state of California, once renowned for education, is now the leader in prison spending. In 2007, California devoted $8.8 billion of the state's general fund to the prison system, and signed into law a bill authorizing another $7.9 billion in spending through lease revenue bonds (Warren et al., 2008). During the 2008 legislative season, Governor Arnold Schwarzenegger recommended a $4.8 billion cut for K–14 education, on top of a $400 million reduction for education in the current year, and a *suspension of the state's minimum funding guarantee* for public schools and community colleges (California School Finance, 2008). Despite the fiscal emergency cited by the Governor as the reason for these proposals, he recommended a 1.7 percent increase in prison spending for 2008 (Californians United for a Responsible Budget, 2008). The following excerpts from an Op-Ed piece in the *San Francisco Chronicle* by the Executive Director of the San Francisco ACLU illuminates the impact on men of color of trading educational opportunities for prison systems.

California will soon spend more on its prisons than on its public universities. It has been projected that over the next five years, the state's budget for locking up people will rise by 9 percent annually, compared with its spending on higher education, which will rise only by 5 percent. By the 2012–2013 fiscal year, $15.4 billion will be spent on incarcerating Californians, as compared with $15.3 billion spent on educating them.

According to a recent report by Northeastern University, the median annual earnings in 2004–2005 of young black men with a bachelor's degree were 2.5 times those of high school graduates and 14.5 times higher than those of high school dropouts. . . . The same study found that 18-to-24-year-old male high school dropouts had an incarceration rate 31 times that of males who graduated from a four-year college. If you're a young black male with no high school diploma, it's worse: You're 60 times more likely to end up behind bars than your classmates who earned a bachelor's degree. . . . Behavior that used to warrant a trip to the principal's office can now result in a trip to jail on charges of assault. Kids not old enough to drive have been arrested for behavior ranging from throwing a temper tantrum to talking during school assemblies and violating the dress code. It's kids of color who bear the disproportionate brunt of these zero-tolerance policies.

Something is clearly wrong when the government's most effective affirmative-action program is the preference people of color receive when entering not college, but the criminal-justice system. (Harris, 2007)

These statistics are especially compelling in that they demonstrate the circular pattern of the problem: by draining resources from communities, incarceration erodes educational institutions and community services that promote well-being and serve to prevent future incarceration. As states support prisons, they lose the ability to fund health, mental health, substance abuse, employment, educational, child welfare, and housing programs (Dyer, 2000). Current incarceration policies destabilize communities and are causes, not outcomes or solutions for criminal justice problems.

PRISONS WITHIN NATIONAL, GLOBAL, AND POLITICAL CONTEXTS

Moving to the exosystem and macrosystem/global level of the ecological framework provides a sobering glance at the relationships between the prison-industrial complex, corporate profits, and global politics. Building and running prisons is a growth industry, one that continues to be funded by state budgets while other services are cut. The number of prisoners in private prisons grew more than 2,000 percent between 1987 and 1996, and the census of private prisons rose from 3,122 to 78,000, a 2,000 percent increase (Sarabi & Bender, 2000). Privately-run facilities are estimated to contain 100,000 (Hallett, 2006) to 130,000 inmates (Sarabi & Bender, 2000). The two largest companies, the Corrections Corporation of American and Geo (formerly Wackenhut), are given state and federal subsidies to build and maintain prisons, and claim that they save the states money over publicly run prisons (although the reality of this claim is disputed, and some studies suggest they save no money at all (Erlich, 1995). The sale of tax-exempt bonds to underwrite prison construction has been estimated to be $2.3 billion annually (Davis, 2003), a boon to Wall Street investment firms. Telecommunication companies profit from public telephones in prisons, where they charge inmates and their families fees higher than the going rate on the "outside." Families may pay up to $22 for a 15-minute call on phones that are often their only source of communication with loved ones (Drug Policy Alliance Network, 2001, Erlich, 1995).

Prison labor has also become a profitable commodity within the federal and state penal systems as well as for private corporate interests. Companies such as IBM, Motorola, Compaq, Microsoft, Honeywell, and Texas Instruments use prison labor (Drug Policy Alliance Network, 2001) where inmates may be earning only $60 total for a month of full employment (Erlich, 1995). Products such as jeans called "prison blues" sold at Nordstrom are manufactured in Oregon prisons. Most of the wages go to the prison, not the prisoner (Erlich, 1995). Erlich reports that some prisons are exporting their products to Asia in order to circumvent U.S. laws that prevent prisons from selling products domestically, unless inmates are paid the prevailing wage. Those products are sold on Asian markets and find their way back to the U.S. or on other global markets. Thus, while the U.S. government is criticizing the Chinese government for using prison labor in manufacturing cheap goods for export, U.S. prisons are using prison labor both for exportation and for goods sold in the U.S. Federal Prison Industries manufacture clothing, file cabinets, electronic equipment and military helmets, once distributed only to federal agencies but now also sold to private companies. Their sales are $600 million annually and rising, with over $37 million in profits (Whyte & Baker, 2000). Arizona has re-initiated the road gang.

Although U.S. prison officials call the work voluntary, there is ample evidence that inmates have the opportunity for reduced sentences for participating and risk solitary confinement and loss of privileges, such as use of the library, when they do not.

Western and Pettit (2000) argue that prison labor actually takes jobs away from unskilled workers seeking jobs in society. They provide data to show that, starting in the 1990s, the substantial increases in incarcerated men working in prison labor competed with and contributed to the unemployment and low wages of those outside of prison. Lockhart Technologies, Inc. is an example of prison labor taking jobs from the community. The company closed its circuit board plant in Austin Texas, laid off 150 workers, and re-opened in a state prison. Customers include IBM, Compaq and Dell. The company pays the prison the federal minimum wage for each laborer, 20 percent of which the inmates receive with the other 80 percent going for room and board, victim restitution, and other fees. No benefits are paid by the company, unlike their former operation in the community. Erlich (1995) interviewed Leonard Hill, the owner of Lockhart Technologies, and discovered that prison labor built the company a new factory assembly room for which they pay $1 per year rent and receive tax abatement from the city. "Normally when you work in the free world," says Hill, "you have people call in sick, they have car problems, they have family problems. We don't have that here." Hill says the state pays for workers' compensation and medical care. And, he notes, inmates "don't go on vacations" (Erlich, 1995).

Using prison labor to break unions or replace civilian jobs for lower wages is not new. Historian Paul Lucko, interviewed by Erlich (1995), recounts the story of the building of the Texas State House in 1995. The contractors forced prison laborers, who were mostly African American, to haul the granite for the state house under construction. The unionized granite cutters objected to the use of prison labor and boycotted the project. Sixty-two granite cutters were imported from Scotland to complete the project.

CORPORATE PROFITS, POLITICAL LOBBYING, AND THE INCARCERATION BOOM

The Western Prison Project and Western States Center (Sarabi & Bender, 2000) investigated the relationship of political campaign contributions to state legislative prison policies. Their report concluded that private prisons are a major political factor in the incarceration boom. They assert that (1) prisons are "big business" and like any other corporation with vested financial interests they strive to profit and grow; (2) the private prison industry exerts increasing influence on criminal justice policy directly by writing model criminal justice legislation in collaboration with the American Legislative Exchange Council and through targeted campaign contributions in key states. Legislation tends to recommend long sentences and stiff penalties not only for serious crime, but for relatively small drug offenses and technical parole or probation violations. Their report details their strategies and success across many states.

HISTORICAL CONTEXT OF INCARCERATION FOR BLACKS: BACK TO RECONSTRUCTION

Historical context, a meta-level in this framework, plays an important role in an ecological analysis. History tells us that neither (1) attempts at social control through the spawning of increasingly punitive and repressive criminal justice legislation, nor (2) the link between exploiting prisoners for profit and incarceration are new. Following the Civil War, the Southern states enacted legislation that criminalized a wide range of nonviolent activities as a means of social control of newly freed slaves. As incarceration rates rose, so did the costs of maintaining prisons. Many states contracted prison labor with private entrepreneurs who then housed the inmates. The inmates were then forced to labor for former slave owners on the plantations on which they had been slaves, except under more brutal conditions. While slave owners had previously held a vested financial interest in keeping their slaves alive, they and the prison contractors worked their prison labor literally to death.

Private prisons were banned in the early 1900s because of deplorable conditions, brutality, and corruption. They did not emerge again until former U.S. President Ronald Reagan privatized governmental services as part of the Reagan Revolution. Since that time, criminal justice legislation has boomed, the private prison industry has moved into 28 states, and incarceration has boomed (Sarabi & Bender, 2000). In what can be called either hubris or irony (or both), it has been reported that Geo/Wackenhut even tried to sell investors on a plan to convert a former slave plantation in North Carolina into a maximum security prison (Drug Policy Alliance Network, 2001).

WHITE PRIVILEGE, RACISM AND AVERSIVE RACISM AND THE INCARCERATION OF AFRICAN AMERICANS

The narrative of the Jena 6 is emblematic of how white racism and white privilege feed into criminal justice inequities for African Americans. In Jena, Louisiana, after obtaining permission from the school principal, black high school students began to sit under a shade tree in the school yard that previously had been the domain solely of white students. Three nooses were found hanging from the tree the following day. The principal recommended expulsion of the three white students responsible for the nooses, but the Superintendent reduced the action to a three-day suspension, for what he described as a "youthful stunt." Black parents and students alike were upset by the Superintendent's characterization and unwillingness to place the nooses in a more accurate historical context. Parent voices were rebuffed; the students protested by holding a sit down under the tree. The police and the District Attorney (DA) soon appeared; the DA threatened the black students, saying, "he could make [their] lives disappear with the stroke of a pen." Racial tensions heightened over the next few months. The academic wing of the building was burned. Serious fights between white and black students broke out. During one episode, a black student was attacked and beaten with beer bottles; a white student was apprehended and was charged with simple battery. In another, black students attacked a white student who was witnessed verbally taunting them. Six black students were charged with attempted second-degree murder. At trial, the charges were reduced but only to second-degree aggravated battery and conspiracy. One of the students was charged as an adult. He was found guilty by an all-white jury and faced up to 22 years in prison until a court of appeal dismissed the charges stating that he should never have been tried as an adult (Baron, 2007).

McIntosh (1988) identifies white privilege as a system of unearned advantages obtained and maintained by whites through direct and indirect acts of racism. These acts perpetuate a system of social stratification and oppression. In the Jena 6 example, the first challenge to white privilege was the black students' attempts to upset the hierarchy by integrating the ground beneath the shade tree. The response at that point was an overt act of white supremacy in the form of nooses, which was then denied as anything but a prank. When threats, symbolic and overt, did not silence the black community, tensions continued to escalate until violence erupted. At that point, the power of the criminal justice system landed clearly on the side of white privilege: unequal treatment was accorded the white and black transgressors. For beating a student with beer bottles, a white student was charged with simple battery; for an altercation that involved no weapons (a legal requirement of the charges brought by the District Attorney), black students were charged with attempted murder and later aggravated assault.

Pewewardy and Severson (2003) report how white privilege influences the policies and privileges that then contribute to inequities and racial disparities in the criminal justice system. They argue that the dominant (white) culture has manipulated issues of race and crime by "de-emphasizing critical social issues, such as structural unemployment, and misrepresenting the relationship between race and crime" (p. 55). The disproportionate incarceration of African American and Hispanic peoples stems from racist practices designed to maintain white privilege through social control. Societal voices, such as the media, by selective focus and by creating and then reinforcing racial stereotypic, preserve the structural inequities. The authors cite Buenor Hadjor's (1995) work showing how both those who control media images and those who shape public policy use the language of law and order to increase the racial divide. Attention is deflected from the real problems associated with poverty and focused on crime filtered through race. Punishment and social control rather than remediating social inequities becomes the solution.

Clark (2001) accurately describes this process of white privilege:

One tactic of oppression is the implicit denial of oppression by making its infra-structure as invisible as possible. The longer race or gender oppression can be plausibly denied or shielded or masked, the better for the oppressors. Not only is it beneficial to deny the facts of oppression, it's beneficial to deny their intended results, the privileges such oppression confers, and the mechanisms by which such oppression is created, maintained, extended. The denial of White privilege, like the denial of racism itself, serves the interests of those who enjoy it.

It should not be surprising, then, that so many White people are so confused about what racism is; such confusion reinforces the status quo and sets the bar of justice and social change far too low. White people want to and do claim that racism is (only the) overt expression of racial bigotry or prejudice, and that such overt expression is socially impermissible. And so it is in situations and contexts, normally, where black people are really present because they have some social or institutional power—but these are rare in the South, as I rediscovered.

This patterned White response—so remarkably uniform as to merit analysis—obfuscates in two ways: first, by trying to make racist social structures and institutions invisible by directing critical attention away from them and onto the failings of individuals; second, by falsely claiming that bigotry and prejudice are unuttered and unutterable. (p. 1)

AVERSIVE RACISM

Clark's (2001) analysis is a lucid explanation of aversive racism (Gaertner & Dovidio, 2005) and how it operates to penalize racial/ethnic minorities within the criminal justice system. The premise of aversive racism is that regardless of our intentions or even conscious beliefs about racial equality, we (whites) hold stereotyped and biased beliefs about blacks, ideas that of which we may be unaware, but that nonetheless hold severely negative outcomes for blacks, and other people of color. We often:

adopt, without question, cultural stereotypes and justifying ideologies for group inequalities that reinforce group hierarchy . . . discrimination will occur when an aversive racist can justify or rationalize a negative response on the basis of some factor other than race. Under these circumstances, aversive racists may engage in behaviors that ultimately harm Blacks, but in ways that allow them to maintain their self-image as non-prejudiced. (pp. 317–318)

Because we don't want to recognize white privilege or racism, we avoid understanding the implications and maintain our ignorance of the ways in which exploitation of racial groups continue. The "unconscious" views we may harbor of white superiority cannot be changed or challenged because we deny their existence and do not examine them in the face of new information. Instead of questioning the spurious associations between race and crime that have permeated society, we strongly hold onto beliefs that punishment must be deserved if meted out by our legal system. In a study of aversive racism in the criminal justice system, Hodson, Hooper, Dovidio, and Gaertner (2005) reveal that under circumstances of greater legal ambiguity, black defendants were found to be guiltier, given longer sentences, seen as less likely to be rehabilitated, and more likely to re-offend.

INCARCERATION DISPARITIES: CALL FOR ACTION

Social activists within psychology as well as in the broader society have increasingly called for a social agenda drawn from an integrated analysis of oppression. Feminist Women of Color have led the way in voicing the need for social action built on understanding multiple sources of inequity (Greene & Sanchez-Hucles, 1997; Landrine, 1995; Russo & Vaz, 2001). For decades, Angela Davis (2003) has pressed for coalitions to address fundamental and interconnected oppressions. In psychology, Russo and Vaz (2001) have urged us toward "diversity mindfulnesss":

The egalitarian ideals of feminist psychology mandate what we call "diversity-mindfulness." It involves the process of perceiving and processing a multiplicity of differences among individuals, their social contexts, and their cultures. Diversity-mindfulness from a feminist perspective incorporates the feminist values of diversity, egalitarianism, and inclusiveness into critical analyses. It also recognizes the need for complex, context-based viewpoints. (p. 280)

The ecological framework is compatible with "diversity mindfulness." It delineates those interconnections, as in this analysis of incarceration, where it also underscores the interactions between causes and effects that go beyond understanding the impact of any event on the individual or the community. Because of the numbers of poor whites, rural whites, persons with serious mental disorders increasingly caught up in the criminal justice system, the intersections of racism, poverty, global capitalism, age, sexism, and disability are exemplified in the case of incarceration. Incarceration levels in the United States for all groups are shocking, particularly compared to the rest of the world. I have focused on the racial/ethnic disparities within this system, because men of color, increasingly women of color, and communities of color are more endangered and in crisis.

We must use "diversity mindfulness" to recognize the devastation occurring in black communities around incarceration, and to abolish the new slavery that has taken root in the United States. In keeping with the feminist adage, "the personal is political", I will end with the following anecdote so well known to mothers and fathers of young men of color.

A colleague's son, who is African American, lives in the same small San Francisco Bay community in which I live. He tells me that he is regularly stopped on his way home from work late at night for "speeding," which typically means driving about 28 mph in a 25 mph zone. Not only is he pulled over but he is actually ticketed for going two or three miles over the speed limit. What must this be like for this young man? We are all well-acquainted with the shootings that occur, with the explanations of "thought I saw a weapon" when none was present. No matter how frustrating or unfair these stops, this young man's life depends on his remaining calm, acquiescent, and polite. Alone on the street late at night, he cannot question the motives or the tactics of the police who stop him. His life depends on his ability to kowtow. This young adult male increasingly has difficulty leaving his house and has left his job because of social anxiety and panic attacks. However, this young man is living in a police state, one that is invisible to me in my daily lived experiences. Scapegoating and suspicion follow him and other young black men throughout U.S. society. Are his fears the result of social anxiety or realistic fear of unpredictable danger?

REFERENCES

Amnesty International. (2003). *United States of America: Death by discrimination—the continuing role of race in capital cases.* Retrieved June 20, 2008, from http://www.amnesty.org/en/library/info/AMR51/046/2003.

Ballou, M., Matsumoto, A., & Wagner, M. (2002). Toward a feminist ecological theory of human nature: Theory building in response to real-world dynamics. In M. Ballou & L. S. Brown (Eds.), *Rethinking mental health and disorder: Feminist perspectives* (pp. 99–144). New York: Guilford.

Baron, M. (2007). The Jena 6 (Jena Six) and Louisiana racial tensions. *The Post Chronicle.* September 4, 2007. Retrieved June 27, 2008, from http://www.postchronicle.com/cgi-bin/artman/exec/view.cgi?archive=30&num=101615.

Buenor Hadjor, K. (1995). *Another America: The politics of race and blame.* Boston: South End Press.

California School Finance. (2008). Retrieved June 29, 2008, from http://www.californiaschoolfinance.org/tabid/182/Default.aspx.

Californians United for a Responsible Budget. (2008). Retrieved June 28, 2008, from http://www.curbprisonspending.org/Fact%20Sheet%20on%20Gov's%20Budget%202008.pdf.

Clark, K. (2001, January 8). My white problem—and ours. Retrieved June 30, 2008, from http://monkeyfist.com/articles/734.

Davis, A. (2003). *Are prisons obsolete?* New York: Seven Stories Press.

Death Penalty Information Center. (2008a). Innocence cases: 2004–present. Retrieved June 20, 2008, from http://www.deathpenaltyinfo.org/article.php?did=2341.

Death Penalty Information Center. (2008b). Race of death row inmates executed since 1976. Retrieved June 20, 2008, from http://www.deathpenaltyinfo.org/article.php?scid=5&did=184#defend.

Death Penalty Information Center. (2008c). Native Americans and the death penalty. Retrieved June 20, 2008, from http://www.deathpenaltyinfo.org/article.php?did=2646#deathrow.

Death Penalty Information Center. (2008d). Women and the death penalty. Retrieved June 22, 2008, from http://www.deathpenaltyinfo.org/article.php?did=230&scid=24.

Drug Policy Alliance Network. (2001). *A new slavery.* Retrieved June 29, 2008, from http://www.drugpolicy.org/communities/race/anewslavery/.

Dyer, J. (2000). *The perpetual prisoner machine: How America profits from crime.* Boulder, CO: Westview Press.

Erlich, R. (1995). Prison labor: Workin' for the man. *Covert Action Quarterly, 54.* Retrieved July 3, 2008, from http://www-unix.oit.umass.edu/~kastor/private/prison-labor.html.

Gaertner, S. L., & Dovidio, J. F. (2005). Understanding and addressing contemporary racism: From aversive racism to the common ingroup identity model. *Journal of social issues, 51,* 615–639.

Greene, B., & Sanchez-Hucles, J. (1997). Diversity: Advancing an inclusive feminist psychology. In J. Worell & N. G. Johnson (Eds.), *Shaping the future of feminist psychology: Education, research, and practice* (pp. 173–202). Washington, DC: American Psychological Association.

Hallett, M. A. (2006). *Private prisons in America: A critical race perspective.* Urbana, IL: University of Illinois Press, 2006.

Harris, M. (2007). Prison vs. education spending reveals California's priority. *San Francisco Chronicle,* May 29, 2007. Retrieved June 30, 2008, from http://www.sfgate.com/cgi-bin/article.cgi?f=/c/a/2007/05/29/EDGGTP3F291.DTL.

Hodson, G., Hooper, H., Dovidio, J. F., & Gaertner, S. L. (2005). Aversive racism in Britain: Legal decisions and the use of inadmissible evidence. *European Journal of Social Psychology, 35,* 329–344.

Human Rights Watch. (2000). Punishment and prejudice: Racial disparities in the war on drugs. Retrieved June 22, 2008, from http://www.hrw.org/reports/2000/usa/Rcedrg00-01.htm.

Information Please. (2007). Death row exonerations, 1973–2008. Retrieved June 20, 2008, from http://www.infoplease.com/ipa/A0908211.html.

Jackson, J. (August 20, 1999). Keynote address. Annual Meeting of the American Psychological Association, Boston, MA.

Kozol, J. (2005). *The shame of the nation.* New York: Random House.

Landrine, H. (1995). *Bringing cultural diversity to feminist psychology; Theory, research, and practice.* Washington, DC: American Psychological Association.

Marsella, A. J. (1998). Toward a "global-community psychology": Meeting the needs of a changing world. *American Psychologist, 53,* 1282–1291.

Mauer, M. (1999). *Race to incarcerate.* New York: The New Press.

New Yorkers Against the Death Penalty. (2008). Retrieved June 20, 2008, from http://www.nyadp.org/main/faq#2.

Nicolaides, S. (Producer), & Singleton, J. (1991). *Boyz in the Hood* [film]. Culver City, CA: Columbia Pictures.

Pewewardy, N., & Severson, M. (2003). A threat to liberty: White privilege and disproportionate minority incarceration. *Journal of Progressive Human Services, 14,* 53–74.

Porter, N. (1995). Supervision of psychotherapists: Integrating anti-racist, feminist, and multicultural perspectives. In H. Landrine (Ed.), *Bringing cultural diversity to feminist psychology; Theory, research, and practice* (pp. 163–175). Washington, DC: American Psychological Association.

Russo, N., & Vaz, K. (2001). Addressing diversity in the decade of behavior: Focus women of color. *Psychology of Women Quarterly, 25,* 280–294.

Sarabi, B., & Bender, E. (2000). The prison payoff: The role of politics and private prisons in the incarceration boom. Western States Center & Western Prison Project. Retrieved June 27, 2008, from http://www.tgsrm.org/pdfdocs/Privatization%20of%20Prisons%20-%20Profit.pdf.

Simon, D. (Director, Producer), & Nobles, N. K. (Producer). (2002). *The Wire* [TV series]. Baltimore: HBO.

U.S. Department of Justice. (2008). Blacks were almost three times more likely than Hispanics and five times more likely than whites to be in jail. Retrieved June 23, 2008, from http://www.ojp.usdoj.gov/bjs/glance/jailrair.htm.

Vargas, L. A., Porter, N., & Falender, C. A. (2008). Supervision, culture, and context. In C. A. Falender & E. P. Shafranske. (Eds.), *Casebook for clinical supervision: A competency-based approach* (pp. 121–136). Washington, DC: American Psychological Association.

Warren, J., Gelb, A., Horowitz, J., & Riordan, J. (2008). One in 100: Behind bars in America 2008. Pew Center on the States. Retrieved June 22, 2008, from http://www.pewcenteronthestates.org/uploadedFiles/One%20in%20100.pdf?sid=ST20080228030162008.

Whyte, A., & Baker, J. (2000). Prison labor on the rise in U.S. Published by the International Committee of the Fourth International. Retrieved July 3, 2008, from http://www.wsws.org/articles/2000/may2000/pris-m08.shtml.

Winfrey, O. (2007). *Failing grade.* Retrieved June 30, 2008, from http://www.oprah.com/slideshow/oprahshow/oprahshow1_ss_20060411/3.

CHAPTER 11

Psychotherapy as Liberation: Multicultural Counseling and Psychotherapy (MCT) Contributions to the Promotion of Psychological Emancipation

Allen E. Ivey and Carlos P. Zalaquett

> Liberation is a praxis: The action and reflection of (people) upon their world in order to transform it.
>
> —Paulo Freire (1972, p. 66)

Since its inception in the second half of the twentieth century, Multicultural Counseling and Therapy (MCT) has been revolutionary; it has produced both theoretical analyses recognizing the limitations of individually focused psychotherapy and psychotherapeutic propositions emphasizing a so-called culture-centered focus.

The increasing recognition of counseling as a sociopolitical endeavor (Sue & Sue, 2008) and the individual as a multicultural being (Pedersen, 1997) led to questioning traditional models of counseling that place the responsibility for problems solely on an individual, family, or group. MCT suggests that traditional theories and techniques are based in a limited cultural frame, and are insufficient to provide answers to the problems and needs of many clients.

MCT recognizes that individuals exist in contextual/cultural contexts and propose that a cultured-centered emphasis should be placed in our individually focused counseling theories. Ivey (1993, 2000) has consistently noted that our failure to help clients understand that their difficulties and problems are the logical result of developmental, social, and contextual history. Psychotherapy and counseling in U.S. culture take a naive point of view emphasizing the individual, while simultaneously failing to consider context and environment. As a result, much of today's therapy unwisely blames the individual.

Psychotherapy as liberation is an essential notion within the broader MCT frame and constitutes a core aspiration of its psychotherapeutic propositions. Liberation psychotherapy draws its tenets from many authorities in cultural identity theory (e.g., Arredondo, 1999; Brown, 1959; Cross, 1971, 1991; Daly, 1973; M. Daly, May 1993, personal communication; Fanon, 1963; Freire, 1972; Hardiman & Jackson, 1997; Helms, 1990, 2007; Jackson, 1975, 1990; Pedersen, Draguns, Lonner, & Trimble, 2008; Sue & Sue, 2008; and White & Parham, 1990), and focuses on helping clients learn to see themselves *in relation* to their cultural/contextual influences. The traditional emphasis on the individual self is replaced by *Self-in-relation* (Miller, 1991; Montero, 2007).

the construction of knowledge resides not in the individuals, but in the relations between individuals. No one can be or do without someone else; both the One (I) and the Other (You, She, He, They) are constructed in the relationships they exist in. Relationships are being constructed in a dialectical movement as, simultaneously, they are constructing their builders. The introduction of this ontological and epistemological foundation in liberation psychology is part of its development. (Montero, 2007, p. 518)

The following examples demonstrate the importance of self-in-relation. Consider the African American client who comes to therapy to learn stress management techniques to control his hypertension. Liberation psychotherapy would support and utilize stress management because we know that these cognitive-behavioral techniques can be both emotionally and physically beneficial, but would consider these techniques insufficient.

Knowing the negative physical and psychological consequences of oppression in African Americans, liberation psychotherapy would consider necessary to help this client examine his cultural context and consider how the constant barrage of racist acts in society contribute to his concerns. Likewise, Latino teenagers who consult high school counselors because anxiety is negatively affecting their academic performance may also need to speak about the anti-immigrant sentiments openly expressed by most in their schools.

Liberation psychotherapy is inspired by the work of Paulo Freire (1921–1997). His concept of critical consciousness (*conscientizacào* in Portuguese) (Freire, 1972), originally applied to education, suggests that one of the major purposes in counseling and psychotherapy is to liberate people to awareness of themselves in social context. Freire's methods for generating critical consciousness and Ivey's (2000) developmental therapy are part of MCT skills and techniques for facilitating client cognitive/emotional liberating processes.

Philosophically, MCT is also inspired by the radical contextualists Brown, Daly, Fanon, and draws from the many experts and the burgeoning literature on cultural identity theory (Cross, 1971, 1991; Hardiman, 1982; Hardiman & Jackson, 1997; Helms, 1990, 2007; Jackson, 1975, 1990; Ponterotto, 1988; Sue & Sue, 2008).

Despite the fact that MCT demonstrates the centrality of contextual/ cultural factors in our work with clients, professionals have been reluctant to accept that their own behaviors and their institution/agencies policies are often acontextual, culturally insensitive, and even oppressive. Consequently, this chapter revisits and brings together theory and practice, and reflection and action, to further move the field toward a culture-centered praxis, one which is truly sensitive to cultural and contextual aspects of human development.

THEORETICAL FOUNDATIONS OF MCT AND LIBERATION

[We are] beings of relations in a world of relations.
—Paulo Freire (1972, p. 41)

MCT offers a new conceptual frame for our theory, research, supervision, and practice. MCT demands that we reflect on the human condition in social context and work to change inhumane systems. This demand is now addressed in professional ethic guidelines. Section A.6 of the Ethics Code of the American Counseling Association states that counselors will advocate on behalf of clients to "to examine potential barriers and obstacles that inhibit access and/or the growth and development of clients, and . . . to improve the provision of services and to work toward removal of systemic barriers or obstacles that inhibit client access, growth" (2005, p. 5).

MCT requires that we address the inequalities observed in our societies, which are frequently overlooked due to factors such as individualistic perspectives (Prilleltensky, 2008) and classist attitudes (Smith, 2005), to determine how they impact our clients. No longer can we "blame the victim" by stating that personal issues reside solely "in the person." As a liberating process, MCT seeks to inform individuals as to how the social and historical past, present, and future affect cognition, emotion, and action (Ivey, 2000).

The process of *conscientizacào* as defined by Freire (1972) is essential: "*conscientizacào* refers to learning to perceive social, political, and economic contradictions, and to take action against the oppressive elements of reality" (p. 19).

This cognitive and emotional process helps clients become aware of the dynamic relations they have with the world, of their critical capacity to address oppressive relations, and of their negative contextual condition (Montero, 2007).

This collaboration between counselors and clients includes attending, problematizing, and dialoguing. During problematization (Freire, 1972), the person begins to question what has been unilaterally taught or depicted as essential social views of the world, and begins to realize that these views represent only one way to conceptualize their contextual situation. This process of questioning and rejecting leads to emotional, cognitive, and action changes because relevant aspects of the clients' daily life are redefined and reorganized. Clients' newly constructed views of self, the world, and their dynamic relationship enable them to transform their lives and world. In turn, this on-going process of transformation helps create more knowledge and action, and empowers the client to generate a new life (Montero, 2007).

Liberation is not imparted; it is generated by clients needing it and therapists facilitating it. This collaboration between counselors and client acknowledges and accepts the existence of a cultural context with varying worldviews.

According to Ivey (1995, 2000), traditional theories of psychotherapy fail to consider, or minimally address contextual/cultural dimensions. Psychoanalytic approaches have been criticized by Norman O. Brown (1959) for their abandonment of social context in favor of social adjustment and individual insight. "Human consciousness can be liberated from the parental (Oedipal) complex only by being liberated from its cultural derivatives, the paternalistic state and the patriarchal God" (p. 155).

Humanistic and cognitive-behavioral theories, too, have met with severe criticism for similar reasons. Lerman (1992) points out that humanistic theories "failed to recognize that no person constructs their own reality without external influences" (p. 13). She criticizes hallowed concepts such as self-actualization and autonomy as middle-class products that simply aren't relevant to many cultural groups, especially those for whom power rests in others. It is difficult for one to be "self-actualized" while being controlled by another culture. While recognizing that cognitive-behavioral approaches do consider context, Kantrowitz and Ballou (1992) comment that "individuals are expected to improve their adaptive capacities to meet the environmental conditions, which serve to reinforce the dominant (male) social standards" (p. 79).

Feminist theory argues that patriarchy is a central condition of these theories. The negative effects of the controlling patriarchal metaphor are well documented by the radical feminist Mary Daly (1973, 1978). She comments in 1993:

In my analysis, racism is not exactly a "variation" of patriarchy. Rather, I see patriarchy as the root and core of all forms of oppression, including racism, sexism, classism, and speciesism. It would not be accurate to say that I "develop gender as the central issue." I find this kind of language inadequate to describe the atrocities against women and all oppressed beings on this planet.

In effect, traditional counseling and therapy theory are white, male, Eurocentric, and middle-class in origin and practice. Therapy can be described as centrally concerned with maintaining "patriarchy" or the status quo.

Racism, a particularly virulent form of patriarchal domination, has been explored by Fanon (1963). Racism may be described as a form of colonialism in which oppressors actually inscribe a mentality of subordination in the oppressed. This enables oppressors to use the labor and life of the oppressed for their own ends. In *The Wretched of the Earth*, Fanon (1963) comments on the importance of the oppressed to find their own voice and have the language to name and describe their condition. Asante (1987) also points out the importance of naming one's self as a way to learning new actions—"it is a liberating act, the intellectual equivalent of a slave's wave of good-bye to (the) master from the North side of the Ohio River" (p. 115).

Prilleltensky (2008) warns us that well intentioned and compassionate therapies may have unintended consequences:

The idea of internalized social prescriptions has direct implications for the self-perception of people with psychological problems. Although coercion has not disappeared from the treatment of the mentally ill, we have today treatment methods characterized by kindness and compassion. However humanitarian, this turn is not without side effects, for it shifts responsibility for problems and solutions inward. In the absence of apparent coercion, and in the presence of overt caring, there is nobody but oneself to blame for difficulties and lack of progress. (p. 120)

The philosophers and theorists of contextualism operate in a very different world. Hallowed words representing old solutions such as "self-actualization" and "doing one's own thing," and "individualism" become new problems to be solved. From this frame of reference, traditional counseling and therapy, to paraphrase Eldridge Cleaver, are more problem than solution.

Despite being controversial and many traditionalists refusing to change, we continue to move toward a renewed view in our field. MCT is now recognized as a major and relevant fourth force in the helping field. True to its tenets, MCT is not formed by one "famed" individual or a small group of key "gurus" as is frequently observed in the popular individualistic therapies such as client-centered, cognitive-behavioral, and psychodynamic. Many authors promote the renewal of counseling (Arredondo, 1999, 2002; Cheek, 1976; Cheatham & Stewart, 1990; Fukuyama, 1990; Ivey, Simek-Morgan, Ivey, & D'Andrea, 2006; LaFromboise & Graff Low, 1998; Locke, 1990, 1992; Myers, 1988; Parham, White, & Ajamu, 1999; Pedersen, 1997, 1999; Pedersen & Ivey, 1993; Pedersen et al., 2008; Sue, Ivey & Pedersen, 1996; White & Parham, 1990; Wrenn, 1962, 1985). Professional journals, in turn, have provided full issues for them to present their multicultural views and research (for example, see the *Journal of Counseling and Development*, 2008, Vol. 86). The general theme of these and other authors is that cultural issues need to take their place as the center of a totally redefined and liberatory psychotherapy.

PSYCHOTHERAPY AS LIBERATION

Good theory leads to good practice and promotes good research (Ivey, 1995). At issue, however, is the definition of the "good." The "patriarchal" "goods" and "shoulds" of our past history in counseling and therapy promote an individualistic, expert-based, and top-down relationship. Psychotherapy of liberation cannot remain hierarchical with firm distinctions between helper and helpee, counselor and client, or therapist and patient. Liberation psychotherapy stresses the importance of generating a more mutual, culturally sensitive approach to counseling and therapy. The term "client colleague" is introduced to further promote a liberatory psychotherapy relationship.

Traditionally, we think of the helping professions as generous and giving. Freire (1972) states that:

True generosity consists precisely in fighting to destroy the causes which nourish false charity. False charity constrains the fearful and subdued the "rejects of life" to extend their trembling hands. True generosity lies in striving so that these hands—whether of individuals or entire peoples—need to be extended less and less in supplication, so that more and more they become human hands which work, and working, transform the world. (p. 29)

To take these theoretical ideas into practice, Freire presents the concept of *cointentional education* in which problems are posed and two people work together *intentionally.* Feminist theory, which focuses on *self-in-relation* (Miller, 1991) and egalitarian relationships, provides a concrete path of therapeutic action in which the client colleague becomes a partner, exploring with the other. Developmental counseling and therapy (DCT; Ivey, 2000) talks about co-construction of reality in which two people work together to find new meaning and new ways of being. The person who "helps" may learn as much as the person "helped."

According to Freire (1972), "Liberating education consists in acts of cognition, not transferals of information" (p. 67), which become a dialogue between and among individuals. He decries "banking" education in which "deposits" are made in the student and calls for "problem-posing" education in which we work together on presenting, discussing, and sometimes resolving contradictions and issues. A liberating psychotherapy will help individuals and groups become intentionally conscious of themselves and conscious of consciousness itself.

LIBERATORY INFLUENCE OF CULTURAL IDENTITY THEORY

Cultural identity theorists cited earlier are central in elaborating counseling and psychotherapy as a liberatory process. These theories are liberating in that they focus on the expansion of consciousness—learning how to see oneself and others in relation to cultural context. Cultural identity theory has its roots in the black and African American consciousness movement of the 1960s and, more recently, the feminist, gay/lesbian, and other group liberation movements. The liberation that comes with consciousness of self-in-relation leads to a broader form of self-concept, which Cross (1991) terms reference group orientation (RGO). It could be argued that the RGO provided by the black identity movement has done more for African American mental health than all other existing theories of human change put together. Feminist theory has done much the same for women as has the gay/lesbian movement (Ivey, 1995).

Cultural identity theory can be traced back to its early roots in Plato's Allegory of the Cave (Cornford, 1941/1982). Plato clearly lists four level/stages of consciousness that parallel both cultural and identity theory. Briefly, slaves are encapsulated in the cave without awareness of the Other and of oppressive forces holding them in chains. Through a gradual process, the slaves are led out of the cave to face the light of truth and their own oppression.

This evolution of consciousness is the basis of liberatory therapy—helping clients to see themselves in a social context—the fourth stage/level of cultural identity theory. Ivey's (2000) Developmental Counseling and Therapy (DCT) will be presented later as it offers specifics for the liberation of consciousness and ACTION against oppressive elements in the world.

Cultural identity theory, then, enables us to frame counseling and psychotherapy as consciousness development, the generation of more complex cognitions and behaviors as one comes to see oneself in context. Although, there are varying models within the cultural identity theory group, Ivey and Payton (1994) select five stages of consciousness-development as central. These levels are drawn from Freire (1972) and Jackson and Hardiman (1983).

One seldom finds a "pure" type and most client colleagues will be mixtures of stages just as we are ourselves. Jackson and Hardiman (1993) also point out that each stage seems to have an entry point, a consolidation phase, and a time for exit as new data force the individual to accommodate to new perspectives. Parham (1989) notes also that it is possible to recycle through the separate stages several times in a lifetime as one discovers new issues of identity and discrimination, and builds new awareness.

OPPRESSIVE OR REVOLUTIONARY ACTION?

Traditional therapy and counseling tend to be oriented toward oppressive action. Many counselors inadvertently may be engaging in oppression (Sue & Sue, 2008). Freire's theory of oppressive action below illustrates what occurs when a therapist ("the-rapist") acts on clients. Note that the language of therapy orients us as dominant elite to act on clients or patients. And, as part of the action, whether we use humanistic, behavioral, or psychodynamic formats, we tend to bring the client "back to reality." In this typical model, the client receives knowledge from the expert. Societal context is not considered in this current frame of reference, except as therapists and counselors as "experts" define it.

Actors-Subjects
(dominant elites)

Object—the reality   *Object*—the oppressed
reality to be preserved   (as part of reality)

for
Objective—the preservation of oppression

(Freire, 1972, p. 131)

To concretize the above diagram, consider the cognitive-behavioral therapist who meets with a holocaust survivor or a homeless Iraq veteran who manifest clinical depression. Fairly effective treatment procedures can be established with this framework to help these clients feel better. Medication can also ease the process. Freire would term this type of therapy oppressive as it fails to inform the client colleagues of how the depression is a logical result of developmental history and oppressive social conditions. Effective education and therapy seek to work with client colleagues to consider how oppressive conditions contribute to present reality. This *naming* of social context is a collaborative act between counselor and client colleague.

Freire also talks of a theory of revolutionary action in which inter-subjectivity—a framework of equality—surrounds the educator-student relationship. Feminist theory (e.g., Ballou & Gabalac, 1984) is the prime current example of how psychotherapy can become liberating rather than encapsulating. Note that the counselor or therapist works *with* the client colleague in this model. Both learn together how they might transform reality—interaction of the pair in the helping relationship replaces action of the therapy *on* the client as occurs in traditional helping models.

Intersubjectivity

Subjects-Actors   Actors-Subjects
(revolutionary leaders)   (the oppressed)

Interaction

Object   Reality   Object
which mediates   to be transformed   which mediates

for
Objective   Humanization   Objective
                    as a permanent
                    process

(Freire, 1972, p. 131)

Psychotherapy as liberation demands two (or more) people working together to examine their relationship with each other *and* their social context. What is the effect and impact of the social environment on individual thought and action? Armed with personal and contextual information, two (or more) can work together to transform reality. The holocaust survivor and the homeless Iraq veteran learn how social contextual issues of anti-Semitism and society's lack of affordable blue-collar jobs and housing contribute to their so-called emotional distress or DSM-IV diagnostic classification (for additional examples see Zalaquett, Fuerth, Stein, Ivey, & Ivey, 2008). In addition, the client colleagues are encouraged to work toward confronting social conditions that may be causative of their issues. It is not enough to learn that one has been a victim, one can benefit from attacking the source of victimization. If the problem is not in the individual, we also need to challenge external social/contextual stressors. Both therapists and client colleagues can benefit through a therapy that also seeks to address environmental causes of individual distress.

AN IMPORTANT CAVEAT ABOUT ESTABLISHING EMANCIPATORY DIALOGUE IN PSYCHOTHERAPY

Intrinsic difficulties hinder the communication of people that are dramatically different from each other (Guareschi & Jovchelovitch, 2004). We need to remember that the communication of client colleagues and therapists is shaped by the contextual/cultural dimensions of both members. These factors are more visible in our interaction with diverse clients. For example, the homeless Iraq veteran may reject the help of the counselors because he may believe that the ulterior motive behind this help is to remove him from the streets. Thus, despite our desire to establish a dialogical communication to increase *conscientizacào* to reduce oppressive conditions in which the client lives, this may remain an ideal (Guareschi & Jovchelovitch, 2004).

Cultural representations of help as intentions and actions realized by professionals and representations of clients as passive recipients of counseling influence the participants' views. Thus, client colleagues' participation depends on how they perceive and respond to our efforts. True dialogue is difficult to achieve. Guareschi and Jovchelovitch (2004) offer the "law of silence" as an example of such difficulties. This "law" operates in members of some groups to protect themselves and present you with an expected identity. The authors suggest utilizing both, verbal and nonverbal, communication with client colleagues because speech can be used to hide and silence can be used to reveal during the interaction.

MCT theory facilitates establishing a true dialogue. Achieving dialogical communication places both participants in a position of changing him or herself and the other, and leads to the development of a productive alliance between individuals from different cultural contexts and levels of expertise (Freire, 1972; Guareschi & Jovchelovitch, 2004).

CASE EXAMPLE OF MCT THEORY IN PRACTICE

Assume you are working with a low-income Puerto Rican woman who suffers from *ataques de nervios*. These are best described as epileptic-like seizures that have an emotional base and function in Puerto Rican culture. U.S. psychology originally pathologized these events as hysteria or thought them actually to be physical in origin (Rivera-Arzola, 1991). We now know that such events are a normal part of dealing with trauma and grief in traditional Puerto Rican culture. The following passage is a direct quote from Cheatham, Ivey, Ivey, and Simek-Morgan (1993, p. 114–115) and is used by permission. Parts that are not direct quotes are in italics.

The client colleague is a single parent, twenty-five years of age with two children. (*As once was common in Puerto Rico,*) she has been sterilized with only minimal information given to her before she gave consent. She has suffered physical abuse both as a child and in more recent relationships. Following is an example of how multicultural counseling and therapy might use cultural identity development theory to facilitate *conscientizacào* and the generation of critical consciousness.

Acceptance—diagnostic signs. The client colleague enters counseling hesitatingly as her *ataques de nervios* are increasing in frequency. A physician has referred her to you believing that the fainting spells are psychological in origin as no physical reasons can be found. You discover that she blames herself for the failures in her life. She comments that she is "always choosing the wrong man" and states she should have been sterilized sooner and thus fewer children would be born.

Acceptance—helping interventions and producing dissonance. Your intervention at this stage is to listen, but following Freire (1972, pp. 114–116), you can seek to help her codify or make sense of her present experience. You use guided imagery as you help her review critical life events—the scenes around sterilization, the difficulties of economic survival when surrounded by others who have wealth, and actual discrimination against Puerto Ricans in her work setting. . . . Through listening and perturbing with dissonant images, the move to a more critical consciousness is begun. But, at the same time, she needs help. Attending to her immediate needs, you help her find food and shelter and in finding work. You teach her basic stress management and relaxation, but especially you listen and learn.

Naming and resistance—Diagnostic signs. At this point, the Puerto Rican client colleague may become angry for the responsibility or "fault" which she believed was hers is now seen as in the oppressive environment. Her eyes may flash as she talks about "them." An emotional release may occur as she becomes aware that the decision for sterilization was not truly hers, but imposed by an authoritarian physician. The woman may want to strike back wherever possible against those who have oppressed her. In the early stages of naming, she may fail to separate people who have truly victimized her from those who have "merely" stood by and said nothing.[1]

Naming and resistance-Interventions to help and produce dissonance. Early in this stage, you are very likely to do a lot of listening. You may find it helpful to teach the client colleague culturally-appropriate assertiveness training and anger management. There may be a delayed anger reaction to traditional sex roles. Later, this client colleague may profit from reality therapy. However, the therapy must be adapted to her relational Puerto Rican heritage. You may support constructive action on her part to change oppressive situations. In the later stages of work with her, you may want to help her see that much of her consciousness and being depends on her *opposition* to the status quo and that she has given little attention to her own real needs and wishes. *At this point, identifying and naming contradictions between self and society may be especially important.*

Reflection and redefinition—Diagnostic signs. It gets very tiring to spend one's life in total anger towards society and others. The consciousness-raising theories find that at this stage the client colleagues often retreat to their own gender and/or cultural community to reflect on what has happened to them and to others. Responsibility is now seen as more internal in nature, but keen awareness of external issues remains. You may note that the client colleague at this stage is less interested in action and more interested in understanding self and culture. There may be a great interest in understanding and appreciating her Puerto Rican heritage and how it plays itself out in North America.

Reflection and redefinition—Interventions to help and produce dissonance. Teaching client colleagues the cultural identity development theories can be useful at this stage as they help explain issues of development in culture. In addition, culturally appropriate theories such as feminist theory may be especially helpful, although they are useful at all consciousness levels. Cognitive-behavioral, psychodynamic, and person-centered theories may be used if adapted to the culture and needs of the person. *The reflective consciousness is still considered a form of naive consciousness by Freire as much of the emphasis is on the individual with insufficient attention given to systemic roots of difficulties.*

Multiperspective integration—diagnostic signs. The Puerto Rican client colleague draws from all previous stages as appropriate to the situation. At times, she may accept situations, at other times be appropriately aggressive and angry, and later withdraw and reflect on herself and her relationships to others and society. She is likely to be aware of how her physical symptoms of *ataques de nervios* were a logical result of the place of women in her culture. She is able to balance responsibility between herself and society. At the same time, she does not see her level of *conscientizacào* as "higher" than others. She respects alternative frames of reference.

Multiperspective integration—Interventions to help and produce dissonance. You as helper may ask the client colleague to join with you and your group to attack some of the social justice issues which "cause" emotional, personal, and financial difficulty. The Puerto Rican woman may establish a family planning clinic with accurate information on the long-term effects of sterilization or she may establish a day-care center. The woman is clearly aware of how her difficulties developed in a system of relationships and balances internal and external responsibility for action. In terms of introducing dissonance, your task may require helping her with time management, stress management, and in balancing the many possible actions she encounters. You may also arrange to see that she has accurate feedback from others about her own life and work. *You do not merely encourage her to work to transform the system. You also work with her to facilitate the process. You and your client colleague are now working together to produce cultural change in oppressive conditions.*

In summary, MCT as presented here provides specific actions that can lead to critical consciousness and *conscientizacào*. The example of the Puerto Rican woman could be changed to represent a middle-class woman, a gay male, or any of a variety of culturally distinct client colleagues. Particularly relevant for broader practice of counseling and therapy is Pfefferle's (1989) developmental concepts of long-term psychological problems. She states that depressed client colleagues typically see themselves as responsible for their problems in the early stages and only gradually move to the awareness that depression was generated in a systemic context. Rigazio-DiGilio (1989) and Rigazio-DiGilio and Ivey (1990) find that systematic questioning of depressed client colleagues leads to a critical consciousness. In this new state of awareness, the client colleagues are able to balance responsibility for self and others in a more constructive fashion.

As observed in the example, above, psychotherapy as liberation has much to offer individuals and the growth process. Our problem is our tendency to focus too much of our efforts at the Platonic belief and thinking stages—thus our emphasis on behavior and cognition. We have given insufficient attention to sensorimotor reality and direct client colleague experience; and, more seriously, we have failed to consider the systemic issues underlying the client colleague's world.

We have restricted counseling and psychotherapy unnecessarily in our search for self-actualization and individual change. No longer is it adequate to situate problems solely *in the individual.* The time has come to increase our attention to the direct experience of the individual through immediate sensorimotor reality and consider how that reality is affected by systemic contextual/cultural issues. Armed with this knowledge it may or may not be appropriate to utilize traditional humanistic, cognitive-behavioral, and psychodynamic strategies we have in the past.

Let us now turn to some examples of specific verbal skills and strategies that may be useful to client colleagues and ourselves in the process of *conscientizacào* or critical consciousness.

THE SKILLS AND STRATEGIES OF *CONSCIENTIZACÀO*

Ivey (1993, 2000) suggests some specific skills and questions that may be used to help the client colleague move from each level of consciousness to the next. The following are based on the steps of Freire's *conscientizacào*. You will note the use of narratives and storytelling in the systematic sequence.

Just reading the following list will be next to useless for you. We urge you to find a colleague and practice the questioning sequence together one by one. We know that this series of questions, adapted to client colleagues' individual differences, has positive results. Please give it a try. *Understanding is not enough—this requires concrete action in the here and now.*

Moving from naiveté to examination of acceptant behaviors, feelings, and thoughts. Tell me about your life. I'd like to hear a story about a time when you felt one-down, out of control, depressed/oppressed, or helpless. Tell me you see the life and story of others, who may be oppressors.

Moving from acceptance to naming and resistance. What is your image of a situation? What are you seeing? Hearing? Feeling? Locate the feeling in a specific place in your body. What is your image of the other or the context? Use the same sensorimotor questions to elaborate the image and the bodily feelings that are associated. *How would you **name** that image, feeling, or experience?*

Helping client colleagues to expand their understanding of naming and resistance and to move to the next stage or level. We usually identify a client colleague as a person who has developed a well-defined anger at the system (although this anger may be injurious to health). We also tend to find that client colleagues at this level have identified their sense of self as built *in opposition* to the other. For example, African Americans are *not* white European-Americans, women are not men, differently abled are *not* able—the locus of control is often external rather than internal.

Some useful techniques to help individuals cope and progress include listening carefully to the concrete details of the stories of oppression, and presenting stress management and cognitive-behavioral therapy to help the person cope with "reality." Assertiveness training may be useful to help the client colleague start work toward reforming the system. Also, it is important to start confronting the external control, thus facilitating the development of a stronger sense of self-in-relation.

Some specific questions to facilitate movement to the next stage.

1. Tell me a story of what happened. What happened first, next, and how did it end? Note the emphasis on linearity and cause-and-effect in storytelling. Here we are applying some basic principles of applied behavioral analysis and rational-emotive therapy to client colleague images and stories so that they can understand them better. As a therapist, you can help your client colleague—"If you say X, then what is likely to be the consequence?" The skill of logical consequences may be useful as well.
2. After this review of the story, how would you *name* or think about the story now? Can you name your thoughts and feelings?
3. Have the client colleague tell several concrete stories in linear detail, then ask for reflection. As you look back on your story, what occurs to you? What is its meaning? What do you make of it?

Helping client colleagues to expand their understanding of reflection and redefinition and also move to dialogic, multiperspective stage or level. Whereas the concrete naming and resistance stage tends to focus on action, this stage tends to emphasize reflective thought. Freire (1972, p. 75) discusses action and reflection as two parts of true praxis. Too extensive an emphasis on action leads to "activism" with insufficient attention to the reasons and purpose of action. Too extensive an emphasis on reflection leads to "verbalism" with little or no action.

The reflective consciousness is an important part of cultural identity theory with obvious strengths and weaknesses so well outlined by Freire. The cognitive, the humanistic, and the psychodynamic orientations are renowned for their verbalism and emphasis on thought as opposed to action. Behavioral psychology, of course, has received many attacks for insufficient reflection. It is small wonder that the cognitive-behavioral revolution is upon us, but even this approach has limitations as it gives insufficient attention to experiencing the systemic issues faced in a multicultural society.

Reflection offers a time to build a sense of self-in-relation to cultural context and develop a stronger sense of internal locus of control. A woman, for example, may be expected to start defining herself uniquely as a woman rather than in opposition to men. A Latina/Latino will define her or himself on the basis of personal and cultural norms.

Techniques useful in expanding self and cultural awareness are group consciousness raising programs such as those widely used in the early stages of feminist or other cultural support groups. Traditional cognitive and behavioral psychological theories can be useful, but only if the theories are culturally shaped and adapted. Confrontation techniques within the interview and group are particularly important as contradictions are identified. This is the basis of later true dialogical thought.

Characteristic questions useful at this time include:

- What is common to your stories? What are the patterns?
- How do we think about these stories and how could we think about them differently?
- Which of your behaviors and thoughts are yours? Which are those that come from your cultural surround and past life history?
- How do family stories and family history relate to your conception of self? Or your cultural background? Or, how the two relate?
- What parts of you are driven internally? What parts are driven by external forces? And, how can we tell the difference?
- Standing back, what inconsistencies can we identify?

Continuing and expanding multiperspective integration. Here we are looking for true praxis—the integration of thought and action. The individual or group here freely draws from and sees the value in all other stages and levels, but clearly see self in social/family/historical contexts. The ability to take multiple perspectives on data is central to this stage, but this contains the seed for a major problem as it is easy for the individual or group to become enmeshed in possibility and fail to act on new cognitions and emotions.

Supporting development at this stage are community and network efforts in which the individual or group seeks out new goals and actions.

The individual at the multiperspective level will be able to see many points of view *and* take action, as appropriate to the situation. The transforming consciousness seeks to move toward action and to make a difference in the world.

Following are some questions that may help individuals and groups at the multiperspective integration stage:

- As we look back on all we've talked about and/or done, what stands out for you? How? Why? How do you/we put together all we've talked about? *These questions help the individual or group look back and reflect on their own cognitive and emotional operations. These questions may also help reorganize old thought patterns leading to a new perspective on old situations.*
- What rule(s) were you (or the other person or group) operating under? Where did that rule come from? How might someone else describe that situation (another family member, a member of the opposition, someone from a different cultural background)? How do these rules relate to us now?
- How might we describe this from the point of view of some other person, theoretical framework, or language system? How might we put it together using another framework?
- What does our family, our educational, our work history say about the development and operation of oppression?
- What shall we do? How shall we do it together? What is *our* objective and how can we work together effectively? Or, equally likely, perhaps the client colleague wishes to manage his or her own affairs and take action as a leader in her or his own right.

Perhaps the last question is the most important. It is the one that reminds us most specifically of praxis—the importance of integrating our thoughts with specific actions.

The questions above can be introduced, as appropriate, to any counseling or therapeutic situation. The goal is to help the client colleague see her or his issues in social and historical contexts. This is not to take responsibility for action away from individuals, but to help them understand that they are not alone in their issues and that full resolution of conflicting situations usually involves some action and awareness of social context. The stoic model of much of cognitive therapy—"it is not things, but what we think of things that is important"—clearly does not hold here. Thought and action must become a unified whole. From this vantage point, much of traditional counseling and therapy supports the status quo and needs serious reconstruction.

The egalitarian, dialogical touch is also important in this framework. With clearly defined goals and specific techniques and questions, it would be all too easy to fall into a hierarchical client-counselor or patient-therapist model. Thus, as often occurs in feminist therapy, goals should be established jointly with the client colleague, constant joint review of the value of each session needs to be undertaken, and goals jointly rewritten as needed. The dialogical therapist or counselor tends not to be formally wedded to a specific procedure and all techniques and strategies are open for review and modification.

SOME FINAL WORDS

Psychotherapy as liberation entails a radical revision of helping theory. The developmental psychology of cultural identity theory is basic to the framework. It is a framework that focuses on self-in-context and self-in-relation.

Humanistic, psychodynamic, and cognitive-behavioral theory have brought us many ideas and innovations. We need not discard them, but we need to review them anew as culturally derived phenomena.

Our reflection on the foundations, tenets, and practices of psychotherapy as liberation reveals the fantastic progress we have made toward integrating cultural identity theory more directly into helping practice. Nonetheless, much more needs to be accomplished. We hope the ideas reviewed here will continue to facilitate our progress toward a more culturally-sensitive approach to the profession of helping and the pursuit of client colleagues' psychological liberation.

NOTE

Copyright Allen E. Ivey 1994. This chapter is a revision and update of a previous chapter published in J. Ponterotto and others *Handbook of Multicultural Counseling and Therapy*. Thousand Oaks, CA: Sage. This new version is copyrighted © by Allen Ivey and Carlos Zalaquett (2009) and presented in this book by permission of the authors.

1. "Not to decide is to decide." This was a popular poster of the 1960s attributed to the theologian Harvey Cox. MCT raises difficult issues about responsibility for change. Many good people have not victimized directly, but by their silence may also share a responsibility for the hurt of others. Reparation of one's inaction may at times be as important as confessing complicity in direct hurts.

REFERENCES

Arredondo, P. (1999). Multicultural counseling competencies as tools to address oppression and racism. *Journal of Counseling and Development, 77*, 102–108.

Arredondo, P. (2002). Counseling individuals from specialized, marginalized and underserved groups. In P. Pedersen, J. G. Draguns, W. J. Lonner, & J. E. Trimble (Eds.), *Counseling across cultures* (5th ed., pp. 241–250). Thousand Oaks, CA: Sage.

Asante, M. (1987). *The Afrocentric idea*. Philadelphia: Temple University Press.

Ballou, M., & Gabalac, N. (1984). *A feminist position on mental health*. Springfield, IL: Thomas.

Brown, N. (1959). *Life against death: The psychoanalytic meaning of history*. Middletown, CT: Wesleyan University Press.

Cheatham, H., Ivey, A., Ivey, M., & Simek-Morgan, L. (1993). Multicultural counseling and therapy. In A. Ivey M. Ivey, & L. Simek-Morgan (Eds.), *Counseling and psychotherapy: A multicultural perspective*. Boston: Allyn & Bacon.

Cheatham, H., & Stewart, J. (Eds.). (1990). *Black families*. New Brunswick, NJ:
Transaction.

Cheek, D. (1976). *Assertive black . . . Puzzled white*. San Luis Obispo, CA: Impact.

Cornford, F. (Trans.). (1941/1982). *The republic of Plato*. Oxford: Oxford University
Press.

Cross, W. (1971). The Negro to Black conversion experience. *Black World, 20,*
13–25.

Cross, W. (1991). *Shades of black*. Philadelphia: Temple University Press.

Daly, M. (1973). *Beyond God the father*. Boston: Beacon.

Daly, M. (1978). *Gyn/ecology: The metaethics of radical feminism*. Boston: Beacon.

Fanon, F. (1963). *The wretched of the Earth*. New York: Grove Wheatland.

Freire, P. (1972). *Pedagogy of the oppressed*. New York: Herder and Herder.

Fukuyama, M. (1990). Taking a universal approach to multicultural counseling.
Counselor Education and Supervision, 30, 6–17.

Guareschi, P. A., & Jovchelovitch, S. (2004). Participation, health and the development of community resources in southern Brazil. *Journal of Health Psychology, 9,* 311–322.

Hardiman, R. (1982). *White identity development: A process oriented model for describing the racial consciousness of White Americans*. Unpublished dissertation,
University of Massachusetts, Amherst.

Hardiman, R., & Jackson, B. W. (1997). *Conceptual foundations for social justice
courses, teaching for diversity and social justice*. New York: Rutledge.

Helms, J. (1990). *Black and white racial identity*. Westport, CT: Greenwood.

Helms, J. (2007). *A race is a nice thing to have: A guide to being a white person or understanding the white persons in your life*. Hanover, MA: Microtraining

Ivey, A. E. (1993, January). Psychotherapy as liberation. Presentation to the Round
Table on Cross-Cultural Counseling, Columbia University, New York.

Ivey, A. E. (1995). Psychotherapy as liberation: Toward specific skills and strategies in multicultural counseling and psychotherapy. In F. G. Ponterotto,
J. M. Casas, L. A. Suzuki, & C. M. Alexander, (Eds.), *Handbook of multicultural counseling* (pp. 53–71). Thousand Oaks, CA: Sage.

Ivey, A. E. (2000). *Developmental therapy: Theory into practice*. Hanover, MA:
Microtraining.

Ivey, A. E., & Payton, P. (1994). Towards a Cornish identity theory. In P. Payton (Ed.),
Cornish studies: Two (pp. 151–163). Plymouth, UK: University of Exeter Press.

Ivey, A., Simek-Morgan, L., Ivey, M., & D'Andrea, M. (2006). *Theories of counseling and psychotherapy: A multicultural perspective* (6th ed.). Boston: Allyn &
Bacon.

Jackson, B. (1975). Black identity development. *Journal of Educational Diversity and
Innovation, 2,* 19–25.

Jackson, B. (1990, September). Building a multicultural school. Presentation to the
Amherst Regional School System, Amherst, MA.

Jackson, B., & Hardiman, R. (1983). Racial identity development: Implica-
tions for managing the multiracial work force. In R. Vitvo & A. Sargent
(Eds.), *The NTL managers' handbook* (pp. 107–119). Arlington, VA: NTL
Institute.

Kantrowiz, R. E., & Ballou, M. (1992). A feminist critique of cognitive-behavioral therapy. In L. S. Brown & M. Ballou (Eds.), *Personality and psychopathology: Feminist reappraisals* (pp. 70–87). New York: The Guilford Press.

LaFromboise, T., & Graff Low, K. (1998). American Indian children and adolescents. In J. Gibbs & L. Huang (Eds.), *Children of color: Psychological interventions with culturally diverse youth* (pp. 114–147). San Francisco, CA: Josey Bass.

Lerman, H. (1992). The limits of phenomenology: A feminist critique of humanistic personality theories. In M. Ballou & L. Brown (Eds.), *Theories of personality and psychopathology*. New York: Guilford.

Locke, D. (1990). A not so provincial view of multicultural counseling. *Counselor Education and Supervision, 30,* 18–25.

Locke, D. (1992). *Increasing multicultural understanding.* Newberry Park, CA: Sage.

Miller, J. (1991). The development of women's sense of self. In J. Jordan, A. Kaplan, J. Miller, I. Stiver, & J. Surrey (Eds.), *Women's growth in connection* (pp. 11–26). New York: Guilford.

Montero, M. (2007). The political psychology of liberation: From politics to ethics and back. *Political Psychology, 28*(5), 517–533.

Myers, L. (1988). *Understanding an Afrocentric world view: Introduction to an optimal psychology.* Dubuque, IA: Kendall/Hunt.

Parham, T. (1989). Cycles of psychological nigrescence. *Counseling Psychologist, 17,* 187–226.

Parham, T. A., White, J. L., & Ajamu, A. (1999). *The psychology of Blacks: An African centered perspective* (3rd ed.). Upper Saddle River, NJ: Prentice Hall.

Pedersen, P. (1997). *Culture-centered counseling interventions: Striving for accuracy.* Thousand Oaks, CA: Sage.

Pedersen, P. (1999). *Multiculturalism as a fourth force.* Philadelphia: Brunner/Mazel.

Pedersen, P., & Ivey, A. (1993). *Culture-centered counseling and interviewing skills.* New York: Praeger.

Pedersen, P. B., Draguns, J. G., Lonner, W. J., & Trimble, J. E. (Eds.). (2008). *Counseling across cultures* (6th ed.). Thousand Oaks, CA: Sage.

Pfefferle, S. (1989). Depression as a response to systemic factors. Unpublished paper, University of Massachusetts, Amherst.

Ponterotto, J. (1988). Racial consciousness development among White counselor trainees. *Journal of Multicultural Counseling and Development, 16,* 146–156.

Prilleltensky, I. (2008). The role of power in wellness, oppression, and liberation: The promise of psychopolitical validity. *Journal of Community Psychology, 36,* 116–136.

Rigazio-DiGilio, S. (1989). *Developmental theory and therapy: A preliminary investigation of reliability and predictive validity using an inpatient depressive population sample.* Unpublished doctoral dissertation, University of Massachusetts, Amherst.

Rigazio-DiGilio, S., & Ivey, A. E. (1990). Developmental therapy and depressive disorders: Measuring cognitive levels through patient natural language. *Professional Psychology: Research & Practice, 21,* 470–475.

Rivera-Arzola, M. (1991). *Differences between Puerto Rican women with and without ataques de nervios.* Unpublished Doctoral Dissertation, University of Massachusetts, Amherst.

Smith, L. (2005). Psychotherapy, classism, and the poor. *American Psychologist, 60*, 687–696.

Sue, D., & Sue, D. (2008). *Counseling the culturally different* (5th ed.). New York: Wiley.

Sue, D. W., Ivey, A. E., & Pedersen, P. B. (1996). *A theory of multicultural counseling and therapy.* Pacific Grove, CA: Brooks/Cole.

White, J., & Parham, T. (1990). *The psychology of blacks.* Englewood Cliffs, NJ: Prentice-Hall.

Wrenn, C. (1962). The culturally encapsulated counselor. *Harvard Educational Review, 32*, 444–449.

Wrenn, C. (1985). The culturally encapsulated counselor revisited. In P. Pedersen (Ed.), *Handbook of cross-cultural counseling and therapy* (pp. 323–329). West-port, CT: Greenwood.

Zalaquett, C. P., Fuerth, K., Stein, C., Ivey, A. E., & Ivey, M. B. (2008). Reframing the DSM from a multicultural and social justice. *Journal of Counseling and Development, 86*, 364–371.

Appendix: Key Questions

CHAPTER 1

What is the history of the social justice movement? What theoretical frameworks support current conceptualizations of social justice? What empirical support exists for social justice theories and practices? What are the strategies that can be used to take action based on social justice scholarship and principles? What are the future directions of social justice theories, research, and practice?

CHAPTER 2

How can well-intentioned people inadvertently and subtly discriminate and contribute to racial disparities?

CHAPTER 3

Examine your own beliefs and experiences of heterosexuality or homosexuality. What impact would your own orientation have on working with GLBT clients, students or staff?

CHAPTER 4

How can we promote an informed, humane, socially just and comprehensive immigration policy based upon this nation's historical lessons learned about how it has dealt with race and ethnicity?

CHAPTER 5

What does the term *gerodiversity* mean? What are the issues faced by elders of minority groups/minority groups among older adults? How can psychologists meet the needs of minority older adults?

CHAPTER 6

What can counselors, educators, employers, and health care professionals do to identify and address systemic forms of injustice toward individuals with disabilities in their own organizations and communities?

CHAPTER 7

How can military personnel be served with culturally relevant health care if information about injuries is based on self-diagnosis?

CHAPTER 8

What are some of the cultural issues counselors should consider when working with ethnic minority women during the trauma recovery process?

CHAPTER 9

What are the cultural-development-sociopolitical issues that are key factors of challenge and oppression for older women, and especially older, ethnic minority women in the United States today?

CHAPTER 10

Describe the role of white privilege in the current racial/ethnic disparities in incarceration in the United States.

CHAPTER 11

Why is "dialogical communication" so important for multicultural therapists?

About the Editor and Contributors

JEAN LAU CHIN, EdD, ABPP, is professor and dean of the Derner Institute for Advanced Psychological Studies at Adelphi University in Garden City, New York. Prior to her current position, she held executive management positions as Systemwide Dean of the California School of Professional Psychology at Alliant International University; president, CEO Services; regional director, Massachusetts Behavioral Health Partnership; executive director, South Cove Community Health Center; and co-director, Thom Child Guidance Clinic. She is a licensed psychologist with over 35 years of experience in education, health, and mental health services. Her prior faculty appointments included: associate professor at Boston University School of Medicine and assistant professor at Tufts University School of Medicine. Dr. Chin is an educator, administrator, clinician, and scholar. She has published extensively, with 10 books, many chapters and articles, and over 200 presentations in the areas of diversity and cultural competence; ethnic minority, Asian American, and women's issues in health and mental health; and leadership. Her most recent books are: *Women and Leadership: Transforming Visions and Diverse Voices* (2007) and *Learning from My Mother's Voice: Family Legend and the Chinese American Experience* (2005). She serves on many national and local boards including: the Advisory Committee for Women's Services and the Eliminating Mental Health Disparities Committee for Substance Abuse Mental Health Services Administration, U.S. Dept of Health and Human Services; Board for the Advancement of Psychology in the Public Interest of the American Psychological Association; board member of the National Asian Pacific American Families Against Substance Abuse; and president of the National Council of Schools and Programs of Professional Psychology.

ROSALIE J. ACKERMAN, PhD, is a clinical and research neuropsychologist and computer consultant in the Research & Development Division of ABackans DCP, Inc., in Akron, Ohio. The focus of her teaching has been on the importance of applying psychological and neuropsychological assessment skills to the delivery and monitoring of culturally diverse clinical clients. She has taught face-to-face graduate level clinical psychology and neuropsychology at the University of North Carolina at Chapel Hill and The Pennsylvania State University. Her counseling psychology degree was obtained from Iowa State University; her clinical psychology internship was a neuropsychology track at the University of Nebraska, University of Nebraska Medical Center, and Nebraska Psychiatric Institute. Dr. Ackerman and Dr. Martha E. Banks currently provide an interface to neuropsychological and rehabilitation information through a professional Web site (http://abackans.com/), as well as an award-winning Web site of resources for victims of domestic violence (http://abackans.com/dvresour.html). Dr. Ackerman's hospital-based and private clinical practices included individual, group, family psychotherapy, and neuropsychological assessment and rehabilitation of patients across the lifespan. Dr. Ackerman has provided neuropsychology assessment, treatment, and forensic consultation for victims of intimate partner violence and currently conducts neuropsychological and rehabilitation research. She has treated more than 4,000 clients, which is a indication of clinical success. Dr. Ackerman has participated in several projects including the development and major revision of the Ackerman-Banks Neuropsychological Rehabilitation Battery© and the Post-Assault Traumatic Brain Injury Interview & Checklist©. She has also conducted statistical analyses, consulted, and taught APA-sponsored workshops in Nigeria and Canada as well as more than 180 invited workshop presentations in the United States.

Dr. Ackerman is licensed as a psychologist in North Carolina, Pennsylvania, and Ohio and was on the National Register of Health Service Providers in Psychology. She is a fellow of three divisions of the American Psychological Association, the Society for Women in Psychology, the Division of Trauma Psychology, and Rehabilitation Psychology. These recognitions are reflective of areas of her expertise as reflected in more than 200 publications. She teaches in the new online program at the California School of Professional Psychology (CSPP) at Alliant International University, teaching dissertation and comprehensive doctoral programs (PsyD) in clinical psychology with face-to-face teaching at specified intervals. Dr. Ackerman's research includes health disparities and generating individualized treatment options experienced by women, multimodal biofeedback and neuropsychological rehabilitation, people of color with disabilities, stress and trauma experienced by women of color and women with disabilities, and increasing community awareness about victims of violence and disabilities from head injuries.

NANCY LYNN BAKER, PhD, ABPP, is a director of the Forensic Psychology Concentration at Fielding Graduate University. She is also a former president of the Society for the Psychology of Women (APA's Division 35) and former chairperson of APA's Committee on Women in Psychology. Previously, Dr. Baker served for eight years in the Department of Neuropsychology at a large community hospital. Dr. Baker has a long interest in issues of discrimination and prejudice, particularly as they manifest through sexism, racism, class bias, and heterosexism, and in the interplay of these issues with one another.

MARTHA E. BANKS, PhD, is a research neuropsychologist in the Research & Development Division of ABackans DCP, Inc., in Akron, Ohio and a former professor of Black Studies at the College of Wooster, where her courses included "Black Women in Contemporary America," "Rubrics of Black Psychology," and "First Year Seminar: Should I Call My Bank, My Parents, or My Lawyer? Seeking Answers about Health Disparities." Prior to her retirement from the Brecksville Veterans Administration Medical Center, she served as clinical psychologist, trainer and developing consultant of the Mental Health Package in the computerized medical record, Federal Women's Program coordinator, and hospital-wide trainer in sexual harassment. She has been instrumental in the development and revision of the *Ackerman-Banks Neuropsychological Rehabilitation Battery*© and the *Post-Assault Traumatic Brain Injury Interview.*

ANNIE BELCOURT-DITTLOFF is an American Indian research and clinical faculty member at the University of Colorado at Denver's American Indian and Alaska Native Programs (enrolled tribal member: Blackfeet, Chippewa, Mandan, and Hidatsa). She is a clinical psychologist and her research priorities include trauma, posttraumatic stress reactions, risk, resiliency, and psychiatry within the cultural context of American Indian populations. She has provided clinical services serving diverse clientele in a variety of settings; most recently completing an internship with the Department of Veterans Affairs Medical Center in Denver, Colorado, working with war veterans and addressing post-trauma reactions. Dr. Belcourt-Dittloff has conducted multiple, grant-funded, collaborative research projects with American Indian communities These projects have provided experience in both quantitative and qualitative analysis and were aimed at the investigation of factors, including posttraumatic stress disorder, trauma, cultural resiliency, spirituality, adversarial or posttraumatic growth, and psychosocial factors involved in depression and suicidal ideation. She has presented her research findings to numerous national conferences and tribal communities, and has published in peer reviewed journals including *American Psychologist* and *Educational and Psychological Measurement.*

THEMA BRYANT-DAVIS is an assistant professor of psychology at Pepperdine University. In 2007 the American Psychological Association awarded her the Emerging Leader of Women in Psychology Award for her scholarship and clinical work on violence against women. Her research expertise is in the cultural context of trauma, particularly child abuse, partner abuse, sexual assault, and the societal trauma of racism. Dr. Bryant-Davis is author of the book *Thriving in the wake of trauma: A multicultural guide* and she is also published in the journals *The Counseling Psychologist, Professional Psychology: Research and Practice, and Trauma, Violence, and Abuse*. In addition, Dr. Bryant-Davis serves on the Editorial Board for the journal *Psychological Trauma: Theory, Research, Practice, and Policy*. On a global level, Dr. Bryant-Davis was selected as an American Psychological Association representative to the United Nations where she provided education, advocacy, and monitoring of Member States' mental health policies for three years; she currently serves as the Global and International Issues Chairperson for the Society for the Psychology of Women.

HEEWOON CHUNG earned her master's degree in education and psychology from Harvard University, Graduate School of Education and her B.S. in developmental psychology from Cornell University. She is currently pursuing her doctorate in clinical psychology from Pepperdine University. Her research is in the areas of trauma caused by sexual assault and intimate partner violence in the United States as well as in international settings.

JOHN F. DOVIDIO, who is currently professor of psychology at Yale University, previously taught at Colgate University and at the University of Connecticut. At Colgate, he served as provost and dean of the faculty. His research interests are in stereotyping, prejudice, and discrimination; social power and nonverbal communication; and altruism and helping. Much of his scholarship has focused on "aversive racism," a subtle form of contemporary racism. He is currently president of the Society for Personality and Social Psychology, as well as past president of the Society for the Psychological Study of Social Issues and former chair of the Executive Committee for the Society for Experimental Social Psychology. He has published over 200 articles and chapters; is coauthor of several books, including *Emergency intervention; The Psychology of helping and altruism; The social psychology of prosocial behavior;* and *Reducing intergroup bias: The Common Ingroup Identity Model;* as well as coeditor of *Prejudice, discrimination, and racism; Power, dominance, and nonverbal behavior;* and, *On the nature of prejudice: 50 years after Allport*. He is currently editor of the *Journal of Personality and Social Psychology—Interpersonal Relations and Group Processes* and coeditor of *Social Issues and Policy Review*.

TERRI ERBACHER, PhD, earned her degree at Temple University and, after teaching at her alma mater, is currently a clinical assistant professor in the School Psychology Program at the Philadelphia College of Osteopathic Medicine (PCOM). Dr. Erbacher is a certified school psychologist and licensed psychologist, currently working primarily with adolescents. Dr. Erbacher is also extensively trained in crisis management and intervention, and serves as part of multiple crisis teams. Suicide prevention amongst diverse populations is a particular area of research interest for Dr. Erbacher. Her interest in topics of diversity began early on while working in urban and suburban districts in New York and the Philadelphia. Cross-cultural research is of particular interest as her doctoral dissertation focused on a cross-cultural examination of child abuse and corporal punishment laws, attitudes and practices. Previous courses taught include diversity issues in family therapy, disabling conditions, and linguistic issues. Since joining PCOM, Dr. Erbacher has advised the Culturally Aware Psychology Students (CAPS) Committee, working with students and colleagues to promote the awareness and education of diversity. Other areas of research interest and practice include adolescent group therapy, health psychology (mind-body relationships), grief and outreach to the newly bereaved.

PAMELA F. FOLEY is assistant professor of counseling psychology at Seton Hall University. She teaches courses in assessment, vocational theory, and statistics. Further, she serves as practicum coordinator for the PhD program in counseling psychology, and as on-site supervisor for a doctoral prepracticum rotation at the university's Office of Disability Support Services. Before joining Seton Hall in 2001, she worked at the University of Medicine and Dentistry of New Jersey, where she was responsible for both individual therapy and group-based addiction treatment in a managed-care setting. Dr. Foley is licensed in New Jersey both as a psychologist and as a professional counselor. Professional psychology is a second career for Dr. Foley. After receiving a BA in biology and chemistry from Skidmore College and an M.S. in technical writing from Rensselaer Polytechnic Institute, she spent 15 years in a variety of management roles at Bell Labs and AT&T. During this time, she created and delivered group training on a variety of topics, including diversity, the Americans with Disabilities Act, team building and conflict management, process quality management, and layoff survivor syndrome. She also developed and implemented customer satisfaction survey and data analysis methods for AT&T International Services groups in Europe, the Pacific Rim, and the Americas regions, and she completed an Executive Education Program in International Business at Thunderbird: The American Graduate School of International Management. Dr. Foley's current research interests are in workplace and career issues, cultural issues, and the intersections between them. She has published and presented her work at national conferences, on multiple topics including anger in the workplace, the effects of cultural variables on career decisions, religion as a dimension of identity, and disability status as both a dimension of identity and a social justice issue. Dr. Foley serves as an executive committee member for the National Institute for Multicultural Competence, as a member of the Committee on Legislative Affairs for the New Jersey Psychological Association, as the Seton Hall Campus/Training Representative for the APA Federal Education Advocacy Task Force, and as an ad hoc reviewer for *The Counseling Psychologist* and *Career Development Quarterly*. She is a member of APA Divisions 17 and 45, and has served as a program reviewer for both. She is also a member of the Latino Psychological Association of New Jersey, the American Counseling Association, the National Career Development Association, and the New Jersey Association of Cognitive Behavioral Therapists.

SAMUEL L. GAERTNER (BA, 1964, Brooklyn College, PhD, 1970; The City University of New York: Graduate Center) is professor of psychology at the University of Delaware. His research interests involve intergroup relations with a focus on understanding and reducing prejudice, discrimination and racism. He has served on the editorial boards of the *Journal of Personality and Social Psychology, Personality and Social Psychology Bulletin,* and *Group Processes and Intergroup Relations*. Professor Gaertner's research has been supported by grants from the Office of Naval Research, the National Institutes of Mental Health and currently, the National Science Foundation. Together with John Dovidio, he has shared the Gordon Allport Intergroup Relations Prize in 1985 and 1998, and in 2004, the Kurt Lewin Memorial Award (a career award) from the Society for the Psychological Study of Social Issues, Division 9 of the American Psychological Association.

CAITLIN GILMARTIN graduated in 2008 with her MS degree in counseling and clinical health psychology from Philadelphia College of Osteopathic Medicine (PCOM). She is currently enrolled in PCOM's EdS program in the school of psychology.

ALLEN E. IVEY is Distinguished University Professor (Emeritus), University of Massachusetts and Courtesy Professor, University of South Florida, Tampa. A *Phi Beta Kappa* graduate of Stanford University, he earned his doctorate at Harvard University. A board certified diplomate in Counseling Psychology, Ivey is past president and fellow of the Society of Counseling Psychology, a fellow of the Society for the Psychological Study of Ethnic Minority Issue, and a fellow of the Asian American Psychological Association. He is author or coauthor of over 40 books and 200 articles, translated into 20 languages. He conducted original work on the multicultural implications of microskills in 1966–1974 and has been increasing his work in multicultural studies ever since. Ivey currently focuses on "Psychotherapy as Liberation" and on generating a theoretical/practical approach to working with so-called pathology and *DSM-IV-R* from a positive developmental framework. Among his many awards are an APA Presidential Citation, the ACA Professional Developmental Award, and he was honored as an *Elder of Multicultural Psychology* at a recent National Multicultural Conference and Summit. Most recently, the Japanese Microcounseling Association has been approved by the government as a recognized scientific organization. It has its own journal specialized in Ivey's writing.

MICHIKO IWASAKI, PhD, is a senior fellow in the Department of Psychiatry and Behavioral Sciences at the University of Washington's School of Medicine. She is a recipient of various awards in the area of minority and aging, including the Summer Research Institute of Geriatric Psychiatry, AARP Andrus Fellowship in Minority Doctoral Leadership, Grantmakers in Aging Fellowship, the APA Minority Aging Network in Psychology Summer Institute, and the APA-CONA Working Group in Cultural Competency. Her research interests include Asian American mental health, dementia care, long-term care policies, geriatric/gerontological education, a social concept of attitudes, and scale development. She received her PhD in counseling psychology at Ball State University. She is bilingual in Japanese and English.

DOUGLAS KIMMEL, PhD, is Professor Emeritus at the Department of Psychology, City College, C.U.N.Y., and has a private practice in Hancock, Maine. He was chair of the Association of Gay Psychologists (1977), president of the Society for the Psychological Study of Lesbian, Gay, and Bisexual Issues: Division 44 of the American Psychological Association (1987–1988). He also served on APA's Committee on Gay, Lesbian, and Bisexual Concerns (1980–1983), and the Board of Social and Ethical Responsibility (1983–1986) focusing on ageism issues. His textbook, *Adulthood and Aging* (1974, 1980, 1990), included sexual orientation and an interview with a gay man. He is coeditor of *Psychological Perspectives on Lesbian, Gay, and Bisexual Experiences* (1993, 2003) and coeditor of *Lesbian, Gay, Bisexual, and Transgender Aging: Research and Clinical Perspectives* (2005). He is currently chair-elect of the APA Board for the Advancement of Psychology in the Public Interest. His Web site is www.tamarackplace.com/kimmel

KEN MARTINEZ, PsyD, has been a licensed clinical psychologist for 30 years and has worked in the behavioral health field in a variety of capacities: clinician, university faculty, state administrator, consultant, technical assistance provider and volunteer. He is currently principal research analyst and mental health resource specialist with the Technical Assistance Partnership for Child and Family Mental Health (TA Partnership) at the American Institutes for Research. The TA Partnership operates under contract with the Center for Mental Health Services (CMHS) to provide technical assistance to system of care (SOC) communities funded by the

Comprehensive Community Mental Health Services for Children and Their Families Program. It assists communities to develop and implement a broad array of community-based, culturally and linguistically competent, family-driven, youth-guided and strength-based services to improve outcomes for children with serious emotional disturbance. Dr. Martinez is lead for the TA Partnership's Cultural Competence Action Team that published the Web-based document, *The Cultural and Linguistic Competence Implementation Guide* and several other cultural and linguistic competence related products. Dr. Martinez was the State Children's Behavioral Health Director in New Mexico and has extensive experience in policy, administration and program development. He is also clinical assistant professor of psychiatry at the University of New Mexico Health Sciences Center. He was chair of the National Association of State Mental Health Program Directors (NASMHPD), Children, Youth and Families Division and is currently on the board of directors of the National Latino Behavioral Health Association, the National Alliance of Multi-Ethnic Behavioral Health Associations and founding member of the National Network to Eliminate Disparities in Behavioral Health; the Advisory Board for the Research and Training Center for Children's Mental Health at the Florida Mental Health Institute; the Expert Advisory Panel for the Cultural Competence Center of Excellence at Nathan Kline Research Institute in New York State as well as several other advisory groups. He was on the 2004 and the 2008 Planning Committee for the Rosalynn Carter Annual Symposium on Mental Health at the Carter Center and is a member of the SAMHSA sponsored Outcomes Roundtable for Children and Families. Dr. Martinez is working on the advisory committee, under the leadership of Jane Knitzer, on *Unclaimed Children Revisited,* a strategic policy initiative on the 25th anniversary of Dr. Knitzer's original publication, *Unclaimed Children.*

T. J. McCALLUM, PhD, is an assistant professor of psychology at Case Western Reserve University in Cleveland, Ohio. He is a member of the clinical area and the adult clinical track. He is also a faculty associate at the Case Center for Aging and Health. He received his PhD in clinical psychology with a specialization in aging from the University of Southern California in 2002. Dr. McCallum received his BA from the University of California at Berkeley in 1989, and earned an MA in lifespan development from Columbia University in New York City in 1991. He completed his clinical internship at the Stanford University/Palo Alto Department of Veteran's Affairs in the geropsychology track. Dr. McCallum also spent one year at the University of California at San Francisco in the Health Psychology Program before taking up the position at Case Western Reserve. His research interests include ethnicity in dementia caregiving, psychological and physiological stress response in older adults, cognitive-behavioral caregiver stress reduction programs, and the relationship between religiosity and mental and physical health outcomes among older African Americans.

ENMANUEL MERCEDES is an enthusiastic young man with a great passion for diversity and personal development. Manny, as his friends call him, is currently a fourth year doctoral student at Seton Hall University's counseling psychology program. Manny is also a fulltime Student Development Specialist, working with First Generation College students. The oldest of three siblings, Manny was born in the Dominican Republic and a lifelong resident of Newark, NJ. He was the 2006 Dorothy D. Palmer Fellow in the Study of Optimal Aging in Women.

MARCIA MOODY, PhD, was born in Flint, Michigan, and currently resides in Ann Arbor, Michigan. She earned a doctorate in counseling psychology from the University of Wisconsin–Madison. Dr. Moody currently serves as the director of the Center for Teaching and Learning at Walden University. Prior to this appointment, she served as the assistant dean for curriculum management in Walden's College of Social, Behavioral, and Health Sciences. She was also formerly an assistant professor in the Counseling Psychology Department at the University at Albany SUNY and has worked as a counselor at the University of Wisconsin-Madison Counseling and Consultation Center. Her teaching and research interests include multicultural counseling, internationalization, spirituality and religion, adult development and aging, ethics, psychology of women, and group counseling.

NINA NABORS, PhD, currently serves as associate dean for the School of Psychology at Walden University. Prior to this appointment, she served as assistant dean for faculty development in the College of Social, Behavioral, and Health Sciences at Walden University. Dr. Nabors began as a part-time faculty member at Walden in the School of Psychology in August 2001. Dr. Nabors served as an associate professor in the Psychology Department at Eastern Michigan University 1999–2005. Her research interests include rehabilitation psychology, psychology of women, multicultural psychology, womanist/feminist therapy, women with disabilities, and she has numerous publications and presentations on these topics. Professionally, Dr. Nabors is a licensed psychologist in the state of Michigan and board certified in rehabilitation psychology.

WYNNE E. NORTON's research interests are focused on integrating social psychology theory and health behavior. To date, her work has focused on developing, implementing, and evaluating HIV prevention interventions with a variety of populations, including U.S.-based college students, PLWHA in clinical care in the United States., HIV-positive military personnel in Mozambique and Uganda, and HIV-positive injection drug users in clinical care. Her work has also spanned across several NIH-funded grants, including an NIMH-funded R01 to develop and implement a computer-based intervention to increase adherence to antiretroviral therapy, and a Pre-doctoral National Research Service Award (NRSA) to fund her dissertation work. Her emerging research interests include health disparities and the dissemination and implementation of health promotion/disease prevention interventions, with a particular focus on evidence-based HIV prevention interventions. To this end, she is one of the co-founders and moderators for the Dissemination, Implementation, and Translation Research in Health Listserv, established in 2007 by CHIP/UCONN and NIMH.

LAURA PALMER, PhD, is an associate professor at the Department of Counseling Psychology at Seton Hall University in South Orange, New Jersey. Dr. Palmer is the chair of the Professional Psychology and Family Therapy Department and the training director of the doctoral program in counseling psychology program at the College of Education and Human Services at Seton Hall University. She also maintains a private practice where she works with children, women and older adults. Dr. Palmer's research interests are in neuropsychology, learning disabilities women's issues and trauma.

ADAM R. PEARSON is a PhD student in the social psychology program at Yale University. He received a BS in biology from Cornell University and an MA in psychology from the University of Connecticut. His research interests include prejudice, stereotyping, and discrimination; the role of emotion in intergroup perception and behavior; and dynamics of everyday race relations.

LOUIS A. PENNER (MA, Miami University; PhD in social psychology from Michigan State University) is professor of family medicine at Wayne State University, where he is also a senior scientist in the Communication and Behavioral Oncology Program at Karmanos Cancer Institute. Dr. Penner also is an associate research scientist in the Research Center for Group Dynamics at the University of Michigan and a Professor Emeritus at the University of South Florida. He is a fellow of the American Psychological Society and the Society for the Psychological Study of Social Issues (SPSSI), Division 9 of the American Psychological Association. Dr. Penner also served as president of SPSSI in 2001, and received the 2005 Distinguished Service Award from that organization. He is a consulting editor for the *Journal of Social Issues, Journal of Personality and Social Psychology, Analyses of Social Issues and Public Policies,* and the *Social Issues and Policy Review.* Dr. Penner has authored or coauthored eight books and about 80 articles and book chapters. His current research interests focus on racial and ethnic disparities in health care and understanding the psychological consequences of cancer and other life-threatening diseases. However, he also remains interested in individual differences in prosocial personality orientations, volunteerism, and prosocial behavior in organizations. He coauthored "Prosocial Behavior: A Multilevel Perspective" in the 2005 *Annual Review of Psychology* and the second edition of the *Social Psychology of Prosocial Behavior*, which was published in 2006. He is the principal investigator on a grant from the National Institute of Child Health and Development and a coinvestigator on two other grants from the National Cancer Institute.

NATALIE PORTER, PhD, professor, California School of Professional Psychology, Alliant International University, has contributed to the research, scholarship, and practice of feminist therapy for over 30 years. Primary areas of interest have included women and leadership, feminist models of supervision, feminist ethics, and the intersection of feminist theory and practice with multicultural, antiracist models. Recent articles and book chapters (singly and coauthored) have included: "Supervision, Culture, and Context," "Developing Transformational Leadership: Theory to Practice," "Contextual and Developmental Frameworks in Diagnosing Children and Adolescents," "Location, Location, Location: Contributions of Contemporary Feminist Theorists to Therapy Theory and Practice," and "Psychological Gender Differences: Contemporary Theories and Controversies." Dr. Porter is a fellow of Divisions 12 (Society of Clinical Psychology) and 35 (Society for the Psychology of Women) of APA. She and Dalia Ducker, PhD, are currently completing data analysis of a study on the impact of gender stereotypes on the perception of women political leaders. In addition to serving as chair of the gender committee for NCSPP, Dr. Porter is past president of APA's Division 35, Society for the Psychological Study of Women and of Division 12 (Clinical) Section on Women (IV).

DEANNA MARIE RYDER graduated in 2008 from the Philadelphia College of Osteopathic (PCOM) Medicine with a Master of Science in counseling and clinical health psychology. While at PCOM, Deanna was very involved in student organizations including Culturally Aware Psychology Students (CAPS) and the National Association of University Women. She was also secretary for the Psychiatry Club of PCOM. Deanna presented at Columbia University's Diversity Roundtable last year with a symposium titled "Cultural Competence and Suicidal Youth: Intervening Sensitively with This Preventable, Community Health Problem."

YVETTE N. TAZEAU, PhD, is a licensed psychologist whose independent practice is in Los Gatos, California. She works with clients across the developmental lifespan, including older adults, to whom she provides clinical neuropsychology and psychotherapy services. As a Latina who is fluent in the Spanish language, she has a particular interest in working with Latino/Hispanic clients for neuropsychological assessment of dementia, cognitive-behavioral therapy, and caregiver issues. As an appointed member/active staff and now retired clinical neuropsychologist for the Alexian Senior Center and Regional Medical Center of San Jose, she provided geropsychology and assessment services for the San Jose community. Her research and clinical training experience includes work at the Palo Alto V.A. Medical Center and its Older Adult Center.

SHAQUITA TILLMAN earned her bachelor's degree from UCLA and her master's degree from Pepperdine University. She is a Graduate School of Education and Psychology Diversity Scholar in the Pepperdine University doctoral program in clinical psychology. She is a member of the American Psychological Association and the Association of Women in Psychology. Her research interest is prevention and recovery from interpersonal trauma, particularly for African Americans.

MASAMI TOKUMO, PhD, obtained her master's degrees in psychological counseling and education from Teachers College Columbia University, and her doctorate in counseling psychology from Seton Hall University. She is currently a post doctoral fellow at Princeton House Behavioral Health, Princeton HealthCare System in Princeton, New Jersey. Her research interests include geriatric psychology, mood disorders, psychotherapy, and cross-cultural counseling. Dr. Tokumo is also a licensed professional counselor.

NARRIMONE VIVID THAMMAVONGSA was born in Ubon Ratchathani, Thailand, and raised in Scranton, Pennsylvania. She received her BA in French (2000) from the University of Scranton and MA in teaching English as a second language (2002) from the School for International Training Graduate Institute in Brattleboro, Vermont. While teaching in the Philadelphia School District, she entered the EdS in school psychology program at the Philadelphia College of Osteopathic Medicine and is expected to graduate in May 2009. Her research interests include experiential learning and multicultural teaching, intergenerational cultural dissonance within Asian American families, and resilience among diverse populations.

YUMA IANNOTTI-TOMES earned a BA in psychology (developmental) from The University of North Carolina at Chapel Hill (UNC). It was at UNC that Dr. Tomes was formally introduced to multicultural psychology and its affects on students, teachers, and administrators in public agencies. After graduating, Dr. Tomes pursued an MA and CAS in school psychology from Appalachian State University (ASU). Finally, Dr. Tomes enrolled at Virginia Commonwealth University/Medical College of Virginia (VCU/MCV) to pursue a doctoral degree in (educational) psychology. At VCU Dr. Tomes received the college's prestigious SCHEV research assistantship in his first year. Additional awards, fellowships, and assistantships were to follow over the next three years. Dr. Tomes has accumulated a diverse range of work experiences in the fields of psychology and education over the last 10 years. Dr. Tomes has worked as a school psychologist for urban school districts; as an assistant professor with Eastern Washington University in the Department of Counseling, Educational, and Developmental Psychology; and currently is the director of the MS in School Psychology Program at the Philadelphia College of Osteopathic Medicine. Dr. Tomes's major areas of interest are crosscultural psychology, multicultural assessment, cognitive/learning styles, psychological/ educational assessments, consultation, and gay/lesbian/bisexual/transgendered issues.

JOSEPH E. TRIMBLE (PhD, University of Oklahoma, Institute of Group Relations, 1969), formerly a fellow at Harvard University's Radcliffe Institute for Advanced Study, is professor of psychology at Western Washington University, a senior scholar at the Tri-Ethnic Center for Prevention Research at Colorado State University, and a research associate for the National Center for American Indian and Alaska Native Mental Health Research at the University of Colorado Health Sciences Center. He has held numerous offices in the International Association for Cross-Cultural Psychology and the American Psychological Association (APA). He holds fellow status in three APA divisions: 9, 27, and 45. He is past-president of the Society for the Psychological Study of Ethnic Minority Issues and a former council member for the Society for the Psychological Study of Social Issues. Since 1972, he has served as a member of scientific review committees and research panels for the following federal agencies: NIAAA; NIDA; NIA; NIMH; National Heart, Lung and Blood Institute; NICHD; NCI; National Center for Research Resources; Risk, Prevention, and Health Behavior, NIH; Center for Substance Abuse Prevention; National Academy of Sciences; NSF; NIDA's Subcommittee on Epidemiology and Prevention Research; and NIDA's Risk, Prevention, and Health Behavior Initial Review Group. Currently, he is a member of NIDA's Health Services Research Subcommittee. Dr. Trimble has generated over 130 publications on cross-cultural and ethnic topics in psychology, including 16 edited, coedited, and coauthored books; his coedited *Handbook of Racial and Ethnic Minority Psychology* was selected as one of *CHOICE* magazine's Outstanding Academic Titles for 2004. His recent books include (with Celia Fisher) the *Handbook of Ethical Research with Ethnocultural Populations and Communities*, and (with Paul Pedersen, Juris Draguns, and Walt Lonner) *Counseling Across Cultures, 6th Edition.* He has received numerous excellence in teaching and mentoring awards for his work in the field of ethnic and cultural psychology, including: the Excellence in Teaching Award and the Paul J. Olscamp Outstanding Faculty Research Award from Western Washington University; APA's Division 45 Lifetime Achievement Award; the Janet E. Helms Award for Mentoring and Scholarship in Professional Psychology at Teachers College, Columbia University; the Washington State Psychological Association Distinguished Psychologist Award for 2002; the Peace and Social Justice Award from APA's Division 48; and the Distinguished Elder Award from the National Multicultural Conference and Summit in 2007.

LINDA R. WALTER has her MEd in special education and is A.B.D. at Seton Hall University in the educational leadership, management and policy program. She has been a teacher, director of special services and principal and has worked for the New Jersey Department of Education. She is currently the director of disability support services at Seton Hall and an adjunct professor there and at Kean University. She has appeared on the *Today Show* four times and on MSNBC, and has been quoted in the *Washington Post, New York Times, USA Today*, and several other papers. She has also served as a keynote speaker at several conferences, has presented workshops at national conferences, and has presented five audio conferences at the national level.

ERIC WATSON graduated in 2008 from Philadelphia College of Osteopathic (PCOM) Medicine with a Master of Science in counseling and clinical health psychology. While at PCOM, Eric was a student member of Culturally Aware Psychology Students (CAPS) and presented at Columbia University's Diversity Roundtable in the Spring of 2008 with a symposium titled "Cultural Competence and Suicidal Youth: Intervening Sensitively with This Preventable, Community Health Problem."

LAUREN WEBB is currently enrolled in the EdS in school psychology program at the Philadelphia College of Osteopathic Medicine and is expected to graduate in May 2009. She has worked with diverse populations in prisons and schools in the Pennsylvania counties of Philadelphia, Lower Moreland, and Central Bucks. She is a member of the National Association of School Psychology and participates in the Cultural and Linguistic Diversity Ambassadors of Recruitment Program. She wishes to promote change through leadership and cultural understanding as an advocate in the field of school psychology.

TANIA CZARNECKI WISMAR is pursuing her PsyD in clinical psychology at the Philadelphia College of Osteopathic Medicine. Upon completion of her degree in 2010 she hopes to use her voice as a psychologist to continue advocating for underserviced and at-risk populations.

MIGUEL YBARRA, PhD, currently resides in Austin, Texas. He earned his BA and MEd in psychology and counseling/guidance respectively from Texas State University–San Marcos and his PhD in counseling psychology from the University of Wisconsin–Madison. He is currently the director of the Clinical, School and Counseling Psychology Programs at Walden University. Dr. Ybarra is particularly interested in research that focuses on college student success; persistence decisions of students in college; issues related to students of color; and the intersection of mental health and physical health, especially among communities of color. He is currently licensed for the independent practice of psychology in the State of Texas and enjoys training and education of doctoral students in psychology. He particularly enjoys teaching diagnosis and assessment, theories of personality, and multicultural counseling/psychotherapy, supervision, and supervision of supervision.

CARLOS P. ZALAQUETT graduated from the Catholic University of Chile with a degree in clinical psychology. He completed his master's degree in clinical psychology at Sam Houston State University and his doctoral degree in psychology at the University of Texas in Austin, Texas. Currently, he is an associate professor in the Department of Psychological and Social Foundations of the College of Education at the University of South Florida. He is the coordinator of the Clinical Mental Health Program and The Graduate Certificate in Mental Health Counseling, and serves as director of the Successful Latina/o Students Awards and the Mental Health in Schools, a Grassroots Initiative. He is also the executive secretary for the United States and Canada of the Society of Interamerican Psychology. Dr. Zalaquett has received many awards, including the USF's Latinos Association's Faculty of the Year Award and Tampa's Hispanic Heritage's Man of Education Award. He is an internationally recognized expert on mental health, diversity, and education and has conducted workshops and lectures in seven countries. He is the author or coauthor of more than 50 scholarly publications and books, including *Evaluating Stress: A Book of Resources,* Volumes I and II, with Dr. Richard Wood; *Las Habilidades Atencionales Basicas,* with Drs. Allen Ivey, Mary B. Ivey, and Norma Gluckstern; and *Intentional Interviewing and Counseling,* 7th edition, with Drs. Allen Ivey and Mary B. Ivey.

Index